THE EMERGENCE OF JAPAN'S
FOREIGN AID POWER

THE EMERGENCE
OF JAPAN'S
FOREIGN AID POWER

ROBERT M. ORR, JR.

COLUMBIA UNIVERSITY PRESS
New York

Columbia University Press
New York   Oxford
Copyright © 1990 Columbia University Press
All rights reserved

Library of Congress Cataloging-in-Publication Data
Orr, Robert M.
The emergence of Japan's foreign aid power / Robert M. Orr, Jr.
p. cm.
Includes bibliographical references.
ISBN 0–231–07046–2
ISBN 0–231–07047–0 (pbk.)
1. Economic assistance, Japanese.
2. Economic assistance, American.
I. Title.
HC60.O78 1990   338.9'152—dc20   90–30301
CIP

Casebound editions of Columbia University Press books are Smyth-sewn
and printed on permanent and durable acid-free paper

Printed in the United States of America

c 10 9 8 7 6 5 4 3 2 1
p 10 9 8 7 6 5 4 3 2 1

To My Wife, Miko

CONTENTS

1. Approaches to Policymaking   1

2. Aid Politics and the Decisionmaking Structure   19

3. Aid Policy Evolution, Philosophy, and the Role of the
   Private Sector   52

4. Translating the Policies: Regional and Multilateral
   Bank Emphasis   69

5. Foreign Pressure: The Role of the United States   103

6. Conclusions: The Meaning of the Process   137

   Bibliography   161

   Index   173

ACKNOWLEDGMENTS

Writing the acknowledgments in some ways presents the most difficult of tasks since there are so many people who contribute to an
undertaking such as this. The biggest fear is always that someone will
be left out. I am grateful to all who advanced my understanding of a
very complex subject: the formation of Japanese foreign aid policy.

But there are several people who guided me, offered advice or
simply gave me opportunities to study this topic from a different
angle, that bear mentioning. Among those are former and current
officials in the U.S. Agency for International Development. In particular I wish to express my gratitude to Jon Holstine, Fred Schieck,
Robert Halligan, Ambassador Julia Chang Bloch and Lori Forman.
All them played some kind of role in how I came to see an aspect of
U.S. or Japanese foreign aid questions.

Words cannot express the debt of gratitude I owe toward several
members of the Department of International Relations at Tokyo University who taught me much about the Japanese style of decisionmaking and foreign policy. In particular, I would like to acknowledge the
invaluable guidance offered by Akio Watanabe. Others who con-

tributed to my analysis in one form or another were Seizaburo Sato, Takafusa Nakamura, Susumu Yamakage, and Akihiko Tanaka. Jim Foster, Bill Brooks and Hans Klemm of the U.S. Embassy in Tokyo encouraged me and were great sources of knowledge concerning a variety of Japan-related policymaking issues.

I was fortunate to benefit from the advice and guidance from many non-Japanese scholars as well. In particular, Alan Rix and Dennis Yasutomo, both authors of groundbreaking contributions to our understanding of Japanese foreign aid, were very supportive and many of their comments at various stages of this book's draft have been incorporated. Susan Pharr was also a source of insight and encouragement.

Michael Chinworth and Chris Nelson were very helpful in clarifying some non-aid related ideas. I am extremely grateful to the East-West Center in Honolulu. Seiji Naya and Bruce Koppel in particular were a great source of information, support, and encouragement to me.

There were many in the Japanese aid system who cooperated with me in pursuing this study. Yoichi Aki, Hideaki Domichi, and Akira Moriga spent a lot of time with me discussing issues related to foreign aid. Hiroshi Matsumoto of the Association for the Promotion of International Cooperation helped to open many doors for me in the Japanese aid establishment. Needless to say, none of the above are responsible in any way, shape or form for the conclusions I have reached.

A special word of thanks to Marc Gallichio of Villanova University for getting my publication ball rolling with Columbia University Press. Kate Wittenberg is a great editor to work with.

I wish to thank my parents, Robert and Marylouise Orr, and brother, Alex, for their constant faith in me. I only wish that my father were alive to see the publication of this book. Lastly, I am very grateful to my wife, Miko. Without her love, support, and understanding, not to mention insights, it is doubtful that I could have gotten much beyond the first page.

THE EMERGENCE OF JAPAN'S
FOREIGN AID POWER

1

Approaches to Policymaking

I n 1964, at the time of the Tokyo Olympics, Japan was just becoming known as an economic miracle. Nonetheless, received foreign aid was still playing an important role in the nation's development. Prior to the Olympics, the bullet train or *shinkansen* had been completed as a showcase for the "new Japan." The train system, which was billed as the fastest in the world, was built as a World Bank loan project. In fact, Japan was the second largest recipient of World Bank loans after India in the year that Tokyo was host to those very same Olympics. Much of the highway structure that surrounds Tokyo today was originally constructed through this form of assistance. In 1990, Japan will pay back the last of those World Bank loans and finally come off the debtors list.

In 1989, Japan's foreign aid budget emerged as the largest in the world, overtaking that of the United States. Although it is still the second largest in terms of disbursements, when the 1989 figures are calculated they may show that Japan has become the largest donor in that category as well.

Global awareness of Japan's foreign aid clout was most visibly demonstrated during the funeral for Emperor Showa in Tokyo on February 24, 1989. Representatives and heads of state from 158 nations were present, making the occasion the best attended state funeral in world history. Many of those attending the funeral were from developing nations that either receive significant Japanese foreign aid funds or hoped that their presence would translate into a positive response when aid was requested. For Tokyo, the huge response to the funeral was the clearest indication of the importance with which many countries have come to regard Japan.

For many nations the provision of overseas economic aid is rooted largely in the colonial heritage of the western powers as well as in the missionary experience. Although the term *foreign aid* does not appear in newspaper accounts until after World War II, governments did transfer funds to colonial administrations on concessional terms under the rubric of grant-in-aid, or budgeting subsidy, until the dismantlement of the great European colonial holdings. Collectively these funds were designated as "infant colony subsidies."[1]

Paul Mosley defines overseas aid as "money transferred on concessional terms by the governments of rich countries to the governments of poor countries."[2] This would include funding for the purposes of creating economic development projects. As such, foreign aid has developed into a major enterprise: in 1985 aid constituted roughly one-third of all capital flows into the third world as a whole.

Post–World War II foreign aid programs trace their origins to the U.S.-sponsored Marshall Plan introduced in 1947. The plan, more formally known as the European Recovery Program, set the tone for the basic rationale of most U.S. foreign aid in the post–war period. The program was intrinsically linked to U.S. security concerns in Europe in the wake of Communist guerrilla activity in Greece and Turkey. In addition, America needed markets, and a flattened Europe could not provide this commercial outlet.

Using a rationale that would also act as the underpinning of Japanese aid policy fifteen years later, Under Secretary of State William Clayton said in 1947, "Let us admit right off that our objective has as its background the needs and interests of the people of the United States. We need markets—big markets—in which to buy and sell."[3] America would go on to pump $18.6 billion into Western Europe between 1949 and 1952. This was followed by similar programs for Asia and the creation of an institutionalized foreign aid program by the United States.

With the gradual economic and political recovery of Western Europe and Japan, the stage was set by the late 1950s for other donors to play a role in economic development. Increasingly, aid efforts became focused on the poorer nations of the southern hemisphere. While the United States continued to be the dominant donor, by 1961 the Development Assistance Committee (DAC, originally known as the Development Assistance Group) of the Organization for Economic Development Cooperation (OECD) would come into existence in order to attempt to coordinate donor activities vis-à-vis developing nations. Japan became a member of the DAC upon its foundation.[4]

The Japanese aid program developed out of post–World War II reparations to countries occupied by the imperial army. It is an aid program that, on the surface at least, has had seemingly little developmental rationale. Initially a minor aid donor, by the end of the 1970s Japan had risen to become the fourth largest in the DAC in terms of absolute volume.

This book argues that a key to understanding the Japanese aid program rests in its complex decisionmaking process. Four ministries have responsibility for each and every yen loan that is extended. The principal members are the Ministry of Foreign Affairs (MOFA), the Ministry of Finance (MOF), the Ministry of International Trade and Industry (MITI), and the Economic Planning Agency (EPA), which has the weakest authority of the four. Further, the system has two main implementing arms, the Overseas Economic Cooperation Fund (OECF) responsible for yen loans and the Japan International Cooperation Agency (JICA) in charge of grant assistance. The Japan Export–Import Bank plays a role in economic development through the provision of nonconcessional credits. Each ministry approaches the aid process largely from its own parochial interests and therefore policy is subject to intense bargaining.

The emergence of Japan as one of the principal donors has occurred at a time when U.S. and Japanese policymakers are wrestling with questions related to global economic realignment and burden sharing. As a result, the foreign aid activities of the United States and Japan have become part of a web of issues that are frequently taken up by policymakers on both sides of the Pacific.

The subject of this study is how foreign aid policy is formulated in Japan. As part of the process, I will explore how the United States exercises influence on the Japanese foreign aid program. In order to delineate the parameters I will primarily address bilateral concessional official development assistance (ODA) since heretofore this has been the preferred manner in which aid has been extended by many donors.

While this research is not based upon any elaborate theoretical structure, it utilizes several basic analytical tools. My analysis relies heavily upon the "bureaucratic politics" approach to understanding policymaking accompanied by several amendments which tie this assessment more closely to Japanese foreign aid decisionmaking. The American role is defined through the "transgovernmental relations" approach originally discussed by Keohane and Nye. I have nonetheless modified this concept in order to demonstrate the linkage between bureaucratic politics and transgovernmental relations. It is important to point out, however, that there are times when aid questions rise out of the bureaucracy and into the Diet, the Liberal Democratic Party, and the cabinet. How and why this occurs is also addressed.

Obviously, it is necessary to examine the policy "outputs" of the system. What is the role of the private sector in Japan's ODA policy, how do we characterize its philosophical underpinnings, and how has it changed since the inception of the program? I will discuss the regional emphasis of the government's policy including reference to the major country-specific programs. In addition, the functional aspects of the program will be addressed such as program versus project aid, tied aid, and local cost financing policy.

There are conditions that allow for a U.S. role in the aid process of Japan that go beyond simple political analysis. Historical and psychological factors arguably establish the mind-set that allows for this influence. At the same time, I must emphasize that the role of the United States in Japanese governmental decisionmaking is by no means unique to this bilateral relationship.

As a prelude to examining the process by which the United States influences foreign aid policy in Japan, we must come to terms with several factors underlying Japanese foreign policy. Sato Seizaburo has argued that there are five basic attitudes that characterize the way in which Japan has viewed foreign policy over the last one hundred years: (1) a strong sense of belonging to Japan and the Japanese race coupled with deep-rooted feelings of inferiority; (2) an intense concern with improving the country's international status; (3) a deep anxiety over being isolated internationally; (4) a desire to conform to world trends; and (5) an emotional commitment to Asia, which has resulted in a policy that emphasizes the region.[5] I believe all these propositions can be seen to influence the means by which Japan formulates foreign aid policy. Factors one through four have helped to provide the psychological climate for an American role in the aid process. Japan's wartime experience and its aftermath only served to deepen the nation's sense of inferiority and vulnerability.

Japan suffered total defeat during World War II. The collapse of the Japanese empire and subsequent eight-year rule by the United States helped to create a special kind of relationship between the two nations. This was abetted by the fact that the occupation was, in historically relative terms, largely benevolent to the occupied. Thus, a "big brother–little brother" relationship was established early on, capsulized in the Japanese term *amae* which describes a dependent relationship in which there exist mutual responsibilities. The big brother must be understanding and protective of the little brother. The little brother must have a feeling of loyalty to the big brother.[6] The essence of the development of this relationship was not only linked to America's strength compared to that of Japan; it was also closely connected with America's global position, which was second to none both in military and economic terms.

John Dower shows that the Japanese characterized the United States during World War II as a demon *(oni)*. The *oni* in Japanese folklore is evil but possesses the capacity both to destroy and to bear gifts. The United States thus emerged from the war with the power of giftgiver while being simultaneously dangerous.[7] The role of the United States in the Japanese decisionmaking process has been somewhat like the *oni*. When *gaiatsu* or outside pressure is applied to Japan and there is no domestic support, U.S. arm twisting can be greatly resented although not always successfully resisted. However, when there exist elements within the Japanese government that support the American position, the United States can appear as a benevolent interloper liberating the supporting ministry from an intransigent and conservative bureaucratic foe.

This relationship was augmented by the special security arrangement that developed after the occupation. It is a relationship very much like the other aspects of the "transgovernmental" connection between the United States and Japan that we will examine. Although there existed domestic opposition to the first and second bilateral security treaties, U.S. backing of the treaties' supporters was a determining factor in achieving acceptance of the military arrangement.

Trade relations emerged as the principal bilateral concern in the 1970s and 1980s as America's balance of payments deficit soared. The raw red ink coupled by what was viewed as an assault on key American industries stiffened Washington's negotiating posture with Tokyo. Threats of Congressional legislative action have had a major stimulative effect on successive administrations' efforts to exert pressure on the Japanese government to curtail exports from a variety of sectors. This pressure has been comparatively less visible on aid issues. And, of course, aid has been a far less visible element in Congressional oversight of the relationship.

In recent years, there have been a number of studies published that address various aspects of the Japanese foreign aid program. In Japanese, Higuchi Sadao has put forward arguments basically in line with the Foreign Ministry's view of foreign aid. While he describes the "four-ministry system," he does not take into account the fact that the Foreign Ministry's aid policy is often the result of the bargaining process with other ministries, nor does he address the role of politicians who become involved in the process when aid comes to be viewed as a critical issue.[8]

Dennis Yasutomo focuses on the strategic orientation of Japanese aid. The concept of "strategic" aid has ominous implications for some Japanese aid planners not the least because the term *senryaku* has a seemingly more bellicose connotation in Japanese. Given Japan's experience in World War II and the sensitivity of other Asian nations to the notion of any kind of Japanese strategic concept for the region, this term is never employed by Japanese government officials publically, although it is sometimes used in private bilateral negotiating fora over aid with the United States. Consequently the term lacks definition and Yasutomo is unable to provide us with one, we are thus left to wonder about the real intent of the Japanese aid program.[9]

Alan Rix's contribution on the bureaucratic decisionmaking system of the aid program in Japan has come to be regarded as the definitive work on the aid policy process. Rix identified the pitfalls involved in a system in which four ministries must struggle to formulate a consistent policy. He also suggests that this cripples Japan's effort to have a truly effective aid program, if indeed effective economic aid is the ultimate objective.[10] In several ways, this study reaffirms Rix's findings. Nevertheless, none of these writers have sufficiently taken into account the role of external influence. This book will show that the external factor often becomes an integral part of the bureaucratic policymaking process.

It was not too long ago that the principal underlying assumption of decisionmaking was that actors understood concrete objectives and pursued clear-cut interests. This argument forms the heart of the "rational actor" model. It also assumes that political leaders always or at least usually make decisions rationally. This suggests that decisionmakers strive to be consistent and to make the proper choices in narrowly and neatly defined situations. In addition, the most efficient alternatives are logically ranked according to relative value. There are times in which decisionmakers must and are able to approach problems in this manner. However, one must supplement this perspective with one that takes into account more of the day-to-day operations of foreign policy. Furthermore, many of the rational actor models were created in an age of smaller bureaucracy and fail to heed the proliferation of authority within a large governmental apparatus that has been the hallmark of the modern nation-state.

The bureaucratic politics model was developed in order to explain this kind of phenomenon in the formation of policy within the contours of a modern governmental system. The basic premise of bureaucratic politics stems from interest group or pluralistic theories. Pluralist models assume that politics essentially consists of competing organized interests. Government policy is thus understood to be the result of the effective access to political power that all interest groups seek to attain. As Stephen D. Krasner has pointed out, "interest group theories view politics as a vector diagram in which a series of pressures are brought to bear on the state."[11] In the bureaucratic politics paradigm, interest groups are replaced by government entities.

With pluralism as a basis for the disbursement of power within the bureaucracy, the political process becomes competitive rather than consensual. This is enhanced by a wide diffusion of influence and therefore bargaining. By its nature, pluralism lays the groundwork for the creation of a plethora of agencies designed to augment and articulate a tangle of policy interests.[12] A symptom of the effect of pluralism on the governmental structure is a strong sense of divided institutional loyalty which translates into the policy process. This is something with which all industrialized governments have had to contend through the expansion of specialized departments and agencies. Thus, the behavior of public agencies can be viewed through their own organizational interest.

The pluralist policy process has been described as "disjointed incrementalism." This system is constrained because opposing interests or organizations must bargain in order to achieve a mutually supportable position. Pluralist analysis also suggests that weak interests are unlikely to be effectively represented.[13] This is often a result of insufficient constituent support.

Related to the pluralist concept, Graham Allison's bureaucratic politics model hypothesizes intensive bargaining among decision-making entities. There exists no consistent master plan but "conflicting perceptions of national, bureaucratic and personal goals."[14] In other words, policy emanates not from a centralized, objective decisionmaker but from a conglomerate of powerful organizations with different missions, perceptions, and priorities.

Frequently in disagreement, these organizations compete against each other in attempting to forge governmental policy positions. In addition, prior to a major policy initiative, governmental organizations formulate a position; while smaller institutions must go through the same bargaining process on a micro level. As a result, the consensual nature of an ultimate decision must pass through several barriers even before a ministry's overall policy position can be publicly articulated.

At all levels, government officials are likely to examine any policy proposal, at least in part, to determine whether it will increase the effectiveness with which the mission of their particular organization can be carried out. Part of the driving force for bureaucratic conflict is competition over scarce financial resources. To bureaucratic agencies, a larger slice of the budget pie is also a reflection of relative power within the system. For these officials, the organization's responsibilities help to define the nature of the issue as they see it. This concept is colloquially expressed in the U.S. bureaucracy as "Where you stand depends on where you sit." Policy outcomes and decisions tend to emerge from the system and are less likely to be rational. Even though each actor is assumed to optimize his interests rationally, sometimes there is no link with rationality at all.

The more sensitive the issue, the higher it rises in the government. As a caveat to this observation, the higher the issue rises the more completely experts become excluded while senior generalists take over. During the crisis in the Dominican Republic in 1965 which ultimately resulted in U.S. military intervention, an American diplomat observed, "On Friday I was Dominican Desk Officer; by Friday night Secretary of State Rusk was; and by Sunday afternoon President Lyndon Johnson was."[15] During the administration of Harry S. Truman, the President had a plaque on his desk which read, "The buck stops here." This slogan has occasionally been adopted by succeeding Presidents. However, this ignores the reality that the "buck" is forged, shaped, and framed by bureaucratic subordinates. For every highly publicized decision made by a senior foreign policymaker, dozens of smaller ones are made by those in the system.[16]

In the final analysis, decisions are rarely choices between ideal opposites but rather between and among alternatives. Often the decisionmaker is confronted with only two or more relatively unpalatable options and must decide which is best for that particular situation.[17] Frequently these decisions are partial and incremental in nature.

The predominance of bureaucratic politics in formulating foreign economic policy has been noted by several scholars. This is assured for two basic reasons: first, the increased number of bureaucratic participants and other actors involved; second, as a result, unclear jurisdiction because international economic issues traverse domestic lines.

Unlike national security, which has a relatively undifferentiated impact on all segments of society, international economic policy is in itself subtle, complex, and often subject to intractable trade-off relations. For example, reducing tariffs raises income for the society as a whole, but it poses a threat to certain industries which are in relatively weak positions vis-à-vis imports. Because the interests of these industries will be brought to bear on the government in the form of requests for protection, this politicization of economic issues is likely to draw domestically oriented government organizations into the bargaining and debate over international economic issues. Economic interdependence merely exacerbates this politicization. The situation naturally encourages more bureaucratic participants to present different positions. As the number of participants expands, it becomes more difficult to establish a coherent policy. This is further complicated when the merits of a policy are ambiguous and uncertain, as is generally the case in international economic policy. As a consequence, a quick consensus rarely occurs despite a few shared images.

Legislative institutions, the public, and other actors can influence factors in foreign policy. However, it is difficult to see how they weaken bureaucratic politics. Rather, they can act as a catalyst in facilitating bureaucratic bargaining. Bureaucratic organizations have an inherent desire to build governing coalitions with those actors since they realize that actors outside the bureaucracy become a lever to strengthen their own bargaining power and position. I will suggest that this coalition building can also extend beyond national borders. Constituent strength is among the most crucial sources from which government organizations draw power.

Since the Japanese Constitution proscribes a major military role, Tokyo has had fewer diplomatic tools at her disposal than other powers. This has contributed to Japan's low international political profile in the post–World War II years and has limited most international activity to economic fora. Economic assistance has become an important instrument in this activity.

Aid policy formulation is intrinsically linked with budgetary decisions and also with determining how funds are to be spent. Bureaucratic politics is said to dominate the budgetary decisionmaking process and this is certainly true in Japan. Since the distribution of the budget is directly linked to increases or decreases of power and influence of government organizations, most organizations strive to increase their share of the budget. Prior to analyzing the various elements that comprise aid policymaking, let us examine several arguments related to Japanese policymaking in more general terms.

JAPANESE LEADERSHIP AND BUREAUCRACY

The Prime Minister of Japan is under more constraints and possesses less autonomy than the President of the United States. His position is related in part to the nature of parliamentary democracy and to factional politics within the Liberal Democratic Party (LDP) ruling government.

In order to attain his office, the Prime Minister must of course obtain the support of a majority of the Diet. Since 1955 this has meant that he must win by election or through consensus the LDP party presidency. In order to become President, the candidate of one faction usually must establish an alliance with other factions. After this selection is made, the formation of the cabinet is based more upon political balancing among the factions than on merit. As a result, factional leaders or influential politicians who are immediate subordinates or heirs to factional leaders usually preside over important ministries such as the Ministry of Finance, Ministry of International Trade and Industry, or the Ministry of Foreign Affairs. Therefore, the Prime Minister's cabinet is composed of formidable colleagues including political opponents who either lead their own factions or are senior members within those factions. This is in sharp contrast with an

American President's cabinet, whose members are clearly considered as the President's men and women and are regarded as subordinates. The President can and does overrule his cabinet members. While the Japanese Prime Minister exercises ultimate authority, he must weigh this against the potential political costs within the cabinet vis-à-vis his opponents.

The Prime Minister must, therefore, spend a great deal of time on maintaining a balance between the contending factions in the LDP. As a consequence, few Japanese Prime Ministers have formulated their own foreign policy ideas. Sometimes political factions have been identified with different policy orientations; for example, the Nakasone faction was considered more hawkish on defense whereas the Miyazawa faction was in general more dovish. But the main reason for the faction system rests in reciprocal personal political interests.

The Prime Minister's office is also hampered by limited policy research capacity. For this reason he must rely primarily on bureaucrats for specialized information and has been unable to develop much of an independent source of analysis. The three or four leading special assistants to the Prime Minister, in the fields of finance, foreign affairs, and domestic affairs, are selected by their respective ministries to represent them and serve as liaison. Because these assistants will return to their ministries after their assignment in the Prime Minister's office, their loyalty is stronger toward their institutions than to the Prime Minister. In fact, they often attempt to maneuver the Prime Minister to support their ministry's position on particular issues.[18] As Fukui has noted with reference to the cabinet as a whole, "A twenty-man body of politicians has neither the manpower, nor the information nor the skills and experience essential to the performance of policymaking functions."[19] Diet members also maintain few independent research staff members and must rely on the bureaucracy for important policy information.

The Diet's role in foreign policy has, therefore, also been restricted. Although there have been efforts to change this situation somewhat, most of the Diet's control over foreign policy is limited to applying pressure through debates, questioning cabinet members and ranking ministry officials, and issuing resolutions.[20] Furthermore, for all practical purposes, the Diet's actions are the LDP's actions because of the party's long-term dominance over the legislative process.

As I have argued, the bureaucracy is highly pluralistic and competitive. There exists a greater degree of delegation of authority by the legislative branch to the administrative branch. Career government officials play a larger role in making foreign policy than do their counterparts in the United States. While political appointees are a major feature in every American administration, there are few in the Japanese system. Only the Minister and Parliamentary Vice Minister are noncareer appointees to a ministry.[21] Moreover, few Diet members have detailed knowledge of a ministry's operation unless they are former officials of that ministry. Many important policy issues tend to be handled and decided ceremoniously at regularly held cabinet meetings, but in practice they are worked out through bureaucratic discussion and meetings which involve sometimes rather junior career professionals.

The Administrative Vice Minister, the top position for a career official, has tremendous power in terms of advocating the ministry's official views on policy proposals. However, on occasion the ministry is forced to yield to political pressures on highly sensitive issues.

These very characteristics, which are a vital aspect of the foreign policy process in general, also apply to the aid decisionmaking apparatus. Thus, Japanese policy formulation for aid is largely made within the government bureaucracy. It tends to be "routine" rather than "crisis" or "innovative" policymaking and, as such, produces few surprises and little drama. In short, battles are fought, bargains negotiated, compromises made, and decisions reached largely within the framework of the administrative structure.

Nonetheless, there are limits to bureaucratic power. In the foreign aid policy system because of these very same conflicts in interest, no single bureaucratic institution dominates the process. The Foreign Ministry is unable to claim the preeminent position on all policy questions related to aid.[22] It is at this juncture that external forces can be brought to bear to augment the ministry's clout in pushing a policy position through the system.

One of the weaknesses of the bureaucratic politics analysis is that it assumes little or no influence on policy other than from domestic decision makers.[23] The assumption seems to be that policy is forged and debated in an insulated domestic environment. Actually, officials in one state often share common concerns and interests with their foreign counterparts and may, at times, act in concert with these officials against organizations in their own government to achieve some common political purpose. In effect, transgovernmental coalitions form, which means that governmental organizations employ mutually supportive relations with actors in the other country to strengthen themselves in policy debates on the domestic front.[24]

Both transgovernmental relations and bureaucratic politics are particularly at odds with the notion that governments are unitary actors which exhibit the same kind of purposeful characteristics ascribed to individuals.

There are several motives for accepting transgovernmental intervention. In order to forestall action that might have an adverse effect on a government's interest, there may be a preemptive response. In this sense, we can define *preemptive* as delivering of a benefit to a government which may be about to affect the interests of the deliverer in a negative manner. The benefit delivered may be an inconsequential cost to the delivering nation both materially and in terms of bureaucratic dynamics. It might also include a perception by the benefit-delivering nation that some undefinable benefits may be received in return. The case of foreign aid is highly representative of preemptive transgovernmental politics. When Japan proffers an aid package at a critical period in U.S.–Japan trade relations, this is often an action that is perhaps easier for Tokyo to undertake than it would be, for example, to make concessions on a contentious trade issue. The Japanese government assumes that this will be received in Washington as a demonstration of Tokyo's positive intentions and sincerity.

Japanese government officials are often fully aware of the role of transgovernmental relations within their own bureaucratic system. It is not unusual for Foreign Ministry officials to urge the United States to apply pressure in order to bolster the Ministry's position relative to other ministries on many bilateral issues.[25] Higashi notes that both MITI and MOFA "frequently use [foreign pressure] for their own purposes."[26] And T. J. Pempel observes that the "Ministry of Foreign Affairs seems particularly ready to use the United States generally as an ally in advancing its interest against those of other agencies. Citing pressure from the United States and coordinating MOFA efforts with U.S. pushes and pressures provides the agency with a powerful weapon in domestic political battles."[27] A short examination of the effects of transgovernmental relations on defense and trade is instructive in understanding its impact on aid.

U.S.–Japan defense relations are rooted in the U.S.–Japan Mutual Security Treaty. The relationship has often encountered controversy in large part due to article nine in the Japanese Constitution which restricts the military to a limited defensive role. The clause was imposed on Japan by U.S. occupation authorities. Just prior to the eruption of war on the Korean peninsula in 1950, the Americans had a dramatic change of heart. The United States increasingly applied pressure on Japan to play a more direct role in its own defense, thereby contributing to American perceptions of regional Asian security. Following the American withdrawal from Vietnam in the mid-1970s, this pressure was intensified. In 1976, the Cabinet of Prime Minister Miki Takeo adopted a policy prohibiting Japanese defense expenditures from exceeding one percent of the gross national product. Under the Carter Administration, the U.S. strategy toward Japan was publicly to announce specific budgetary goals it hoped Japan would attain. Public browbeating sometimes created stiff resistance. The approach during the Reagan Administration emphasized private over public prodding. In addition, the Administration tried to focus Japan's exertions on its own defense needs and their compatibility with the U.S. strategic counter to increased Soviet designs in the regional equation. Dialogue through a number of bilateral consultative mechanisms was strengthened, the Japan–U.S. Security Subcommittee being among the most noteworthy instruments.

Naturally, in the case of the Japanese government, the Defense Agency has been the most supportive of U.S. requests for a greater military role for Tokyo. Among the ministries, Foreign Affairs is often an ally of the Defense Agency in interministerial debate over the defense budget. In contrast, the mighty Ministry of Finance is usually the most reluctant to support significant increases in defense spending. The ministry is generally supported by public opinion, which would seemingly prefer a deliberate approach to defense spending issues.

The Defense Agency's ability to prevail in policy debates is hindered by its far weaker stature compared, in particular, with the Ministry of Finance. As a result, the Foreign Ministry also plays a critical role, often supporting the Defense Agency. There is also the MITI–industry relationship when it comes to production decisions. To be sure, under the Nakasone Cabinet greater defense and security spending received substantial political support, and this helped to make the defense account, along with foreign aid, a consistent winner of increased budget levels. Nonetheless, while increased spending may be supported for different reasons, playing the "America card" can be a powerful trump in the hands of defense spending proponents should the need arise to use U.S. pressure. Moreover, it is not uncommon for the Foreign Ministry to suggest to U.S. policymakers that increased pressure is needed to break a bureaucratic logjam.[28] For example, in the FSX aircraft case, industry and MITI wanted to build a plane without U.S. coproduction. MOFA fought for a compromise and encouraged U.S. policymakers to be more vocal in order to turn the tide against MITI and its allies.

Similarly, trade relations have been a major arena of transgovernmental relations. With the exception of the Defense Agency, overt as well as subtle pressure from the United States involves some of the same bureaucratic actors in the Japanese system. Also, the Finance Ministry tends to play a smaller role in the trade debate. MITI, of course, has the lead on many trade-related issues but with considerable input from the Ministry of Foreign Affairs. Furthermore, ministries that normally are involved with domestic issues become active if trade relations affect one of their constituencies.

Trade conflict has been a persistent bilateral theme since the emergence of the 1969 rift over textiles, and U.S. pressure has had a key role in Japan's trade policy.[29] As the U.S. trade deficit with Japan descended ever deeper into red ink, the political overtones have grown. With the balance of payments deficit over $50 billion in 1988, comprehensive trade legislation was passed by Congress in an effort to increase the Administration's ability to apply pressure.

Pressure has taken different forms over the years but often involves a U.S. Administration warning the Japanese government of imminent Congressional action unless certain steps are taken to further expand market access for U.S. companies. As Pempel notes, Japanese governmental institutions used U.S. pressure internally in a number of bilateral economic disputes. When capital was liberalized, MOFA's use of U.S. pressure against the Ministry of Finance was crucial in the Foreign Ministry's gaining the upper hand. MITI was able to use the United States as an ally against the Ministry of Post and Telecommunications during negotiations over telecommunications trade issues. The Ministry of Education employed U.S. pressure against MITI over computer software bilateral trade disputes.[30]

The 1969–1971 textile dispute contained several examples of intergovernmental action in which the United States attempted to move the Japanese government to restrict textile exports. The Ministry of Foreign Affairs feared serious damage to the fabric of U.S.–Japan relations if the imbroglio were allowed to continue for a long time. In the fall of 1970, with negotiations at an impasse and with restrictive import quota legislation making progress in Congress, the Japanese government needed to judge how quickly the legislation might pass in order to decide whether they had to make concessions so as to prevent the bill's enactment. Ministry of Foreign Affairs officials concluded that Congress was likely to pass the measure and that President Nixon was likely to sign it. In contrast, believing the legislation was doomed, MITI did not want to make major concessions on textiles and committed themselves to protecting domestic textile interests. MITI officials concluded that a "Christmas tree effect"—the tendency of trade bills to attract a large number of restrictive amendments favoring various domestic interests in order to ensure the widest possible support—would force Nixon to veto the entire trade bill. Destler, Fukui, and Sato Hideo have argued that "what particular bureaucrats predicted would happen in the future was conveniently consistent with their substantive positions. The MITI optimism suggested that an adamant stance was appropriate; the Foreign Ministry's pessimism supported a readiness to compromise if a good negotiating opportunity arose."[31] On a prima facie basis, this may not appear to be a case of transgovernmental relations as there was no perceivable effort by the U.S. government to convince the Ministry of Foreign Affairs to conclude that concessions would be received since the trade bill would pass. The potential U.S. response was nonetheless used as a bargaining chip by the Foreign Ministry in order to move MITI toward a position more amenable to the Americans.

The Nixon shocks of July and August 1971 fundamentally influenced decisionmaking in Tokyo. Nixon's first action was the announcement of his opening to the People's Republic of China without having had prior consultations with Japan. The second step was the adoption of an import surcharge and the floating of the U.S. dollar. These actions together with the September 1971 ultimatum threatening the invocation of import quotas forced the deadlocked bureaucrats in Japan to make concessions to U.S. demands on textiles. These shocks represent the extreme role of the outside intervenor in Japanese politics. In a sense, this is the evil *oni* manifested metaphorically by Commodore Perry's *kurofune*, or black ships, which arrived off Tokyo Bay and practiced the first U.S. Pacific Ocean gunboat diplomacy in an effort to coax the Tokugawa Shogunate to open the doors for commercial discourse. In *Managing an Alliance*, Destler et al. have described the *kurofune* as it relates analogously to internal Japanese decisionmaking as "a symbol of the ostensibly unwanted, but irresistible, external force that can produce policy changes in Japan."[32]

In the same study, it is argued that there exist certain essential preconditions for the United States to influence Japanese trade policy. First, "the action or threat of action must by unambiguously decisive" and thought to be "unavoidable." Second, accommodation to the outside intervenor must have significant advantages over continued resistance; and third, there must be those in the Japanese system that are already predisposed toward accommodation and are able to use it rationally for their own bureaucratic advantage. These observations serve as useful guidelines to understanding initial approaches to the manner in which the United States is capable of influencing foreign aid policy.[33]

However, it is necessary to refine the three points raised by the Destler study. How specifically do policymakers react to outside intervention? Are there different levels of transgovernmental relations which can explain a variety of policy actions and reactions? Three distinct levels appear to be clear in analyzing Japanese foreign aid decision-making. The first is bureaucratic coalition building. That is, ministry A uses U.S. influence as a tool against ministry B in order to achieve its own objectives. In the foreign aid decisionmaking system, the Foreign Ministry is ministry A, using the "American club" primarily against the Finance Ministry (ministry B). Thus, the nature of bureaucratic politics itself—bargaining, conflict, and compromise—produces the opening for the outside intervenor.

A second level can be called *preemptive*. At this level, both bureaucrats and political figures can use foreign aid as a means of demonstrating to the United States that Japan shares both economic and security burdens. Japanese policymakers often assume that an active aid program can slow down if not brake protectionist trade legislation in the Congress. Aid is frequently an area in which the Japanese government feels it is easier to be responsive in lieu of trade concessions. The U.S. side, as well, particularly through the State Department, often refers to Japanese ODA during testimony in the Congress in order to stress Japan's growing global role and to cool Congressional passions.

The third level is direct pressure from the U.S. government on Japan, the response to which is general resistance to the U.S. position. In other words, when there exists no U.S. ally in the decisionmaking machinery, threats may be implied as is often the case in trade relations. With respect to foreign aid, this kind of pressure or *gaiatsu* in its more traditional sense is much less frequent in comparison with trade and defense. Nonetheless, we shall examine one recent important case involving aid and *gaiatsu* related to Japan's mixed credit policy.

As in the case with defense and trade relations, some actors privately suggest to U.S. policymakers that Washington should apply pressure in order to stimulate the Japanese decisionmaking system. The Ministry of Foreign Affairs has been characterized as "one of the deepest and most intimate friends of the United States in the postwar period, arguing consistently within the bureaucracy for close relations with the United States."[34] However, as a younger generation increasingly emerges in the Foreign Ministry which has no recollection of the Pacific war or the occupation, these new officials may be more reluctant to go along with the United States. Some resent what they view as U.S. interference and believe that concessions lead only to more American pressure.[35] Ironically, Japanese policymakers have at times unwittingly encouraged U.S. pressure by denying that concessions can be made to U.S. negotiators but eventually acceding to American demands.

As a result, some American policymakers doubt initial Japanese pronouncements that the government can make no concessions in a given policy area. This problem has begun to surface in the bilateral dialogue over foreign aid cooperation. Occasionally, Japanese decisionmakers will make "symbolic" concessions since they view American policymakers as often preoccupied with symbolism.[36] Foreign aid sometimes meets the symbolic requirements of a concession by increasing ODA levels to countries deemed critical to U.S. strategic considerations at minimal costs.

Bureaucratic politics and transgovernmental relations strike a persistent theme throughout this analysis of Japanese foreign aid policymaking. Foreign aid decisionmaking is highly complex and involves many conflicting interests. Using foreign aid as a tool of Japan, Inc., implies that there is a chairman of the board and consistent policy goals. This study demonstrates quite the contrary. And the very complexity of the system lends itself to transgovernmental coalition building.

2

Aid Politics and the
Decisionmaking Structure

I n Japan, the government bureaucracy continues to play the crucial role in foreign policymaking in spite of the emergence of
political authority in the domestic arena. Therefore, understanding the motivations, power relationships, and behavior of the bureaucracy is indispensable in coming to terms with Japan's highly frac-
tious aid process.

Conflict within Japan's bureaucracy over policy questions is certainly not a recent development. Many studies have pointed to the
fragmentation of foreign policy in the prewar period. Michael Blaker
argued in his study of prewar foreign policy that conflict made systematic foreign policy decisions difficult.[1] In fact, "particularistic
competition continues to be the basic feature of Japanese politics."[2]
These very same characteristics apply to Japan's foreign aid policy
system. As a result, the very nature of the process lends itself to
bureaucratic policy dominance.

Each of the donors in the Development Assistance Committee (DAC)
have systems reflecting various types of bureaucratic arrangements.
Four of the donors have aid ministries. Others have centralized aid

agencies located in their respective foreign ministries. But Japan, as Rix points out, "has no defined political structure for aid but relies on a dispersed administrative pattern to delineate political relationships."[3]

In Britain, the tax system has been characterized as a system that nobody would design and nobody did.[4] This comment could apply equally to the Japanese aid structure. We have noted that three ministries and one agency make up the four ministry decisionmaking system *(Yon Shocho Kyogi Taisei)* which has primary responsibility for yen loan aid policy. Each ministry's position on aid questions is largely related to its respective policy mandates.[5] The group is officially chaired by the Ministry of Foreign Affairs (MOFA), which tends to approach aid from a general foreign policy perspective related to perceived national interests. The commercial aspects of aid within the four ministries are represented by the Ministry of International Trade and Industry (MITI). Another principal is the Finance Ministry, which often takes a financially stringent position on aid issues. The final actor, the Economic Planning Agency, is the weakest and has a somewhat more vague agenda relating to overseas assistance. This structure considers each and every yen loan extended to developing countries. Grant assistance is the purview of the Finance Ministry from an initial budgeting perspective and of the Foreign Ministry which has sole discretionary power. Nonetheless, since yen loans still make up over fifty percent of Japanese ODA, their position is not as strong as it might seem. In terms of yen loans, however, the four ministry system in a sense resembles the permanent members of the United Nations Security Council in that each ministry has a veto.[6]

The dramatic expansion of the aid budget has prompted other ministries to increase their interest in ODA. In April 1989, the Ministry of Health and Welfare created an Office of International Cooperation designed to deal with the growth of the ODA budget related to the health aspects of aid directed at basic human needs (BHN). On agricultural issues, the Ministry of Agriculture and Forestry may provide advice or temporarily transfer personnel to one of the two implementing arms of the aid program. But these agencies are not formal members of the aid decisionmaking system and their influence is therefore marginal. I would characterize the four ministries as senior participants and the others as junior participants. The latter are almost always informed of basic aid policies rather than seriously consulted.

Because Japan's aid program has been almost entirely reactive, most specific aid decisions could be taken only after requests were made. The only time the system has been circumvented is when aid issues have been "kicked upstairs" and politicians have become involved. This does not happen often but has occurred either when there was a domestic deadlock or when there were unstable relations with a prospective aid recipient.

THE DIET AND THE PRIME MINISTER

Until the Recruit Cosmos scandal occurred, the role of the Diet in the 1980s was becoming increasingly more in line with its constitutional designation. This was particularly so since the Liberal Democratic Party (LDP) had become institutionalized partly as a result of having largely been in a position to fashion the political agenda for Japan since 1955. However, for most of this time, the bureaucracy has been the de facto operator of the policy structure. It has been argued that at present decisions increasingly are derived from an LDP–bureaucracy compound.[7] While this is more apparent within the context of domestic politics, it has seemingly not as yet been mirrored in foreign policy in general and foreign aid in particular. Foreign aid largely remains the preserve of the bureaucracy. McNeill reminds us that "politicians from donor countries are generally not particularly interested in foreign aid."[8] Not only have politicians seldom effectively interfered in the aid policy process, but in Japan's case they usually accord the ministries a great deal of respect. Nor for that matter are most Japanese politicians particularly knowledgeable about foreign aid.[9]

There exists no basic Diet-enacted law establishing guidelines and rules for aid along the lines of the U.S. Foreign Assistance Act.[10] While such legislation is occasionally proposed, it has also met the strong opposition of the bureaucracy as well as of segments of the LDP.[11] The Diet has performed only three legislative functions vis-à-vis foreign aid. First, it passes the annual budget allocation for aid and second, the Diet passed a resolution prohibiting aid for military purposes or to regions where it could worsen ongoing conflicts which the bureaucracy has in any case been unwilling to support.[12] And finally, the Diet must also authorize the carryover of undisbursed funds which is included in the budget, but this is done on a pro forma basis.[13]

There are signs that the LDP's interest in ODA policy has increased in proportion to the budget. In November 1988, the LDP created an economic cooperation ministerial conference which on the surface appeared to be a significant expansion in the party's involvement in the aid policy process. The conference is supposed to overcome bureaucratic tangles and expand the LDP's influence over aid policy. Its membership consists of the party Secretary-General, the Executive Council Chairman, the Policy Research Council Chairman, and other high-ranking party members. In addition to the heads of the four ministry system, it will also include, from the cabinet, the Cabinet Secretary, the Ministers for Agriculture, Forestry and Fishery; Education, Health, and Welfare; Labor; Post and Telecommunications; Transport; and Construction, as well as the Directors General for the Science and Technology and Environment Agencies.[14]

Some observers in the Japanese press have speculated that the real intention of the LDP was to expand the role of the party in ODA. In that sense, goes the argument, an "aid caucus" *(enjo zoku)* is emerging. The initial meeting took place on December 13, 1988, and lasted thirty minutes. Discussions with aid officials in the meantime suggest that the conference will have virtually no impact on policy.[15]

Opposition parties within the Diet are also very supportive of foreign aid although they are often skeptical of how aid is used (tied to commercial interests) or of its ultimate objective (satisfy Washington's strategic designs).[16] But in terms of support for the concept of assisting developing nations, the opposition parties remain favorable.

What is more important than Diet-wide discussions are the deliberations, when they occur, within the LDP, particularly in the Policy Research Council and one of its investigating mechanisms, the Special Committee for External Economic Assistance (Taigai Keizai Kyoryoku Tokubetsu Iinkai). Although this has probably been the most active institution on foreign aid in the Diet, it still does not have as much power as the bureaucracy. It was established in 1959 and, while it currently has a fluctuating membership which averages around sixty, only a handful are really active.[17] Committee meetings at which high-ranking bureaucrats must appear are irregular and consequently there appears to be no systematized oversight. When officials are invited, it is usually during times of scandal. In the words of one MITI official, "We get very little interference."[18] The committee's main position is to support the Foreign Ministry and MITI's request for increased aid funds against the Finance Ministry, which usually points to cases of waste in the program.[19] One Dietman who is a member of the committee characterized its influence as "almost none."[20]

Whatever influence does exist over aid policy can manifest itself in different forms. Former bureaucrats who have been elected to the Diet enjoy special networks among their former colleagues.[21] Through these channels they can lobby for aid funding for pet projects, especially if the official being pressed entered the ministry later than the Dietman and assumes the status of "underclassman" *(Kohai)*. Although these lobbying efforts are not always successful, they do occur.

Another source of potential influence on the bureaucracy from the Diet is the parliamentary friendship leagues (country-related *Giin-renmei*). They sometimes attempt to increase aid levels directed at the particular country to which they are closely associated. But in general their influence is not substantial. During the 1950s, when Japan began disbursing reparation payments to countries that had been occupied by the imperial army, there was reportedly considerable collusion between aid recipients and politically conservative financial interests. Periodically, accusations surface in the press that this practice still continues, but it is very difficult to prove and perhaps much more difficult to undertake. During the time of the Kishi administration when this was supposed not to have been unusual, Japan had no formal aid structure. With the four ministry system plus the implementing mechanisms that the system has currently, these kinds of highly visible and questionable practices are more easily deterred, especially in view of the international recognition of Japan's aid efforts. But the stories continue, such as the construction of a large luxury hotel in Bangladesh funded by OECF yen loans that was supposedly supported by the highest circles in the LDP.

One analyst sees factions within the LDP as having special relationships with certain developing countries and being able to influence the flow of aid funds toward their countries of interest. In this scenario, the former Nakasone faction established special links with countries in the Oceania region while the Abe faction influences the provision of aid to South Korea, Thailand, and Burma. The former Tanaka faction was characterized as having strong ties with China and Indonesia and, by implication, influence on Japanese foreign aid policy in favor of those countries.[22] This presumably carried over to the Takeshita faction. However, LDP members as well as officials in the bureaucracy play down the significance of factional relationships and their impact on aid policy.

I noted earlier the various contending factors that a Japanese Prime Minister must handle. These all tend to hinder his role as a foreign aid policymaker. In addition, foreign aid is usually not ranked very high on the agenda of most Prime ministers. Nonetheless, he can influence which countries will receive ODA, often as subtly as by selecting which developing nations he intends to visit. A Japanese Prime Minister almost always brings promises of new or increased aid on visits to these countries. In fact, the practice is known as *Omiyage Gaiko* or souvenir foreign policy throughout the corridors of Kasumigaseki.[23] But even countries slated for visits are often proposed based on perceived Foreign Ministry priorities.

In an effort to develop a more cogent approach to the security aspects of aid and defense, Prime Minister Suzuki established the Comprehensive Security Council based on a study undertaken by the Ohira Administration in 1981. It was, however, not designed to have a policy role but rather to serve as an open forum for discussing aid and security questions.[24] It is therefore, as characterized by one former member, more of a "debating society" with very little policy significance.[25] The aid budget, of course, must be annually approved by the Diet. Whereas USAID Congressional budget requests list aid by country or international organization, Japanese budget items are listed by implementing agency. After the Diet passes the budget, the ministries divide the funds according to region and country. Although the Diet has no veto power over which countries are to receive aid, it can make the bureaucracy do a considerable amount of explaining about why certain countries should be receiving aid. The Diet can actually have more influence over the aid budget prior to its formal consideration through private meetings with government officials.[26] The Prime Minister and the Cabinet can also increase aid budget levels if they have strong convictions as to the utility of doing so. As Japan has gone through three doubling plans and is in the process of a fourth, Cabinet-level decisions on aid levels have often been necessary to maintain the momentum against the more frugal Finance Ministry. Both MITI and the Foreign Ministry have usually welcomed intervention at this level since it means that aid budget levels will exceed the funding caps imposed by the Finance Ministry.[27]

Diet activity in the aid process appears to be most stimulated when scandal occurs. In this sense, Diet members behave not unlike their counterparts in the U.S. Congress. In 1986, scandals prompted Diet investigations of both the Japan International Cooperation Agency (JICA) and the Overseas Economic Cooperation Fund (OECF), the pillars of ODA implementation.

The extent of the corruption in the Philippine program was revealed after the fall of Ferdinand Marcos in February 1986. The Diet reacted by creating a special investigative committee. On the first day of hearings by the committee, Dietman Ito Kosuke urged a government audit of all future overseas contracts using Japanese aid funds. The Foreign Ministry rejected this proposal.[28] In general, many Diet members believe that how a recipient uses aid funds should be of no concern to the government unless corruption occurs. One Dietmember characterized aid as "the price Japan must pay to dictators to maintain political stability."[29]

Thus, Diet involvement in the aid process appears to be sporadic and relatively ineffectual. Diet members become most active when public attention spotlights problems in the system and fades when public interest wanes. The Prime Minister can have influence but usually confines his activity to major issues, occasionally breaking up bureaucratic logjams and prodding the Finance Ministry to establish a higher ceiling for the aid budget.

INTEREST GROUPS, THE PRESS, AND PUBLIC OPINION

White has noted that public opinion as an influencing factor on government action or inaction is most important "in those areas of policy in which the public at large is most significantly affected."[30] While Japan has no identifiable "aid lobby" advocating increases in foreign assistance, the percentage of overall public support is quite remarkable when compared with that in other donor countries. In fact, it can

TABLE 2.1. Japanese Public Opinion Toward Official
Development Assistance

	A	B	C	D	E
June 1982	40%	37%	15%	7%	1%
June 1985	37.9%	42.1%	13.3%	5.6%	1%
October 1988	39.5%	44.2%	8.5%	7.2%	0.7%

A: The Government should expand aid.
B: The Government should maintain the present level of aid.
C: No answer.
D: The Government should reduce aid.
E: The Government should stop aid.

SOURCE: Association for the Promotion of International Cooperation and Ministry of Foreign Affairs, *Wagakuni no Seifu Kaihatsu Enjo*, 1989.

be argued that one of the strengths of Japan's aid program has been public opinion, which suggests prolonged support as reflected in table 2.1.

The figures show that over 80 percent of the public supported the present level of ODA in 1988 and that there has been little change in this support through most of the 1980s. The extent to which public opinion influences decisionmaking is a debate that this study is not intended to take up but, as Watanabe Akio has suggested, the fact that the government has deemed it necessary to take the public pulse at all suggests "that society generally considers the problem important, hence policymakers cannot completely ignore it."[31] Public opinion polls are frequently taken in Japan and government agencies compete for public support. Until the 1980's MITI was the sole publisher of the annual white paper on foreign aid giving the public an inflated image of the ministry's influence on policy. Since 1986 the Foreign Ministry has competed for public attention with its own much more comprehensive white paper.

The Foreign Ministry is concerned about the potential rise of negative public opinion. A series of articles in several Japanese newspapers in the winter and spring of 1989 alleging misspent aid funds brought quick denials from MOFA lest the charges fester and create a backlash. Nonetheless, an October 1988 poll taken by the Prime Minister's office indicated that 67.7 percent of 3,000 people surveyed regarded foreign aid as a positive measure. But 41.1 percent of those polled felt that Japanese aid was not benefiting the neediest people while almost 25 percent believed that that assistance was not substantially contributing to recipient nations.[32] In an effort to raise the public consciousness of Japan's aid program, governmental officials created International Cooperation Day in 1986; it is supposed to take place annually on October 6.

There do not appear to be any conspicuous groups which oppose providing foreign assistance in Japan. While there exists widespread support for aid, this support does not appear to be very deep. As a tool for comparing public attitudes between the United States and Japan, it may be useful to characterize the differences between the two as passive positive versus passive negative. The notion of "aid fatigue" has not as yet occurred in Japan. Although there is no great public clamor to increase aid levels, unlike the case with defense spending, foreign aid increases are noncontroversial. The public apparently accepts the idea propagated by the Ministry of Foreign Affairs that aid is the price Japan must pay for smooth relations in a turbulent world.[33]

The operative word here is *price* or, as the MOFA poll in table 2.2 characterized it, *obligation*. In contrast to the passive positive view of Japanese public opinion toward foreign aid, attitudes in the United States appear to be passive negative. Most Americans appear to feel that the United States has shouldered the aid burden for far too long and that it is now time to look inward to domestic needs. The U.S. Congress was able to pass only one foreign aid appropriations measure from 1979 to 1987 largely because of the unpopularity of the program. Nonetheless, opposition to foreign aid does not seem to be deep, as witnessed by the rapid voluntary response to African drought victims in 1984.

Nongovernmental Organizations (NGOs) have only recently been very active in Japan. They frequently criticize the program for not being more sensitive to basic human needs in developing countries. But private donations receive no tax break in Japan since public charity has a limited tradition. The NGO community consists of roughly 270 members. While the U.S. equivalent, Private Voluntary Organizations (PVOs), act as virtual camp followers to USAID, of the $168 million budget used by all NGOs about half came from the Japanese government. As they have expanded, so has their voice. Japanese NGOs are now seeking a co-financing system along the lines of the U.S. and European systems.

Media interest in foreign aid was limited in the past but has noticeably increased. The press intermittently publishes reports on Japan's international pledges to increase aid and on critical foreign comments about Japanese aid. Some newspapers such as the *Asahi Shimbun* have run articles on aid which cite waste and the perception that aid is tied too closely to American security interests.[34] Also from time to

TABLE 2.2. Reasons Given for Providing ODA to
Developing Countries

1,853 surveyed in October 1987	
* Stability of developing countries and peace	42.3%
* Humanitarian obligations	32.7%
* Recycling Japan's trade surplus	26.4%
* Foreign policy	22.9%
* Security of supplies of natural resources	14.6%
* Interdependence	15.9%
* Prevention from international isolation	13.7%

SOURCE: Ministry of Foreign Affairs, *Wagakuni no Seifu Kaihatsu Enjo*, 1989.

time, NHK, the national broadcasting company of Japan, has run programs on the nation's aid policy. The media, like the politicians, are far more interested in the "bright lights" of scandal than in the mechanics of aid policy and therefore both worked overtime during the 1986 revelations about the improper uses of aid funds. Because of the relative lack of interest in the day-to-day operations of foreign aid, bureaucrats have been able to negotiate with very little interference. But this indifference appears to be changing as the emergence of Japan as the globe's largest donor has generated considerable press interest and scrutiny.

Of all interested parties, it is the business world that has the most persistent commitment to aid policy. This is largely because they can receive substantial contracts if policy is directed in areas that coincide with their financial interests. A certain amount of lobbying does occur in Tokyo, but it seems most effective at the recipient country level. The heavy infrastructural emphasis of the Japanese aid program attracts construction companies. In 1986, engineering consulting firms alone did 43.7 billion yen worth of ODA-related business.[35]

The aid system suffers from a lack of trained development specialists and frequently the private sector has moved to fill the void. The quasi-governmental Engineering Consulting Firms Association (Kaigai Konsarutingu Kigyo Kyokai) under the auspices of MITI is the leading edge of the engineering lobbying effort. ECFA subsidizes half the costs for preliminary surveys for aid contracts in developing countries, and their officials have constant contact with government aid bureaucrats. ECFA has fifty-six firms as members, which represents 70 percent of their overseas business on ODA-related projects. The demand for infrastructural projects has diminished somewhat, but member companies are hoping to improve their profit picture through implementing more technical assistance, which is growing at a faster rate than overall ODA.[36] The organization also sponsors seminars and research related to the aid system. For example, from 1987 through 1989, ECFA conducted a major survey designed to improve the foreign aid staffing system.

The domestic industry has been an important supporter of the expansion of bilateral Japanese ODA, particularly in recent years. This interest has been heightened since the yen's dramatic appreciation, which has made Japanese firms less competitive in winning bids from multilateral organizations, such as the World Bank, because tenders are usually designated in dollars. The World Bank reported that in the period from July 1, 1986, to May 31, 1987, less than one percent of the World Bank's bids were won by Japanese firms.

There are still very few foreign firms registered with JICA. Examples are SCAC Japan K.K., the Japanese subsidiary of a Paris-based firm which focuses largely on transportation services and has assisted JICA efforts in Africa, and Bechtel, the large American construction and engineering concern. Interest in Japanese ODA on the part of foreign consulting and engineering firms to a certain degree is a spinoff of the controversy over contract bids for the new Kansai Airport.[37] Nonetheless, large budgets attract business interests. The United Kingdom, in particular, has been aggressive in encouraging its consulting firms to bid on Japanese aid projects. In 1987, the Japanese government signed an agreement by which British Crown Agents would implement a sizable portion of a $500 million relief package that Japan designated for Africa. This agreement was renewed in the summer of 1989.

Direct lobbying also occurs in the Diet by Japanese firms seeking ODA contracts. Often, contracting firms will visit specific Diet members who in turn introduce them to the top bureaucrats responsible for aid policy. Lobbying and interest pressure, although present, are not the primary determinants of aid policy.[38]

Before I discuss the principal power centers of Japanese aid policy, it is important to understand that there exist different kinds of aid policy which require different mixes of decisionmaking actors.

THREE KINDS OF FOREIGN ASSISTANCE

Historically, most ODA decisions have been carried out through the four ministry decisionmaking system since Japanese aid has largely consisted of yen credits. As has been pointed out, this form of aid still constitutes over 50 percent of Japanese ODA. Nonetheless, there has been a gradual shift toward grant and technical assistance, although Japan continues to rank substantially below the DAC average in both forms of more concessional aid. The quality of Japanese aid has been a constant source of criticism from other donors. Normally, Japan provides mainly grants to least developed countries and changes the mix more toward yen loans with middle-income countries. Newly industrialized economies usually receive assistance from the private sector or the Japan Export–Import Bank at commercial rates.

Grant Aid. Grant aid imposes no obligation of repayment on the recipient countries and is extended under six broad categories: general grant aid, aid for fisheries, disaster relief, cultural activities, food aid,[39] and increase of food production.

The Ministry of Foreign Affairs exercises considerable influence over the provision of grants. The ministry, however, does consult on an unofficial basis with ministries that may have a specialty in the kind of grant aid to be disbursed. Nevertheless, the other ministries have no official power on this form of aid. The exception to this is the Ministry of Finance which maintains the ultimate power of the purse. Thus, even in the realm of grant assistance in which MOFA seemingly has policy preeminence, if the Finance Ministry does not accede, a prospective aid policy can be squelched.

Technical Assistance. Technical assistance consists of training, dispatchment of the Japan Overseas Volunteers under JICA, and provision of certain types of technical equipment usually used in training. MOFA also has considerable influence in this aspect of ODA through its supervision of JICA, but even this influence is watered down because of the structural nature of the agency, which is discussed in more detail toward the end of this chapter. The Ministry of Finance, again, has ultimate budgetary authority. Technical aid is normally extended to countries with the lowest income, countries that have debt-servicing problems, and oil-producing countries.

Yen Loans. Yen loans are extended on the premise that the principal will be repaid with interest. Interest rates are pegged below commercial rates according to the development level of the recipient. Many Japanese government officials and observers argue that loan aid encourages more fiscal discipline on the part of the recipients, although such claims are empirically difficult to prove.

Still the more prevalent form of Japanese ODA, all yen loans are subject to intense bargaining in the four ministry process to which we have alluded. The four ministry system is generally regarded as the central battleground for the Japanese aid program. While MITI exercises virtually no influence in the development of aid policy under the other categories, yen loans remain the last area in which MITI can wield some clout. Thus, if the other aspects of ODA continue to expand, MITI could gradually be cut out of the ODA decisionmaking process unless they are able to change the manner in which decisions are reached for the other kinds of aid.[40]

Each ministry approaches ODA policy in tune with its own bureaucratic interests, which are usually dictated by its constituency. Within each ministry, a micro policy debate often takes place over which bureau will be able to maximize its influence on macro policy. Sometimes, bureaus of one ministry will ally against the bureau of another ministry to contest policy formulation. Thus, the entire policy process is complicated by a confluence of competing interests.

BUREAUCRATIC ACTORS

The Ministry of Finance. Bureaucratic politics is one of the dominant features of the budgetary decisionmaking process. Since the distribution of the budget is considered to be directly connected to increases or decreases of power and influence in government organizations, most organizations strive to increase their share of the budget pie. It is largely due to this function that the Ministry of Finance sits at the apex of the Japanese bureaucratic power structure. In 1988, the ministry employed thirty-seven officials to oversee economic aid questions. In their eyes, foreign aid remains largely a budget issue although there has been a gradual internationalization within the ministry. As a result, the Finance Ministry focuses on the effectiveness of the aid program relative to its costs and is perhaps most acutely conscious of problems related to waste. It can therefore be said that the ministry views increases in aid requests in terms of conflicting budgetary priorities and generally urges caution in extending highly concessional aid terms lest other countries seek to improve their conditions. If it does not agree to raise the funding ceiling, there are few recourses that the other ministries can take other than to stimulate direct political intervention from the Prime Minister or develop a sufficiently strong consensus by relying on foreign pressure to jell the system.

Incrementalism in Japanese budget making is more prevalent than it is in the United States. Revenues that become available each year are portioned out in relatively equal terms. As a result, each ministry receives approximately the same proportion as in the preceding fiscal year.[41]

The Finance Ministry also requires that ODA not be increased in an unrestricted manner. Many of the newly industrializing economies (NIES) such as South Korea and Singapore, which have rather high economic growth rates as well as GNP per capita, are beyond the development stages of many poorer nations and therefore should be less dependent on aid. Finance Ministry officials rather consistently oppose aid for such countries, desiring to screen potential applicants for financial reasons. Finance officials often feel that MOFA bureaucrats are not stringent enough with recipients and simply accept inflated aid requests.

The three bureaus most directly involved with foreign aid questions are Budget, International Finance, and Finance. In the Budget Bureau, the Examiner *(Shukeikan)* in charge of MITI, MOFA, and the Economic Planning Agency (EPA) is directly responsible for budget appropriations. The Budget Examiner can have final say on the fate of many aid projects and thus exercises powerful authority. He views aid mainly in cost–benefit terms. In the past, most Budget Bureau staff members had limited experience or exposure to foreign countries in their careers and were referred to as the domestic faction (Kokunai-ha). But as Japan's aid program went through its series of doubling plans, the personnel in the bureau became more closely attuned to what other industrialized countries expected from Japan.[42]

Prior to the 1980s, Budget Bureau officials were rarely convinced of the utility of overseas aid. Aid policy was viewed only as a budget issue and Budget officials did not grasp the multiple implications of economic aid to less developed countries (LDCs). This was partly because Budget Bureau officials tended to perceive aid in day-to-day terms rather than examining the larger picture. Having been so preoccupied and imbued with budgetary constraints in the course of their careers, they were unable to appreciate the significance of LDC demands. The Bureau also viewed aid policy as a mere extension of domestic, public and social welfare policies since foreign aid was part of this overall budget portfolio. Since the late 1970s, international cooperation has been a separate account.

However, as I have suggested, there have been some changes, and in actuality the Budget Bureau has moved much closer to the views of MOFA on aid questions today. In fact, MOFA officials report that conflict can occur just as often, and sometimes more so, with the other bureaus in the Ministry of Finance. This is because, as the importance of ODA has increased, Finance Ministry bureaus with mandates more closely aligned with MOFA have developed a greater "turf consciousness" *(nawabari ishiki)* than before.[43]

The Financial Bureau is responsible for compiling the Fiscal Investment and Loan Program (FILP or Zaisei Toyushi) which is used as a supplement to the national budget. Sometimes known as the second budget, FILP includes government pensions, postal savings, insurance funds, and bond issues as well as a small portion of the General Account (Ippan Kaikei). Items that cannot be totally funded by the General Account are covered by FILP. It is usually two-fifths as large as the regular budget. The size of the FILP is determined each year along with the General Account. Ministries that wish to use the funds submit requests which are cut and then appealed during the revival negotiations period. Because FILP funds make up a significant portion of OECF's account, negotiations over their request can be quite critical to the OECF's overall budget.[44]

The Second Fund Planning and Operation Division of the Financial Bureau is in charge of deciding the allocation of these financial resources. At the request of the Budget Bureau, this division reviews each aid program requested in the budget preparation. It is often very concerned with the overall rapid increase of ODA expenditures. Both the Budget and Financial Bureaus are somewhat cautious over softening the concessionality of aid terms or extending the repayment period on loans.

In the past, the International Finance Bureau was viewed as the most liberal and amenable to aid requests. Staff members of the bureau were often referred to as the international faction (Kokusai-ha) of the ministry. Since the bureau is in charge of international monetary matters, it is quite concerned with Japan's foreign exchange and its balance of payments. Japan's huge foreign surplus has been, of course, the subject of severe criticism by other industrialized nations. Partly as a means of deflecting criticism, the bureau is seen as an advocate of increased aid spending aimed at reducing the surplus. The bureau staff also tends to regard tied aid warily and to support multilateral over bilateral assistance. The reason for the bureau's reluctance to support tied aid is that it cancels out the response to criticism of trade policy because of the increased exports generated by the procurement of aid-related equipment. In principle, under untied aid, non-Japanese corporations have at least a chance to outbid their Japanese competitors. Multilateral aid is untied and more easily and quickly disbursed. The combination of these factors helps to explain why the bureau supports untied and multilateral aid.

In the past, it was the International Finance Bureau that viewed aid questions more in line with MOFA. But as suggested above, this has changed because of the expansion of the aid budget as well as the bureau's policy competition with MOFA. Nonetheless, the bureau sees itself as a mediator between MITI, MOFA, and the ministry's Budget Bureau.[45]

Within the International Finance Bureau, the Overseas Investment Division is in charge of multilateral aid. The Overseas Public Investment Division is in charge of bilateral aid and usually acts as the representative of the ministry in formulating ODA loan policy in the four ministry system. The division will also coordinate the dialogue between the ministry's Budget Bureau and the other ministries. On the basis of requests put forth by MITI and MOFA, this division often acts to create modi vivendi and to strike compromises among the other ministry bureaus involved in the aid process.

Intrabureau discussions in the ministry take place on an ad hoc basis when a relevant issue comes up. On problems regarded as more important and intractable in nature, the issue is bucked up to a Ministry Council (Shogi) where it may ultimately be resolved.[46]

The strong pluralism of the four ministry decisionmaking system is reflected in the sectionalism and decentralization of the Finance Ministry bureaus. Relations between the bureaus can become rather hostile and it is not unusual for them to vie with each other over policy, each attempting to maximize its own interests. The outcome of the power struggle among these bureaus usually favors the Budget Bureau.

Annual budget negotiations among the ministries start in September for the fiscal year beginning April 1. Earlier cabinet decisions based on Finance Ministry recommendations set ceilings for proposals from all the ministries. Once all these proposals are received, the Finance Ministry chairs interministerial negotiations over the next three months in order to cut the requests down to more acceptable budgetary levels. During the final stages, the ministry reveals the amount of residual funds and the other ministries compete for a share. Since most accounts have been frozen for several years because of Japan's fiscal austerity policies, the principal contenders are usually in the defense and aid areas. This is because Japan has made international commitments to expand these roles. The Finance Ministry finalizes its draft by the end of December and submits it to the cabinet for approval. It is at this juncture that a political decision is usually made to increase the final account figures. Following cabinet approval, the draft is sent to the Diet for passage.[47]

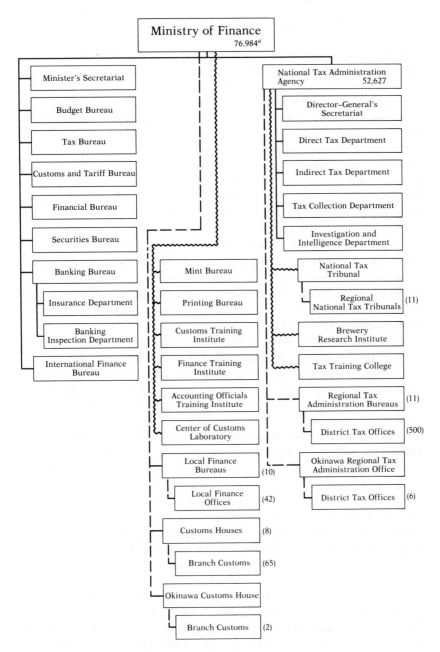

FIGURE 2.1. Organization Chart of the Ministry of Finance

Source: Government of Japan, Administrative Management Agency, *Organization of the Government of Japan* (Tokyo: Prime Minister's Office, January 1986).

The Ministry of International Trade and Industry. MITI has been a prominent actor in Japan's aid policy since the program's infancy in the 1950s. Aid policy formulation is largely the creation of the Economic Cooperation Department in the International Trade Policy Bureau. In 1988, the department consisted of forty-four professionals. They are rotated through and can remain in position a maximum of three years. The senior officer in this department acts as the ministry's representative in receiving requests from the private sector and in particular the general trading companies *(Sogo Shosha).* Trading firms submit development plans to MITI for specific projects sometimes even before the formal requests arrive at MOFA.

Other bureaus, however, can attempt to influence aid policy. For example, the Industrial Policy Bureau may make recommendations related to aid for heavy industrial projects. In other words, the bureau reviews aid proposals from the perspective of long-range heavy industrial planning. The Petroleum Department promotes aid projects that relate to their interests and works with the Economic Cooperation Department accordingly.

As a general rule, MITI determines the extent to which aid will help or hinder Japan's overseas market and domestic industry. Traditionally, MITI has opposed assistance to labor-intensive industries such as textiles for fear it would damage Japan's own struggling industry. MITI, like others in the bureaucracy, has been highly skeptical of the basic human needs approach to aid, preferring large-scale capital projects instead. Because of MITI's commercial emphasis with respect to aid, it enjoys the strong support of business circles. No other ministry has such an extensive and well-established network with the private sector as MITI. Not surprisingly, MITI prefers aid that will help to promote Japanese commerce rather than aid as a means of assisting the development of LDCs. If a major Japanese industry or trading company becomes particularly interested or involved in a certain large-scale aid project, MITI often becomes an ardent advocate for that commercial enterprise in the decisionmaking process.

MITI continues to be very reluctant to support eliminating the practice of tied aid lest it diminish Japanese commercial opportunities. Even as international pressure against the practice mounted, MITI advocated only cosmetic changes. The employment of the "LDC untied" aid policy heralded by the Japanese government allows only developing countries to participate in bidding against Japanese companies. The result under this scheme was that over two-thirds of all procurements still ended up in Japanese hands since the LDCs were usually unable to compete effectively with Japan. The practice of LDC untied aid has gradually been chipped away and accounted for roughly 20 percent of all aid in 1988.

Mainly because of MITI's interest in promoting Japanese commercial interests through aid, the ministry can appear rather insensitive to the needs of the "least less developed countries" (LLDCs). MITI has frequently been an opponent of increasing aid to Africa since much of that assistance is earmarked for BHN projects or emergency food aid, neither of which is on the ministry's policy agenda. In addition, 90 percent of Japan's assistance designated for Africa is in the form of grants rather than yen loans. Not being subject to deliberation by the four ministry system means that MITI can be effectively cut out of the policy process regarding African aid.

MITI's other priorities concerning aid recipients include countries that have an abundance of natural resources, particularly oil. Resource-poor nations are regarded as being of secondary importance. The implications of this policy as well as of commercially motivated aid is that MITI attaches remarkably little political significance to aid. Being an ally or particular friend of Japan in the developing world in a political sense does not mean that that country deserves special favors at the cost of the Japanese economy. Thus, MITI never opposes extending assistance to communist countries based on political grounds. MITI was a supporter of relations with the People's Republic of China for commercial reasons long before MOFA. In line with this position, MITI has wanted to conduct "business as usual" with Socialist Vietnam despite the fact that Japanese basic foreign policy, along with ASEAN and the United States, has been largely opposed to such an approach. MITI seems to feel less anchored by the importance of U.S.–Japan relations in a variety of foreign policy spheres than does MOFA, which retains the role of keeper of the bilateral Security Treaty flame. The emphasis on aid for natural resource security explains why MITI is such an eager supporter of assistance to the Middle East.

Changes in Japan's domestic economy and criticism of trade surpluses forced MITI to become more actively concerned with the structural readjustment of Japanese industry beginning in the 1970s. As a result, industries that faced difficulty, such as aluminum smelting and textiles, started seeking structural improvements through economic assistance. While MITI believes that these problems should primarily be resolved with industrial restructuring and modernization, aid-related sales of products from depressed sectors are regarded as a useful interim tool to ease the transition period.[48] Nonetheless, sales of commodities have often been made to recipient countries that were inconsistent with their needs. Yamamoto Tsuyoshi relates an example of this situation with Japanese aid to East Pakistan (now known as Bangladesh). Following a major disaster caused by a typhoon and flood, the Japanese Ambassador requested that Tokyo provide an emergency supply of cotton sheets, alumniferous pans, and rubber boats. In response, the government supplied blankets and chemical fibers (both were useless in the tropical climate) and dried milk (which was not used by the public at that time). Most of the goods were Japanese domestic surplus products from depressed industries.[49]

One long-standing MITI aid policy has changed. MITI had always opposed extending assistance to developing countries' export industries since they could potentially challenge the remaining Japanese labor-intensive industries. However, in January 1987, MITI Minister Tamura Hajime signaled a policy reversal when he pledged a broad range of assistance to Indonesia. The policy is designed to help boost exports of manufactured products.[50] Tamura also indicated in a speech in Jakarta that the government was lowering interest rates on yen credits. All of these changes are connected with the New Asian Industries Development Plan spearheaded by MITI.[51] Part of the bureaucratic significance of this action is that the Foreign Ministry, which usually makes aid-related announcements, had no perceivable involvement in the policy nor was there much support within MOFA for this undertaking.[52] Thus, we are presented with another indication of how Japanese aid policy is hampered by its turf-conscious aid decisionmaking system. A major aid policy initiative heralded by MITI involved very little planning with the Foreign Ministry, and for that matter the basic intent of the policy lacked the ministry's support.

MITI launched another aid scheme in 1989 which in typical fashion is aimed at promoting Japanese commercial interests. The plan calls for extending aid to institutes in certain developing countries to study the infrastructure, work force, wage levels, and needs relating to development. The conclusion of these studies will go to Japanese companies that might have interest in investing in these countries.[53]

But a community of interests between MITI and MOFA does exist on several major issues in aid policy. Despite or perhaps because of MITI's continued support for the commercial applications of aid and its intimacy with those in the business community interested in aid policy, the ministry has been a consistent supporter of increased ODA levels and has frequently allied itself with the Foreign Ministry to press this position with the Ministry of Finance.

While MITI and MOFA continue to view aid generally from two totally different worlds, MITI from the perspective of commerce and MOFA from that of diplomacy, both support increased aid volumes for their own purposes. As for MITI, there is concern that, if Japan does not provide assistance, other donors will do so and thereby will create their own markets, making it more difficult for Japan to compete.

As a consequence, although MITI is often an ally of MOFA in terms of absolute aid volume, it just as often opposes aid to countries that do not fit into what the ministry perceives as Japan's economic interests or aid that does not promote the private sector's commercial interests. This means that countries in which there is little Japanese private sector activity or are non-natural resource producers receive very little aid interest from MITI.

The Ministry of Foreign Affairs. The Foreign Ministry is regarded as the "window" for the receipt of aid requests from developing countries. MOFA is the strongest supporter of expanding aid and is also the ministry most sensitive to foreign criticism. The ministry derives its power from its broad authority and its overview function of the entire aid process as well as the management of diplomatic relations.[54]

MOFA has been in the forefront of the aid policymaking community in attempting to be innovative with overseas assistance. The Foreign Ministry is more likely to use aid as a diplomatic lever, as often with developed as with developing nations. Foreign aid policy within the ministry is developed and coordinated by the Economic Cooperation Bureau, which was created in 1962 and is the largest aid section of any of the ministries. Its several divisions handle loans, grants, technical cooperation, and multilateral aid. The Aid Policy Division is in charge of overall and long-range policy planning. Final aid policy responsibility resides in this division. The International Organization Division is responsible for multilateral aid projects. The Loan Aid Division handles financing aid such as yen loans. Therefore, this division has frequent contact with the OECF and presents MOFA's position at the Four Ministry Conference. The Grant Aid Division deals with grants and training programs. There also exists a division responsible for technical assistance and a Cooperation Development

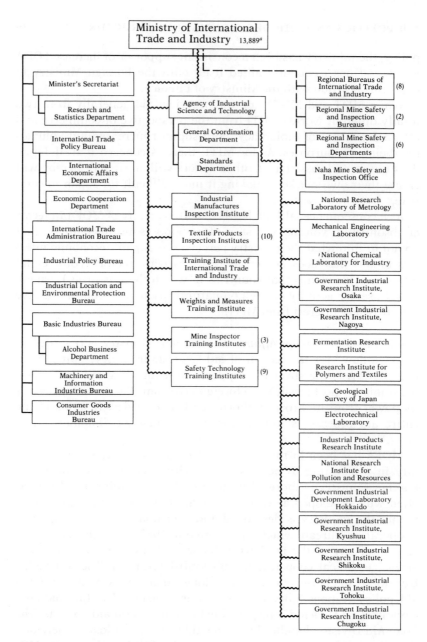

Ministry of International Trade and Industry 13,889[a]

- Minister's Secretariat
  - Research and Statistics Department
- International Trade Policy Bureau
  - International Economic Affairs Department
  - Economic Cooperation Department
- International Trade Administration Bureau
- Industrial Policy Bureau
- Industrial Location and Environmental Protection Bureau
- Basic Industries Bureau
  - Alcohol Business Department
- Machinery and Information Industries Bureau
- Consumer Goods Industries Bureau

- Agency of Industrial Science and Technology
  - General Coordination Department
  - Standards Department
- Industrial Manufactures Inspection Institute
- Textile Products Inspection Institutes (10)
- Training Institute of International Trade and Industry
- Weights and Measures Training Institute
- Mine Inspector Training Institutes (3)
- Safety Technology Training Institutes (9)

- Regional Bureaus of International Trade and Industry (8)
- Regional Mine Safety and Inspection Bureaus (2)
- Regional Mine Safety and Inspection Departments (6)
- Naha Mine Safety and Inspection Office
- National Research Laboratory of Metrology
- Mechanical Engineering Laboratory
- National Chemical Laboratory for Industry
- Government Industrial Research Institute, Osaka
- Government Industrial Research Institute, Nagoya
- Fermentation Research Institute
- Research Institute for Polymers and Textiles
- Geological Survey of Japan
- Electrotechnical Laboratory
- Industrial Products Research Institute
- National Research Institute for Pollution and Resources
- Government Industrial Development Laboratory Hokkaido
- Government Industrial Research Institute, Kyushuu
- Government Industrial Research Institute, Shikoku
- Government Industrial Research Institute, Tohoku
- Government Industrial Research Institute, Chugoku

FIGURE 2.2. Organization Chart of the Ministry of International Trade and Industry

SOURCE: Government of Japan, Administrative Management Agency, *Organization of the Government of Japan* (Tokyo: Prime Minister's Office, January 1986).

Division. Final administrative decisions are often left to the head of the bureau, the Director General, who must coordinate the intrabureau decisionmaking process. However, the principal aid policy efforts are usually carried out by directors and their subordinates. Some Directors General have had careers that have brought them in and out of the bureau. These officials, such as Matsuura Koichiro, who became Director General in 1987, tend to be more active in the policy process.

The Economic Cooperation Bureau gives priority to its policy interests, i.e., to increase aid levels in general, whereas geographical bureaus also tend to give priority to the interests of their constituents, which means the countries with which they must deal on a daily basis. Sometimes these interests are compatible but on occasion they collide. As is the Ministry of Finance, MOFA is highly decentralized and interbureau coordination is often rather ineffective. Further, MOFA has no supreme authoritative body such as a council which can resolve internal differences as do some of the other ministries. This sectionalism can and does hinder the analysis and evaluation efforts of aid programs. As a result, policy pronouncements are often articulated in rather vague terms.[55]

In the past, an assignment in the Economic Cooperation Bureau was not regarded as being very helpful to a diplomat's career. This was partly because being stationed in developing countries was less prestigious and also because Japan's economic aid played a relatively minor role in overall foreign policy. With the increase in importance of aid, the career image of the bureau began to change in the early

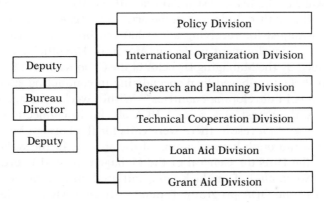

FIGURE 2.3. Organization Chart of the Economic Cooperation Bureau, Ministry of Foreign Affairs

1980s. In a survey conducted in late 1985, the bureau was ranked first as a place in which young diplomats would like to serve.[56] The bureau also does not seem to hinder subsequent choice appointments. The last five Directors General have moved on to important positions within Japan's foreign policy establishment.[57]

A ministry-commissioned special committee published a report in 1985 designed to address several aid policy questions that needed reform.[58] Among the most salient recommendations were: (1) Japan's aid should be less reactive and reliant upon recipient country requests. (2) More consideration should be given to local cost financing and project maintenance. (3) The creation of private sector–academic "pools" for expert consultation should be considered. (4) The use of NGOs should be expanded in implementing aid policy. MOFA has implemented these recommendations with varying degrees of success.

The Foreign Ministry's approach to South Pacific nations in January 1987 appeared to suggest a more vigorous aid posture and a change in the aid-by-request policy.[59] Already before the report's release there appeared changes in Japan's traditional aversion to local cost financing when yen loans extended to an Indonesian project allowed for up to 30 percent financing for local costs.[60] Also, the Foreign Ministry created a Philippine panel in February 1987 which was composed of academicians and government personnel and was vested with the task of formulating proposals for a new aid relationship with Manila.

Occasionally, plans to reform institutions in the Foreign Ministry occur on a more involuntary basis. This is surely the case with JICA in the wake of the bribery scandal that hit the agency in the summer of 1986. The affair culminated in the arrest of a JICA official by Tokyo police in August for receiving a 700,000 yen bribe in relation to an agricultural development project in Morocco. The official was allegedly bribed by the Managing Director of the Chuo Kaihatsu Company, a Chiba Prefecture-based firm specializing in conducting surveys for aid projects in developing countries.[61] Within weeks, the agency was rocked by the arrest of a second JICA official in connection with a bribery case. As a result, there were calls for the Foreign Ministry to institute a thorough housecleaning of the agency. In the wake of the scandal, the Director General of the Management and Coordination Agency (Somu-cho), Tamaki Kazuo, initiated an administrative inspection of the ODA program. Tamaki criticized what he viewed as MOFA's unrepentant attitude, complaining that they never apologized for the corruption scandal. Then Chief Cabinet Secretary Go-

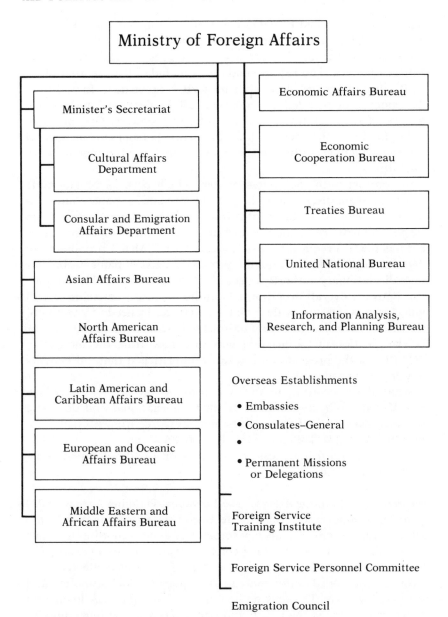

FIGURE 2.4. Organization Chart of the Ministry of Foreign Affairs

SOURCE: *Who's Who in Japanese Government* (I.C.A. of Japan Co., Ltd., 1989).

toda Masaharu echoed Tamaki's comments, citing the "closed nature" of the Foreign Ministry's activities.[62] The following month, JICA submitted a report to the Foreign Ministry suggesting ways to prevent similar episodes. The recommendations included the creation of an audit office under the direct control of JICA's president. In addition, the report recommended an increase in JICA's personnel and a clarification of responsibilities and discretionary powers. One problem highlighted was the need by JICA to borrow personnel from several agencies which, according to the report, contributed to management difficulties.[63]

In contrast with the United States, which permits considerable decisionmaking discretion in large field missions, Japanese aid policymaking remains highly centralized in Tokyo. Survey teams from the government are frequently dispatched after the prospective recipient has made a request for assistance. In 1988, MOFA proposed and MOF for the first time accepted a proposal to give Japan's Embassies more discretionary authority over aid. Although still small in comparison with the overall program, 300 million yen was set aside worldwide for new programs designed to meet basic needs in recipient countries. According to Foreign Ministry officials, one of the reasons for the creation of the account was to demonstrate the increasing flexibility of the program and to ward off criticism that aid benefits only Japanese companies.

What, then, according to MOFA, determines aid policy? Many Foreign Ministry officials commented that international and domestic circumstances as well as requests and pressures from abroad were most influential.[64] This suggests that MOFA's approach to aid has been, at least until now, less concerned with the developmental aspects of foreign aid.

The Economic Planning Agency. The Economic Planning Agency (EPA) is the least important and least effective of the four ministries in the deliberation system. The agency sometimes plays a coordinating role in aid policy and has been rather consistently supportive of expanding and improving foreign assistance, at least from a cost-effective perspective. The Coordination Bureau is responsible for aid policy and has two divisions. The first division is in charge of ODA loans and therefore supervises the OECF and participates in the four-ministry system. EPA's position in the process is often rather ambiguous and its influence is of no real significance compared to that of other ministries. The agency's principal power comes from, in a de jure sense, administering the OECF, but even in that capacity it is really limited because of the stronger decisionmaking competitors involved in aid policy formulation. In fact, it is because it is the weakest actor that it has authority over the OECF. At the time OECF was created in 1961, there was considerable competition over which of the "big three" would have the lead role. After difficult negotiations, the three agreed on EPA as a compromise since it was the least threatening.

One explanation for the weakness of the agency in the aid process is the long-standing practice of transferring MITI and Finance Ministry personnel to key positions in EPA. These officials tend to remain loyal to their home ministries. Many of the important positions in the Coordination Bureau are occupied by either MITI or Finance Ministry transfers.[65]

The EPA does of course have the ability to block an issue in the four ministry system although it never has done so. Nonetheless, the other ministries have on occasion taken their views into consideration, for instance, on lowering the interest rates on yen loans which would hamper an already debt-ridden OECF.

Implementing Agencies. The implementing agencies have been alluded to and are important to discuss not so much for their contribution to Japanese aid policymaking, which is virtually nil on a macrolevel, but because they are a reflection of this cumbersome decisionmaking system.

In the early years of the Japanese aid program, the Export–Import Bank was regarded as an important implementing tool. However, with the creation of the OECF and the Overseas Technical Cooperation Agency, the predecessor of JICA, its activity in aid became much less pronounced. In 1986 and 1987, the role of the Bank in recycling Japan's huge trade surplus again made it a potential actor in economic development. However, there appears to be some confusion over this role in the DAC. In reality, the Bank has never provided bona fide development assistance because its lending rates are not concessional enough to qualify as ODA under DAC guidelines. Consequently, the Bank's activities and structure will not be discussed here since it is not solely a tool for economic development.

The Overseas Economic Cooperation Fund. The Overseas Economic Cooperation Fund developed out of the Asian Development Fund set up in 1957 through the support of Prime Minister Kishi Nobusuke. The Fund was never drawn upon largely because there were no other

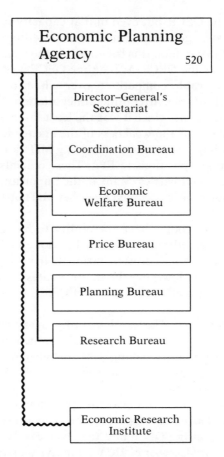

FIGURE 2.5. Organization Chart of the Economic Planning Agency

SOURCE: Government of Japan, Administrative Management Agency, *Organization of the Government of Japan* (Tokyo: Prime Minister's Office, January 1989).

contributing countries outside of Japan and so the idle budget was transformed into the OECF. As I have noted, due to bureaucratic contention, the Fund was folded under the weakest agency. Thus, as Rix has shown, the OECF was "emasculated from the start and made subject to bureaucratic interests rather than to those objectives of international development espoused in the OECF Law."[66]

Originally the OECF only extended loans directly to Japanese corporations engaged in projects in developing countries. In 1966, OECF provided its first government-to-government loan to South Korea.

Since that time, the Fund has been the backbone of Japan's concessional yen loan program.

The OECF has seven departments, two offices, and twelve overseas representative offices including one in Washington which opened in 1980.[67] In 1989, the OECF had thirty-six officers stationed overseas to manage what amounts to more than half of all Japanese aid disbursements. Although it is officially under the supervision of the EPA, the Finance Ministry exerts considerable influence through the budget process. Indeed, the OECF president in 1989, Yamaguchi Mitsuhide, as well as the immediate two past presidents, Hosomi Takashi and Ishihara Kaneo, were former high-ranking officials in the Ministry of Finance. The Finance Ministry, of course, also has authority over one of the OECF's principal funding sources, FILP, which further enhances the ministry's clout in the Fund.

OECF capital is subscribed through appropriations from the General Account Budget, also the responsibility of the Finance Ministry. OECF loans are directly connected to the national budget and operations come under close Finance Ministry scrutiny. The ministry attempts to impose the same concepts of financial accountability on OECF as it does on the Export–Import Bank.

The OECF has had to contend with serious problems in disbursing bilateral loans. Despite the fact that the Fund is regarded as one of the main tools for implementing the various ODA doubling plans, it has continued to be plagued by serious pipeline problems. By 1987, the pipeline had reached 1,690,000 million yen, over four times the total of disbursements in that year. There are several reasons for this dilemma. First, the OECF has inherent organization weaknesses—only 268 staff members in 1988. Second, the decisionmaking process, as has been demonstrated, is extremely cumbersome. This has slowed down decisions on loans. Third, there have been considerable cost over-runs on projects.[68] And finally, OECF officials complain about the inability to identify worthy projects by the recipient country. Some countries absorb yen loans more quickly than others and therefore the pipeline varies from country to country. It is doubtful that this issue will be solved in the short term. In fact, it will most likely get worse before it gets better. As the Japanese aid program mushrooms in overall terms, the problems associated with implementation will no doubt be exacerbated.

The Japan International Cooperation Agency. After a considerable political and bureaucratic battle, the Japan International Cooperation

Agency was created in 1974. Originally, serious consideration was given to merging the functions of the OECF with JICA's predecessor agency, the OTCA. In the early 1970s, many of the government's ministries were seeking to expand their influence in Japan's fledgling aid process. In 1972, the Ministry of Agriculture and Forestry requested funds for the creation of a new agency to promote agricultural development in the third world. MITI, in 1973, also requested funds for the establishment of an aid-related agency under its guidance. The EPA opposed the addition of two agencies that would com-

FIGURE 2.6. JICA Departments and Source of Department Heads

JICA: Japan International Cooperation Agency
MOFA: Ministry of Foreign Affairs
MOF: Ministry of Finance
MPT: Ministry of Posts and Telecommunications
M&W: Ministry of Health and Welfare
MAFF: Ministry of Agriculture, Forestries, and Fisheries
MITI: Ministry of International Trade and Industry

Department	Ministry or Agency
General Affairs	MOFA
Personnel	JICA
Finance and Accounting	MOF
Planning	MOFA
Procurement	JICA
Training Affairs	JICA
Experts Assignments	JICA
Social Development Cooperation	MPT
Medical Cooperation	M&W
Agricultural, Forestry, and Fisheries Planning and Survey	MAFF
Emigration	JICA
Agriculture Development Cooperation	MAFF
Forestry and Fisheries Development Cooperation	MAFF
Mining and Industrial Planning	MITI
Mining and Industrial Development	MITI
Grant Aid Planning and Study Dept.	JICA
Grant Aid Project Management Department Japan Overseas Cooperation Volunteers	MOFA

Source: JICA

pete with the OECF. MOFA sided with the EPA because it was concerned over conflict with the OTCA. However, the Foreign Ministry turned the discussion around and argued that the competition over aid administration was obvious evidence for the need to create a unified aid structure. MOFA, in consultations with the LDP, hoped that the answer to a unified aid system would come in the form of scrapping the OTCA and replacing it with JICA which would be under the Foreign Ministry's control. At one point in the debate, some quarters in the LDP wanted to set up a new ministerial post for economic cooperation. However, then Foreign Minister Ohira Masayoshi opposed the proposal, warning against "double diplomacy" and concerned about interference with his own portfolio. This idea was eventually rejected and a Kokusai Kyoryoku Jigyodan or JICA was agreed upon as a compromise measure which would incorporate OTCA as well as the Japan Emigration Services. The outcome meant that the functions and responsibilities of the OTCA were basically transferred to JICA.[69] The objective of creating an aid ministry or even a more modest Japanese version of the U.S. Agency for International Development was dealt a fatal blow once again by the politics of competing bureaucratic interests. The controversial birth of JICA in microcosm represented all of the problems endemic in Japan's aid system, and this experience has also acted to discourage serious efforts to reform the program despite realization by many Japanese policymakers that it hampers Tokyo's role as a major donor.

As a child of MOFA, JICA presidents traditionally come from the Foreign Affairs Ministry. The agency is the principal implementor of grants and technical assistance, a role that could grow if Japan moves in the direction of other donors and provides a larger ratio of grants.

Technical assistance is the focus of human resources development aid which has increased substantially in recent years. Despite increases in 1987, Japan's net disbursements for technical assistance amounted to $853 million, which ranked fourth behind France, the United States, and West Germany.[70] Another aspect of technical assistance is training, which Japan has doubled since 1980.

One of the most serious problems facing JICA is the extremely large number of "parachute staff," that is, staff members who are designated to head the various offices and departments that make up JICA's structure. Of the eighteen departments in the Agency, JICA career staffers manage to control only seven of the departments. Six other ministries retain control of the other eleven. This has a detrimental effect upon the morale of the career staff members; it limits opportunities for advancement since much of their organization appears to be controlled by outsiders. The internal competition among the department heads has heated in almost direct proportion to the increase in aid funds.[71] Thus, JICA continues to echo the problems in the entire Japanese aid decisionmaking system.

Complicating the decisionmaking process is the fact that there exists almost no cooperation between JICA and OECF in the field. One OECF official told me, "We get better cooperation with U.S.A.I.D. than we do with JICA."[72] A JICA representative noted that USAID often advises JICA of OECF activities in the field.[73]

Abundant Yen, Small Staff. The staffing problem that we see in the OECF and JICA is mirrored throughout the Japanese aid system. While the system is still heavily focused on infrastructure, which is not as labor-intensive as those of other donors that emphasize technical cooperation it is nonetheless an issue over which the Ministry of Foreign Affairs has often expressed concern. Between 1977 and 1987, Japan's ODA increased by 5.2 times while spending per staff expanded 350 percent. In other words, whereas in 1977 aid spending was $1.56 million per staff person, it had reached $5.34 million in 1987. Figure 2.7 compares the spending and staff levels of both USAID and the Japanese aid program between 1977 and 1988.

The conflict over the system that this chapter examines is the principal reason for a lack of consistency in Japanese foreign aid policy. Fukui has noted that Japan's foreign policy apparatus lacks the "internal unity and solidarity that would be necessary [for one ministry] to totally dominate the . . . decisionmaking process."[74] And

TABLE 2.3. Annual ODA Disbursements and Personnel Levels
1982–1988

Personnel	1982	1983	1984	1985	1986	1987	1988
Japan	1287	1324	1372	1424	1452	1496	1539
United States	5406	5273	5168	4904	4668	4667	4695
Disbursements (in $ million)							
Japan	3023	3761	4319	3797	5634	7454	9134
United States	8202	7992	8711	9403	9564	8945	9777

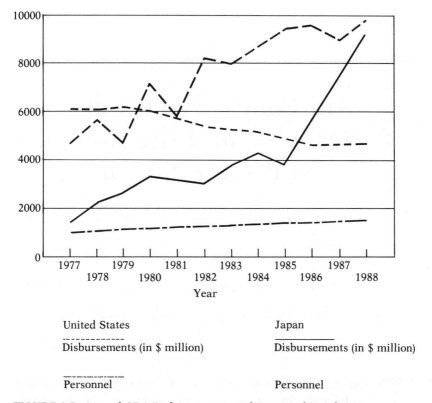

United States

Disbursements (in $ million)

Japan

Disbursements (in $ million)

Personnel

Personnel

FIGURE 2.7. Annual ODA Disbursements and Personnel Levels

John Campbell has argued that "significant policy conflict does occur with notably less conflict resolution than meets the eye."[75] Policy-making in the aid system is consistent with these observations and it is in large part due to this dearth of cohesion that policy emerges in the manner described in the following chapter.

3

Aid Policy Evolution, Philosophy, and the Role of the Private Sector

The speed of Japan's advance toward the pinnacle of aid donors caught many by surprise, including Japanese aid policymakers. In addition to the steady increases in aid above all other budget accounts, two other factors allowed Japan to forge to the top. First, since ODA figures are calculated in dollars at the DAC, the appreciation of the yen since 1985 had the effect of magnifying expenditures. Second was the drop in U.S. foreign assistance in response to budgetary red ink.

In spite of Tokyo's aid volume increases, which have been favorably received in the DAC, several policies continue to draw criticism. Although the share of low-income countries that are the beneficiaries of Japanese aid is above the DAC average, that of least-developed countries is below the average. Ironically, this is because Japan has overwhelmingly focused its ODA on Asia. The DAC continues to urge Japan to extend more assistance to African countries where structural adjustment support is urgently needed.

Japan has also been the target of criticism for what is viewed as its policy of tying aid to commercial interests. Additionally, there is concern over Japan's aid management capacity which has not appreciably altered since the early 1970s, making it questionable whether the system can handle its expanded role.[1]

The aid program evolved through several stages. Conceptually, assisting developing countries in the postwar period began for Japan with the extension of reparation payments to many, but not all, of the nations that had been victimized by Japan's aggressive war in Asia. Japan concluded reparation agreements with Burma in 1955, the Philippines in 1956, and Indonesia in 1958. Even in these cases, influence from the United States had a role. In the face of pressure from Secretary of State John Foster Dulles to extend reparation payments, Prime Minister Yoshida Shigeru argued that Japan could ill afford any indemnities.

But reparations were provided and later technical assistance. As early as 1954, Japan became a donor through the Colombo Plan with a $50,000 contribution. Although formal reparation payments were not provided to Laos and Cambodia, both countries started receiving cash grants from Japan in 1959. India received the first yen loan as part of a contribution to a World Bank Consortium in 1958. Of all the major nations in Asia, China, which suffered more from the Japanese sword than any other, received no reparations. Throughout most of the post–World War II period, Japan's policy toward China was tangled in the Sino-American estrangement. In addition, during much of the 1950s, China remained embroiled in revolutionary fervor and hostile toward a Japan that was so firmly in the American camp. The result was that China did not put forward any claims on Japan. Japanese government officials say that the very generous aid levels that China has received in the 1980s are in part due to the lack of a postwar reparations accord between the countries.

The fact that most of the reparation payments were focused on Southeast Asian countries strengthened the regional bias of Japanese aid for the future. The loss of Northeast Asia as a source for raw materials in the postwar period further enhanced Japan's aid emphasis on Southeast Asia.[2]

With the initiation of these different forms of assistance, the term "economic cooperation" (keizai kyoryoku) became the catchall description for Japan's economic relations with the countries of Asia. The term aid was never employed. Thus, a great deal of confusion developed in the West over what constituted development assistance and what was designed to further Japanese commercial interests. The truth is, as Japan moved away from reparations, all aid was becoming

an explicit tool to promote exports. From the time of the first publication of MITI's white paper on foreign aid in 1958, which was the
only government statement on aid until 1978, Japan unabashedly
linked aid with trade promotion.[3]

As early as 1960, the MITI aid white paper referred to economic
cooperation toward developing countries as the "mission of the world's
industrial nations."[4] According to the paper, Japan would cooperate
in this mission not through concessional aid but by extending commercially tied loans and increasing investment overseas. Thus, economic cooperation was directed toward developing Japan rather than
third-world nations. Also, 1960 saw Japan's admittance into the Development Assistance Group which was later renamed the Development Assistance Committee. Japan's entry into the DAC took place
before she was admitted into the Organization for Economic Cooperation and Development (OECD), which was accomplished through
American sponsorship in spite of the objections of several European
nations.

There was probably another reason why the idea of aid was slow
in being accepted. I would suggest that there is no great tradition of
charity in Japan. This is also reflected in the meager size of the
domestic welfare state, smallest among all industrialized nations. In
the West, besides the colonial experience, the roots of foreign aid go
back to the activities of missionaries in the nineteenth century. To
this day, organizations that remain affiliated in some manner with
Christian causes retain the strongest support for foreign aid in the
West. Many of these organizations make up the PVO community in
the United States and Western Europe. In Japan, this community is
still in its infancy although the 1985 Foreign Ministry report recommended an expansion of their activities.

The overwhelmingly commercially self-serving approach of foreign
aid changed in the 1970s. The real jolt to the system was the 1973 oil
crisis. Prior to the Yom Kippur War, Japan had loyally followed
strong American support for Israel just as many nations in Europe
had. Following the war when the Organization of Petroleum Export-
ing Countries (OPEC) placed an oil embargo on the American allies
that had supported Israel at least morally, Japan's heavy dependence
on energy imports made her most vulnerable.

With very few diplomatic and no military tools in her portfolio,
OPEC quite literally had Japan over a barrel. Crisis decisionmaking
for one of the very few times in postwar history was triggered in
Tokyo, which meant that policies came from the political leadership.

It was decided for the first time to use aid as a diplomatic weapon to restore neutralist credibility in the Arab world. Thus, in December 1973, the month following the embargo's announcement, the Miki Takeo mission was born. Miki, who would the following year become Premier, was dispatched by Prime Minister Tanaka Kakuei to the key oil-producing nations in the region in order to hand out aid packages to placate Arab anger over Japanese compliance with U.S. policy in the region. The mission brought $3 billion in aid pledges to regional oil-producing states and a "distancing" policy toward Israel that still continues.[5]

From this experience, Japan became far more concerned about the stability of her natural resources. Foreign Ministry and MITI officials could effectively join forces on many aid issues to press the ever recalcitrant Finance Ministry to release the budgetary purse strings for aid based on national security. Key energy-producing countries and even nations bordering important natural resource routes became candidates for Japanese foreign assistance. But as the crisis abated, so did interest in foreign aid at the highest reaches of government. Policymaking reverted again to the bureaucratic trenches although concerns about natural resource diplomacy remained. Nonetheless, the consciousness for aid both in the Foreign Ministry and the political world was sufficiently raised that the idea of using it as some kind of foreign policy device was firmly implanted.

The pattern of virtual complete aid concentration on Asia remained throughout the 1960s and the very first years of the 1970s. In 1971, 98.4 percent of Japanese aid went to Asia. The following year, the figure dropped to 88.1 percent, and by the late 1970s the percentage of Japanese ODA provided to the region stabilized between 65 and 70 percent. This gave rise to the 7:1:1:1 regional distribution doctrine unofficially adopted by the Foreign Ministry. In other words, the 70 percent of aid would be earmarked for Asia and 10 percent each for Latin America, the Middle East and Africa.

A succession of events in the late 1970s represent the turning point in Japan's march toward global aid volume leadership. In 1977, Prime Minister Fukuda Takeo announced the first of a series of aid-doubling plans. Despite Fukuda's strong connections with the Ministry of Finance because of his former career, the first doubling plan represented a victory for the Foreign Affairs Ministry. While MOFA was engaged in bureaucratic combat with Finance over a dramatic expansion of aid volume, MITI was attacking the ministry on its flank in order to make sure that Japan did not follow through on several aid untying plans that had been put forward in response to international pressure. MITI was also opposed to MOFA's desire to use aid increasingly as a political tool rather than as a commercial device. International events in 1978 and 1979, however, played right into the hands of MOFA's aid planners.

The Iranian revolution as well as the Vietnamese invasion of Cambodia and later the Soviet War in Afghanistan visibly demonstrated for many in Japan's ministries the direct connection between political stability and secure markets. The dramatic petroleum price increases following the hasty getaway of Iran's Shah reinforced sensitivities over secure resources which had first confronted Japan in the first oil shock. The Vietnamese invasion potentially destabilized all of Southeast Asia, and Soviet Red Army troops in Kabul meant a crisis in United States–Soviet relations with all its attendant dangers.

These events collectively raised the consciousness of strategic interests and encouraged the Ministry of Foreign Affairs to promote a policy more closely aligned with security concerns. How these security interests were to be defined posed another problem. The Finance Ministry remained unconvinced while MITI's definition of security interests remained narrowly focused on the potential impact of international political disruption on the Japanese economy. MOFA officials wanted to pursue a more broadly based policy linked to a certain extent to western security interests. Nonetheless, for domestic consumption purposes, the Foreign Ministry defined the issues as relating to Japanese rather than western security. In a sense, the government described the application of this policy differently to different audiences. To this day, the Ministry has officially not admitted the use of aid with any strategic connotation. As we shall explore in greater detail later, U.S. pressure played an important role in getting Japan to extend aid to countries of importance to western interests as determined largely in Washington.

Continuing pressure on Japan in the DAC to extend more grants oriented toward basic human needs began to have some effect in the early 1980s. Again, MITI and the Finance Ministry opposed emphasis on this form of assistance. MOFA frequently had to wield the "America card" in internal deliberations on the kind of aid projects that would be promoted. While capital projects continued to dominate Japan foreign assistance, Prime Minister Suzuki formally introduced a Japanese BHN approach during a January 1981 speech in Bangkok. In the speech, the Prime Minister indicated that four sectors would receive increasing Japanese government aid support: (1) rural and agricultural development, (2) development of new and renewable energy, (3) human resource development (technical assistance), and (4) promotion of small and medium-sized businesses in developing countries.[6] Throughout this evolutionary process, there have been many changes in policy subject to the pushes and pulls of Japanese bureaucratic politics. Nonetheless, several themes, sometimes contradictory, often poorly articulated, remain constant.

PHILOSOPHY

Government documents sometimes indicate that it is Japan's duty *(Nihon no gimu)* to help poorer countries. As Rix has suggested, this along with other arguments implies that aid is a burden that Japan must bear. Other documents reinforce this impression by referring to aid as the "cost" Japan must pay to help maintain peace. These costs require efforts *(doryoku)* to extend ODA but only when it is economically feasible *(keizairyoku ni miatta).*[7]

Policymakers in Tokyo have often argued that Japan has a special role to play vis-à-vis developing countries as a relatively recent member of the industrial club of nations. The idea of being a "bridge" between North and South is a concept often espoused by Japanese decisionmakers, although specifically what this kind of role entails is never fully explained.

One prominent argument as to the basic tenet of Japanese ODA is that the program is aimed at creating "self-reliance" in developing countries.[8] We can see this approach translated through yen loans which are supposed, as mentioned, to impose discipline on the recipient. In contrast to the U.S. aid program which is more prescriptive in nature, Japan provides fewer guidelines to recipient countries as to how project aid is to be implemented. Japan is seemingly reluctant when extending assistance to encourage its aid recipients to take steps to improve economic efficiency. Tokyo regards such activity as meddling in the domestic affairs of aid recipients. The result of this hands-off approach is that Japanese ODA funds can sometimes be misused. This is compounded by the fact that the ODA program has little experience in project evaluation.

Rather than the needs of the aid recipient countries, Japan's domestic and security needs have figured most conspicuously in policy. In addition, there appears to be a great concern with recognition of Japan's efforts in providing aid not necessarily from developing countries but rather from other donors. Consequently, Japan's foreign aid motives seemingly embrace many of Japan's self-perceived insecurities in the world. Again, as Rix has argued, policy appears "blatantly defensive in nature — defensive of Japan's reputation, of its economic diplomacy, of its resource supplies, its overseas investments and presence, its trade."[9] For this reason, aid policy is sometimes subject to pressures to adapt to perceived changing circumstances brought on by external factors.

The Japanese government has adopted several slogans designed to explain the basic direction of Japanese foreign policy in the post–World War II period. For a time, the term "omnidirectional foreign policy" (zenhoui gaikou) was employed. Although it is practically devoid of meaning in English since theoretically all foreign policy is "omnidirectional," it was supposed to describe a policy of equal benevolence toward all countries, East and West. Given the global alignment and Japan's security relationship with the United States, it was a description never taken very seriously by Tokyo's friends and foes alike. It also did not explicitly address Japan's relationship with developing countries.

"Comprehensive security," which was the slogan given to more strategically oriented aid, was a term almost equally obscure in meaning. Along with defense and diplomacy, aid was designated as a foreign policy tool. As I noted before, when Japanese policymakers meet with their American counterparts, the potential strategic nature of aid is emphasized. When this same policy is described domestically, the strategic connection is vociferously denied. This is in sharp contrast with the American aid program which tends to couch aid in humanitarian terms and in cold war language.[10] The Japanese Foreign Ministry sometimes argues that ideological considerations play no role in whether or not aid should be extended to a given country. But the government has not always been consistent in this policy. Whereas communist governments in Laos and Mongolia receive small amounts of Japanese ODA, Vietnam's aid was cut following Hanoi's invasion of Cambodia. The People's Republic of China with its communist government has been by far the largest recipient of Japanese aid in the 1980s, but Marxist Cuba has never received anything except a few trinkets in the form of technical assistance from Tokyo. Undoubtedly, the lack of Japanese assistance to Havana is largely attributable to Cuba's proximity to the United States. Nevertheless, it does appear that a country's ideological stripes are much less important to Japanese decisionmakers than they are to aid planners in the United States.

Another feature of the Japanese aid program in recent years has been a preoccupation with quantity targets. Since the late 1970s,

Japan has gone through three ODA doubling plans and will achieve a fourth in 1992. These have been praiseworthy objectives that have been widely lauded by members of the DAC. However, quantity increases do not necessarily mean that improvement in quality has been assured. Japan still lags behind almost all the donors in most of the categories used by the DAC to evaluate ODA performance.

THE PRIVATE SECTOR

Since the infancy of Japan's aid program, the role of the private sector has often been criticized by both donors and recipients. The high degree of cooperation between the public and private sectors continues to suggest to some observers that Japanese ODA remains a thinly disguised export promotion program. As such, this aspect of Japanese ODA has been seen as linked with Japan's trade policy. One possible explanation for this practice has been a subconscious desire to recreate the "Japan model" through development. In the Meiji period, it can be argued that foreign threats helped to stimulate Japan's economic development and as a result the private and public sectors were forced to collaborate closely. Adam Smith's clear-cut separation between government and business was never present in Japan as is clear with other aspects of Japanese foreign economic policy.

Despite the variety of actors, as pointed out, the Japanese aid policy bureaucracy is relatively small, and indeed there exists no core of development aid specialists as there is in USAID. Japan has no field missions abroad as USAID does and is usually represented by only two or three professionals from JICA and OECF plus an Embassy official. The seriousness of this problem can be clearly understood if one considers that the aid programs administered by Japan at least in Asia are usually several times larger than those of the United States which often has twenty times the personnel. Because of these problems in administration, it is not surprising that the Japanese private sector has played a pivotal role in ODA implementation.

The private sector in Japan has historically acted as a catalyst and a magnet for concessional aid flows. Japanese aid officials sometimes describe ODA as "seed" money for investments in developing countries. Aid, especially yen loans, demonstrates the government's confidence in a recipient country's stability. This also suggests why aid planners are reluctant to extend much assistance to countries that are experiencing domestic political difficulties. As a result, Japan's largest aid recipients are often countries with which Japan has significant trade interests. One way in which the private and public sectors work closely together is directly related to the kind of aid Japan has tended to prefer: large-scale infrastructural assistance. Large projects of this nature, such as power plants, port facilities, or farm-to-market roads, can make certain locations in a recipient country more attractive for Japanese investors.

As we have seen, Japan's aid administrative structure is subject to considerable conflict between the ministries over policy questions. This has made it difficult for the government to sustain a clear-cut policy. More often than not, policy tends to reflect this process. In addition, the implementing agencies are subject to the same conflict of loyalties as the ministries, consequently agreement over placing personnel overseas has always been stalemated. In practice, this has allowed the private sector a greater role than it might have had under a more centralized aid structure.[11]

A second feature of the system that has encouraged a substantial private sector role in the aid process is the request basis of the program *(yosei shugi)*. This requires that proposals for all aid projects come directly from the recipient government. As the aid program was initiated in Southeast Asia, the *yosei shugi* approach was undertaken to allay fears of the recipients of an incipient reemergence of Japanese imperial policy. *Yosei shugi* is still largely a fundamental precept of the aid system in contrast with that of the United States, which is far more aggressive in proposing aid projects to recipient governments, a legacy of America's role as occupier in postwar Europe and Japan. The request basis policy has allowed Japan to maintain a small bureaucracy because, in theory, it was the recipient governments that would be doing project implementation. In reality, many developing country recipients lack the expertise to plan and execute the large-scale infrastructural projects that are characteristic of the Japanese program and have therefore had to turn to the Japanese private sector for assistance. Furthermore, many of the trading companies most active with developing countries have extensive networks in the Japanese government and are capable of conducting the kind of *nemawashi* or greasing of the system required to get the projects approved in Tokyo.

Competition over projects is, as Pollock notes, rather straightforward. Among engineering companies, this is most critical in the initial stages since the company that undertakes the design will usually have an inside track in determining which companies receive commodity procurement contracts and thus earn consulting fees to supplement their income from the design stage. Contracts are awarded on evaluation based on quality and price. Optimally, a Japanese company seeking an award will wish to be involved in the earliest stages of project identification. Companies may also advise recipients which projects they believe will find the best reception in the Japanese government. The principal objective of the Japanese company is to ensure that the project in which it has invested will be selected. Therefore, the company's strategy is targeted at reducing competitive risks.[12]

The overseas trading companies are very active in this process and therefore also play a crucial role in coordinating the equipment supplier companies that will participate in the project. As a consequence, the success of the project is also related to the effectiveness of the network of subsidiaries that the trading company has established. Increasingly, these subsidiaries include non-Japanese.

Trading companies can have critical roles in many Japanese foreign commercial dealings. The nine largest trading companies in Japan account for 45 percent of Japan's external trade. These companies have a total of at least 1,100 overseas offices with 6,400 representatives. Many of these are located in the developing world and are actively engaged in Japan's aid program. For example, the largest trading company, C. Itoh, receives contracts amounting to between $350 and $400 million annually from Japanese ODA.[13]

Trading companies have been able to take a rather long-term approach to developing and implementing projects. The process, from identification through fruition, can take years to accomplish.

Through their networks, many of the trading companies are well acquainted with key people in a potential aid recipient's government. They are able to determine how a particular project is prioritized in the national economic planning of a developing country. After a project is identified, the company can advise the potential recipient whether it is worthwhile to apply for Japanese development financing.

At this stage, a trading company along with the would-be recipient decides what kind of financing to apply for: nonconcessional Japan Export–Import Bank funding, OECF yen loans, JICA grants, or perhaps private capital.[14] Until the last few years, trading companies have had a considerable advantage in this activity in comparison with foreign competitors.

Because of the historical emphasis by Japan on infrastructural assistance, the construction industry and engineering consultants have played a huge role in implementing Japanese foreign aid. But before examining their activities in developing countries, it is important to understand the clout that the industry has had in Japan.

There are 520,000 construction firms in Japan and they account for 20 percent of the nation's massive gross national product. The five largest are Kajima, Taisei, Shimizu, Ohbayashi, and Takenaka. Sixty percent of the industry's profits are derived from the private sector, 40 percent from government-sponsored public works. In 1986, 68 percent of all public works projects went to construction companies. This, at least in part, attests to the large-scale use of pork barrel by the LDP. Construction is one area in which the party has been able to exercise considerable clout.[15]

Prasert Chittiwatanapong of Bangkok's Thammasat University has pointed out that unlike most countries, in Japan there is no clear distinction between contractors and engineering consulting firms.[16] This parallels "gray areas" in other aspects of Japanese economic activity in which clear distinctions between business and government are often difficult to discern. Often, there are no distinctions to be made. The close-knit relationship between engineering consultants and contractors means that a considerable amount of collusion behind the scenes can take place regardless of whether Japanese aid is officially tied or not. The criticism that is sometimes heard is that if engineering specifications for projects remain tied even though the project itself is not, the collusive relationship described above negates the positive impact of general untying. This is because engineering firms can draw up specifications for a project that only a Japanese construction company, with which it may have a relationship, can meet.

How can such relationships come to be? Mainly through the existence of several associations for contractors and engineering firms which often have members coming from both business activities. The membership of the Overseas Construction Association consists of fifty-six of the largest construction companies with considerable overseas business in Japan. The organization's role is to coordinate the construction activities of its members overseas. This often means that collusion takes place in developing countries among member firms not unlike the *dango* system which is employed domestically. Under *dango* construction work is often divided up among the firms, which makes it difficult for outside bidders even to have a chance at winning a successful contract. The Overseas Construction Association also maintains close contact with Japanese government aid officials in all the ministries. Within the organization, there is the Overseas Construction Promotion Fund which provides low-interest rate financing for preliminary feasibility studies coming out of the Association.

Another important organization is the Japan Federation of Construction Contractors (Nikkenren) which is a member of the powerful Federation of Economic Organizations (Keidanren), the large super-chamber of commerce which acts as a key funding source for the LDP. Through the Keidanren, Nikkenren has easy access to members of the LDP who are associated with the *Kensetsu zoku* or construction caucus. Although caucus members do not have much influence over macro-aid policy, they can have an impact on micro or project-level aid. Sometimes the result can appear, from a development perspective, to be absurd. The largest hotel in Bangladesh was constructed through OECF yen loans largely as a result of LDP's lobbying the ministries. I once sat in an LDP member's office while he lobbied officials in the Finance Ministry for yen loans to build a resort with a golf course in Turkey. The officials listened politely, and it has not been built. While I would argue that the above cases represent the exception rather than the rule, it does suggest the activities that some in the construction industry are willing to promote at the expense of real economic development.

We have already discussed ECFA and its role in the aid system. The International Engineering Consultants Association is another organization worthy of mention. IECA with its fifty-six members comes under the stewardship of the Construction and Transport Ministries. It is mandated to work with third-world countries on their development projects. The membership consists of a mixture of contractors and engineering consultant companies. For example, one of the four members of the Board of Directors is also the Managing Director of the Overseas Construction Association of Japan. Another Board member is a member of JICA's Management Council.[17]

One more organization bears mentioning, largely because of the potential large-scale scope of its activities. In early April 1989, under the auspices of the Keidanren, the Japan International Development Organization (JAIDO) was inaugurated. JAIDO appears to have a multiplicity of roles mapped out for it, but basically it is to marshall the private sector to play a stronger role in coordination with Japanese aid efforts. For example, if OECF yen loans are to be extended to a country to build a factory building, JAIDO would try to organize private sector funds to build a road to the facility. It is also hoped that export earning industries will be promoted and, according to literature produced by the organization, an expansion of their products into the Japanese market. JAIDO is also encouraging foreign investors to participate in the program.[18]

Most of these organizations, and indeed some of the major companies, hire former officials from the government in a practice widely known in Japan as *amakudari* or descent from heaven, which shows the esteem in which the bureaucracy is held. This custom helps to create an "old boys" network.

Thus, it appears that Karel van Wolferen's description of the role of informal networks known as *jinmyaku* in Japan is quite applicable to the Japanese aid system at least at the project level.[19] The interlocking organizations I have described trade information back and forth concerning aid. This is not to say there is no competition. There is, but until the mid-1980s, competition was restricted to Japanese firms.

There is another issue relating to Japan's private sector that is just under the surface in many developing countries with which Japan maintains close relations. There is a perception of insensitivity toward local norms and customs. In a sense, the "ugly American" has been increasingly replaced by the "ugly Japanese" as Tokyo's power has expanded. Chittiwatanapong relates the example of the Ayuthaya History Study Center that was built through a JICA grant. Ayuthaya is an ancient capital of Thailand and holds a cultural value not unlike Kyoto to the Japanese. The grant was to be provided in commemoration of the centennial of Thai-Japanese relations. However, tremendous ill will ensued when JICA insisted that the designs of the building be undertaken by Japanese architects while Thai planners could only be "commentators" on the building specifications. This would be akin to an American company's erecting a building next to a famed historical shrine in Japan and only inviting comments on the design from Japanese architects.

Predictably, Thai architects demanded full participation from the beginning. Prime Minister Nakasone, during a state visit to Thailand, was expected to go to the city and sign the exchange of notes for the project. But the hue and cry over the conditions forced Nakasone to cancel his visit to Ayuthaya. In mid-1988, the Thai side stated flatly that it would not accept the project unless it was handled by Thai architects. JICA relented and as a consequence Japan benefited from a favorable reaction from the Thai public.[20] Nonetheless, brought on by insensitivity, it was an episode needlessly mismanaged by the Japanese. The interaction between construction, engineering, and consultant activities described above has been predominant in the aid system until now. But there are some indications that change may well be under way. This change has not been brought about by any internal dynamic but rather by persistent pressure. As we describe elsewhere in this volume, decisionmaking in Japan often results in a gridlock and requires outside influence to make policy adjustments.

REFORMING TIED AID POLICY

Three factors are forcing Japan to have a much more open bidding system for aid projects. First, there are the effects of general untying. In 1988, according to the Ministry of Foreign Affairs, 77.4 percent of yen loans were generally untied meaning open for universal bidding and 22.6 percent LDC untied for procurement restricting bidders to Japanese and developing country firms.[21] Because of the hand-in-glove relationship of the private sector that I have described, one would normally be suspicious about whether it really matters that aid is formally untied or not. But two other factors have affected the relationship between the private sector and the aid program. The effects of yen appreciation *(endaka)* have lowered the competitiveness of Japanese in bidding on the projects. And finally, the Foreign Ministry, against considerable internal opposition, has slowly moved toward increasing program lending, as opposed to project lending. In the Japanese fiscal year 1987, 27 percent of yen loans were for program aid. In other words, fewer big projects are being funded. An OECF official related to me that when he showed a list of current yen loan projects that were being planned to a representative of a large trading company, the reaction was that the list "didn't look very tasty."[22] In other words, the projects are of less interest to companies. The major Japanese trading company, Nissho Iwai, published an interview in April 1989 in its monthly magazine *Tradepia* with Misawa Hisao, the Director General of its International Cooperation Department, in which he lamented the effects of aid untying. "The government has continued to untie loans every year and has made it more difficult for Japanese enterprises to get business," he commented. "No matter how hard we work to identify a project, there is no longer any guarantee that we will win the order."[23] Thus, the combined impact of these three factors is driving up the cost of competing for Japanese companies. The Overseas Construction Association surveyed its members in 1988 in order to determine the effects of these changes. A decrease in orders from ODA-related construction can be clearly discerned in table 3.1.

The drop in receipts has occurred particularly in the area of yen loans, where much of the general untying has been directed. The construction industry has not taken this lying down. A ferocious lobby has been generated in Tokyo aimed primarily at the Diet in order to encourage a resumption of aid tying. MITI has not been unsympathetic. But as I have pointed out, partly because these is a lack of mechanisms to effect policy, the LDP has been able to have very little influence over these changes. Furthermore, the ruling party is not universal in its support for tied aid.

The effects of aid untying and yen appreciation along with the tremendous increases in the volume of aid have started to lure non-Japanese firms toward testing the water. As mentioned earlier; the most aggressive have been British companies. In the summer of 1988 in London, the British Consulting Firms Association held a seminar in order to educate its members as to the aid process and the precise kinds of needs of the Japanese aid program. The Japanese Ministry of Foreign Affairs along with representatives from OECF, JICA, and the Japan Export–Import Bank participated in the conference. The British Embassy in Tokyo followed this up with a day-long seminar in April 1989 in which British consulting companies gave presentations to their Japanese counterparts showing them just what experience they had had and suggesting ways in which cooperation could take place.

The Australian Embassy in Tokyo sponsored a seminar in November 1988 for Australian consulting firms which included Japanese government participation. In May 1989, USAID organized two conferences, one in San Francisco, California, and the other in Orlando, Florida, in order to educate American companies in the Japanese foreign aid bidding process. Representatives from the trading company C. Itoh, JICA, OECF, and the Japan Export–Import Bank along

TABLE 3.1. Receipts in Billions

	1983	1984	1985	1986	1987
Loans	1,008	344	569	415	361
Grants	442	461	327	507	391
Total	1,450	805	896	922	752

SOURCE: Overseas Construction Association of Japan.

with MOFA made presentations at the meetings. Japanese trading companies responded to invitations with remarkable enthusiasm. Some apparently believe that forging joint ventures with foreign firms in areas in which they have little experience will strengthen their competitive positions under a program which is no longer automatically tied in one form or another.

Despite the opening efforts by Japan, foreign companies have remained skeptical since many large-scale projects still seem to be won by Japanese bidders. But in January 1989, the British General Electric Company won a major contract amounting to $64 million in signaling equipment to be exported to the Thailand State Railway financed by OECF yen loans. GEC outbid Mitsui for the project, something that would have been unheard of just a few years before. The main reason for GEC's successful bid was that they undercut Mitsui's proposal. Mitsui was unable to adjust its price sufficiently because of the appreciated yen. Also, the British arm of Westinghouse had had contracts with the Thai railway system in the past so there was a strong argument for technical compatibility.[24] Nonetheless, this could become a more frequent occurrence if the Japanese aid system continues to open up generally and genuinely.

One key reform undertaken by OECF in 1988 which will work against the "buddy system" of consultants and contractors in Japan is the new rule that allows non-Japanese consultants to tender directly for untied projects funded by the OECF.

Since 1983, contracts have been increasingly won by developing country companies in the area of untied procurement for OECF yen loans. Table 3.2 shows that while European firms have increased their

TABLE 3.2. Procurement Share by Nationalities of
Contractors (percentages)

	JFY82	JFY83	JFY84	JFY85	JFY86	JFY87	JFY88
Local cost	3	3	2	5	3	6	5
LDCs	24	26	22	28	32	41	45
Other							
OECD members	7	6	7	11	14	12	17
United States	8	3	3	4	3	4	5
Japan	57	63	66	52	48	38	27

SOURCE: Government of Japan.

share of OECF contracts, the American percentage has been cut roughly in half.

The percentage of procurement by American companies has been practically halved, so argue many Japanese officials in a familiar refrain, because American firms do not make sufficient efforts. There may be some truth to this simply because the reputation of Japanese tied aid is so widely accepted in the United States. European procurement has increased mainly because their expertise is oriented more toward Africa, a region where Japan is weakest. Chittiwatanapong warns that we must also be careful with Japanese designations as to what constitutes an LDC business enterprise since some have only token management in recipient countries but are actually Japanese subsidiaries.[25] This argument has merit, but even if it is true, the aid funds would in all likelihood be reinvested in the local economy.

It is difficult to imagine even with untying that the Japanese bidding system will be truly open for all. Japanese firms should continue to win the lion's share simply because they have more experience with the system, they are well connected in Tokyo, and their companies do have long experience, especially in the developing countries of Asia. Grants, being Japanese taxpayers' money that is not repaid, no doubt have fewer opportunities for open bidding. As other donors overwhelmingly extend grant aid, this perhaps helps to explain the heavily tied nature of other donors. Favoritism toward the companies of the donor country is hardly peculiar to Japan. While West German aid projects are generally untied at the consulting stage, the project specifications can normally be met only by German companies. The American aid program is practically all tied; Congress would have it no other way. It is often extremely difficult to use non-American-made equipment in projects without seeking a specific waiver for one of the pervasive "Buy American" laws enacted by Congress. When I was in USAID, the mission in Indonesia had tremendous difficulty with the American-made land rovers that had been purchased. In a span of just a few years, the chassis had broken down twice and new vehicles had to be purchased. We became aware that Toyota had built land rovers that were better suited for the terrain in Indonesia. But a special waiver was required to make the purchase. Getting the waiver required passing through a political minefield the likes of which I had not seen before.

4

Translating the Policies: Regional and Multilateral Bank Emphasis

J apan's emphasis on Asia is a notable feature of the ODA program. As I have pointed out, during the 1980s, aid extended to South and East Asia hovered between 65 and 70 percent of the total. Roughly 30 to 35 percent of that total was earmarked for the ASEAN states, which is usually more than the amount of Japanese ODA offered to Africa, the Middle East, and Central and South America combined. While the reparations agreements signed by Japan with many Southeast Asian countries helped to established a bias toward the region, historical and cultural ties also played an important role.

That Japan has an ODA regional preference is not unusual for a donor nation. Almost 70 percent of British aid flows toward Commonwealth countries, while France designates roughly 90 percent of assistance for departments, territories, and former colonies.[1] During the 1980s, the United States has extended roughly 40 percent of its ODA to just two countries, Israel and Egypt.[2] Also, as table 4.1 suggests, Japan has tended to focus less attention on extremely poor countries with long-term growth problems. See also table 4.2.

TABLE 4.1. Japan's Bilateral ODA by Region and by Recipients
of Largest Amounts ($ million)

	BY REGION				
	1980	*1985*	*1986*	*1987*	*1988*
Asia	1,383 (70.5)	1,732 (67.8)	2,494 (64.8)	3,416 (65.1)	4,034.35 (62.8)
Northeast Asia	82 (4.2)	392 (15.3)	490 (12.7)	577 (11.0)	724.64 (11.3)
Southeast Asia	861 (44.0)	962 (37.6)	1,169 (30.4)	1,866 (35.6)	2,196.59 (34.2)
ASEAN	703 (35.9)	800 (31.3)	914 (23.8)	1,680 (32.0)	1,930.21 (29.9)
Southwest Asia	435 (22.2)	375 (14.7)	831 (21.6)	970 (18.5)	1,109.21 (17.3)
Unspecified	5 (0.3)	3 (0.1)	4 (0.1)	3 (0.1)	3.64 (0.1)
Middle East	204 (10.4)	201 (7.9)	340 (8.8)	526 (10.0)	582.52 (9.1)
Africa	233 (11.4)	252 (9.9)	418 (10.9)	516 (9.8)	883.93 (13.8)
Central and					
South America	118 (6.0)	225 (8.8)	317 (8.2)	418 (8.0)	399.29 (6.2)
Oceania	12 (0.6)	24 (0.9)	55 (1.4)	68 (1.3)	93.07 (1.4)
Europe	−1.5 (—)	1 (0.0)	2 (0.1)	2 (0.0)	3.96 (0.1)
Unallocable	1 (1.2)	122 (4.8)	221 (5.7)	302 (5.8)	424.75 (6.6)
Total bilateral					
ODA	1,961 (100.0)	2,557 (100.0)	3,846 (100.0)	5,248 (100.0)	6,421.87 (100.0)

NOTE: The figures in the parentheses indicate the shares (%) of bilateral ODA distributed to each region. Regions are classified according to the standard by the Ministry of Foreign Affairs.

	BY RECIPIENTS OF LARGEST AMOUNTS					
	1970		*1975*		*1980*	
Rank	*Country*	*Amount*	*Country*	*Amount*	*Country*	*Amount*
1	Indonesia	125.84	Indonesia	197.92	Indonesia	350.30
2	Korea	86.76	Korea	87.44	Bangladesh	215.14
3	Pakistan	39.55	Philippines	70.33	Thailand	189.55
4	India	32.73	Malaysia	63.27	Burma	152.46
5	Philippines	19.23	Egypt	50.17	Egypt	122.97
6	Thailand	16.91	Bangladesh	47.05	Pakistan	112.42
7	Iran	11.96	India	46.61	Philippines	94.40
8	Burma	11.94	Thailand	41.21	Korea	76.30
9	China	9.53	Iraq	29.77	Malaysia	65.63
10	Singapore	5.75	Nigeria	27.31	Sri Lanka	44.78

BY RECIPIENTS OF LARGEST AMOUNTS

	1986		1987		1988	
Rank	Country	Amount	Country	Amount	Country	Amount
1	China	496.95	Indonesia	707.31	Indonesia	984.91
2	Philippines	437.96	China	553.12	China	673.70
3	Thailand	260.41	Philippines	379.38	Philippines	534.72
4	Bangladesh	248.47	Bangladesh	334.20	Thailand	360.62
5	Burma	244.14	India	303.94	Bangladesh	341.96
6	India	226.71	Thailand	302.44	Pakistan	302.17
7	Indonesia	160.83	Malaysia	276.39	Myanmar*	259.55
8	Pakistan	151.56	Burma	172.00	Sri Lanka	199.83
9	Sri Lanka	126.91	Turkey	162.39	India	179.46
10	Egypt	125.70	Pakistan	126.69	Egypt	172.90

SOURCES: Ministry of Foreign Affairs, *Japan's Official Development Assistance, 1988: Annual Report.* Also, Ministry of Foreign Affairs, *Wagakuni no Seifu Kaihatsu Enjo,* 1989, V.1.

* Burma officially became Myanmar in 1989.

THE PEOPLE'S REPUBLIC OF CHINA

Economic cooperation with China dates back considerably before the Communist revolution that culminated in 1949. Arguably, the first concrete example of Japanese aid being extended to China was the Nishihara loans. The arrangement, provided by Japanese banks but backed by the government, was designed as a lever to encourage Chinese participation in World War I against Germany. Between 1917 and 1918, seven separate loans totaling 145 million yen for the development of a telegraph system, mines, lumbering, and railroads were agreed upon.[3] Of course, as Japanese involvement in Manchuria expanded in the 1930s, various economic cooperation schemes designed to leverage political concessions out of the fledgling Chinese government were also concomitantly conceived.

Immediately after the second World War, Japan was in no condition to provide economic assistance to any country. And following the victory of the Communists in 1949, Sino-Japanese relations were frozen, at least with the government on the mainland. Opinions within the Japanese government concerning the prudence of maintaining relations with the Nationalist regime in Taipei were always divided, but American pressure to persist with the Taipei connection essentially tipped the balance in favor of the supporters of the government of Chiang kai-shek. Nonetheless, Japan was only a minor aid donor

TABLE 4.2. Ranking the United States and Japan as Donors to Countries with Long-Term Economic Growth Problems, 1987

	United States	Japan
Afghanistan	*	*
Benin	*	*
Bolivia	1	2
Burkina Faso	*	*
Burundi	*	*
Central African Republic	*	3
Chad	*	*
Ethiopia	*	*
Gambia	2	*
Ghana	*	2
Guinea	*	3
Guyana	1	*
Haiti	1	*
Honduras	1	2
Madagascar	3	*
Mali	2	*
Mauritius	*	3
Nepal	3	1
Paraguay	*	1
Rwanda	*	*
Senegal	2	*
Somalia	2	*
Sudan	1	3
Uruguay	*	3

SOURCE: Compiled from Ministry of Foreign Affairs, *Wagakuni no Seifu Kaihatsu Enjo*, 1989, vol. 2.

NOTE: "Long term" is defined as economic growth rates of less than 1.5 percent between 1950–1972 and 1979–1987.

* Denotes ranked fourth and below.

until the early 1970s. By the time Japan began to emerge as an aid power, relations with Taiwan had radically changed. Quickly following the Nixon shocks, the Tanaka cabinet established official relations with Beijing and severed diplomatic ties with Taipei.[4]

Japan's first pledges of economic assistance to the People's Republic of China came under the Ohira government in 1979. The acceptance of aid by Beijing was in itself unprecedented since China had previously refused all offers of economic assistance following the cut-off of the last of Soviet aid in 1960. The rationale for providing assistance embraced several basic interests that Japan has in the region and, to a remarkable degree in the post–World War II era, reflected a foreign policy in which Japan essentially took the lead albeit with assurances to the western powers and ASEAN that their interests would not be trampled upon.[5]

Japan's interest in extending aid to China combines many factors not the least of which are historical ties, cultural affinities, and geographic proximity. Beyond these basic influences are commercial and strategic motives. If we define *strategic* broadly, then perhaps we can, as Brooks argues, attribute most of the rationale for Japanese aid to China to this factor.[6] Story even suggests that Japanese ODA engenders indirect military consequences by bolstering the economy through technology transfer.[7] A close relationship between China and the West is in Japanese interests as it helps to counter the increased Soviet threat in the region and lends credibility to the economic reformist policies of Deng Xiaoping. Providing large amounts of economic assistance promotes these policies.

From 1982 until 1986, China was Japan's largest recipient of economic assistance. In 1988, ODA disbursements amounted to $673.70 million. Of China's fifteen major donors, Japan is easily the largest. Significantly, the United States is explicitly prohibited from extending ODA to China by the Foreign Assistance Act since China is regarded as a "member of the international communist movement."[8] There was consideration given to requesting a Congressional exemption for China in the earliest days of the Reagan Administration, but it was decided that the necessary expenditure of political capital was too high a price to pay, particularly with conservative Republicans in the Senate. Therefore, the United States still lacks an aid program in China although consideration has been given to opening a USAID office to facilitate the transfer of technology. From a strategic perspective, support for a moderate and open China also serves U.S. interests, and as a result State Department and USAID policymakers have consistently encouraged Japan to take the lead in the West's relations with China through foreign aid even though the Commerce Department views Japan's aid presence somewhat suspiciously.

With the provision of the first yen loan package to China in 1979, the countries established two precedents. First, it was Japan's initial multiyear commitment to extend ODA and second, it was the first time that China had decided to accept assistance from a member of the DAC.

Practically all of Japan's ODA to China has been in the form of concessional yen loans administered by the OECF. In an apparent effort to allay western fears that Japan would dominate the potentially lucrative China market through its aid program, procurement has been for the most part generally untied. Assistance in the form of LDC untied loans has actually decreased from an average of 20 percent as a share of the annual loan package to roughly 10 percent in 1985 and 4 percent in 1986.[9]

There have been only two major hitches that have impeded the aid program to China. The first occurred when Beijing discovered in 1982 that it had insufficient local costs to cover procurement for several OECF-supported private sector steel projects. The Chinese were forced to pull back and a number of Japanese companies suffered huge losses. Subsequently, the Chinese government requested that the funds be converted into commodity loans and applied to a petrochemical facility in Daqing and to the first phase of the Baoshan steel complex.[10] The second major interruption in Japanese aid disbursements came in June 1989 following the brutal suppression of Chinese students at Tian-an-mien square. While many nations in the West publically lambasted Beijing, Japan was relatively circumspect, giving rise to the impression that Tokyo was mainly interested in protecting its enormous commercial stakes in China. While the United States curtailed military cooperation with China, Japan employed a potentially more influential device to demonstrate revulsion to the Beijing regime's exercise of violence: Tokyo stopped disbursing foreign aid and refrained from making new commitments. Instead of calling it a "sanction," the Japanese government said that holding back disbursements was necessary in order to protect Japanese aid officials. It is questionable as to what extent Japan would have responded to the crisis had it not been for unified revulsion in the west. Some Western observers criticized Japan's less than virulent public attacks on China. Government officials argued that Japan's wartime record in China made strident statements difficult. In the final analysis and for whatever reason that policy responses were undertaken, I would suggest that Japan's actions were very much consistent with the west.

Beyond bilateral difficulties that have effected aid flows Sino-Japanese relations have occasionally encountered other political problems in the 1980s. China strongly protested changes in history textbooks weakening Japanese culpability in World War II, the official visit of Prime Minister Nakasone to Yasukuni Shrine, and sovereignty questions during a controversy over ownership rights between China and Taiwan of a student dormitory in Kyoto. Pragmatically, China has managed to keep these disputes from spilling over into the economic relationship.

Until Tian-an-mien, one reason for the continuously high level of disbursements to China was the efficient absorption of funds from Japan. In several other countries in Asia, Japan has had to contend with severe pipeline problems due in part to difficulty in identifying worthy projects. This has not been the case with regard to China. Nonetheless, with the first repayments due in 1990 for the initial loans extended in 1980, many Chinese government officials have become less enthusiastic about Japanese project loans.

Japan's grant program in China has been modest. The most noteworthy example of grant aid was the funding provided from 1980 to 1983 to the 1,000-bed-Sino-Japanese Friendship hospital constructed in Beijing. This project alone accounted for almost 57 percent of all grants provided by Japan to China between 1980 and 1985.

ASSOCIATION OF SOUTHEAST ASIAN NATIONS

The nations comprising the ASEAN region are regarded by all ministries, politicians, and the private sector alike as vital to Japan's political and economic interests in Asia. ASEAN receives over half of its bilateral ODA from Japan. The Japanese government assigns priority to Asia in general for many reasons. Beyond historical and cultural ties, economic and strategic interests are also factored into Japan's regional equation. The countries of ASEAN are a major source of raw materials for Japan and are an important market for Japanese goods. The energy sector is regarded as crucial to Japanese interests, a fact reflected by a heavy emphasis on power-related projects in the region. In the 1980s, Japan extended aid to certain countries that border "areas in conflict," thus applying a strategic rationalization.[11] In addition, several ASEAN states straddle two sealanes that are essential for Japan's economy. One is the "petroleum road" which originates in the Middle East and weaves its way through the straits of Malacca. The other is the "iron ore road" which starts in western Australia and proceeds northward to Japan.[12]

The American withdrawal from Vietnam inadvertently pushed Japan into the role of regional leader, at least in an economic sense. In the late 1970s and 1980s, the increased Soviet presence in the region has helped spotlight Japan's role as a stabilizing force. However, many in Japan argue that Tokyo can best play such a role in South-east Asia by providing economic assistance rather than by acting as a military counterweight to Soviet strategic designs.[13]

A consensus among the ministries regards the ASEAN states (with the exception of Brunei) as *Nenji Kyoyokoku,* or countries that automatically receive a consistently high volume of ODA in line with Japanese interests. Japan has been the region's largest donor since 1977.[14] In 1988 Japan provided roughly 30 percent of its overall aid volume to ASEAN, a decrease from 40 to 50 percent of total annual ODA extended by Japan to ASEAN until 1976. See table 4.3.

Every Japanese prime minister since Tanaka Kakuei has placed a great deal of importance on maintaining amicable relations with the members of ASEAN. Some of this initial attention may have been connected with Mr. Tanaka's rather unpleasant reception in several ASEAN capitals when, on a trip to the region in 1974, he was greeted with widespread anti-Japanese protests because of perceived preda-tory commercial practices. The subsequent cabinet of Miki Takeo attempted to devise an "Asian Marshall Plan," but this did not survive beyond his term. Prime Minister Fukuda Takeo's prescription for the economic ills of the region unveiled in Manila in August 1977 included a $1 billion pledge to assist ASEAN regional projects. While this pledge went unfulfilled, Fukuda did later announce the first ODA doubling plan.

The other prime ministers in the 1970s and 1980s have also empha-sized the importance of ASEAN. Prime Minister Ohira Masayoshi reiterated this during his trip to Beijing in 1979, and his successor,

TABLE 4.3. Share of DAC Countries in Total: Top Three Donors to the Major ASEAN States (1987)

Philippines	53.7% (Japan)	32.6% (USA)	13.7% (others)
Thailand	69.4% (Japan)	8.0% (USA)	6.9% (FRG)
Malaysia	78.5% (Japan)	11.0% (Aust)	10.5% (others)
Indonesia	63.1% (Japan)	12.5% (Neth)	24.4% (others)
Singapore	50.6% (Japan)	20.2% (FRG)	16.1% (Aust)

USA: United States of America
FRG: Federal Republic of Germany
Aust: Australia
Neth: Netherlands

SOURCE: Compiled from Ministry of Foreign Affairs, *Wagakuni no Seifu Kaihatsu Enjo,* 1989, vol. 2.

Suzuki Zenko, made ASEAN the venue for his first official visit overseas after taking office. The Suzuki doctrine placed emphasis on increasing the basic human needs content of Japanese ODA as well as
strengthening ASEAN technical training programs in a variety of
sectors. To this end, Suzuki promised, during his 1981 tour of ASEAN,
to construct five technical training centers throughout ASEAN tai-
lored to meet the basic needs of each country. Funding was also set
aside for a headquarters training center in Okinawa which opened in
April 1985. Initially, the Japanese government was confronted with
problems in implementing this program since some of the recipient
governments apparently assumed that the centers were being established solely for the host country's use as opposed to the Japanese
intention of having an integrated ASEAN technical training program.
After some delays, the ASEAN centers were completed and technical
training was initiated.

When Prime Minister Nakasone succeeded Suzuki in 1982, he indicated continued emphasis on aid relations with the ASEAN nations.
Instead of introducing a new doctrine for the region, Nakasone focused on consolidating and trying to fulfill the promises of past cabi-
nets.[15]

Japan's absolute ODA volume to ASEAN has mushroomed. While
private sector investments lagged in the early 1980s, the appreciation
of the yen since 1985 has triggered a massive influx of Japanese
private capital flow. In addition, the general health of most of the
economies of ASEAN have been stronger than global growth trends.
Many ASEAN countries are planning to develop and strengthen their
export industries to serve as the engine of economic growth. In the
past, the nations of Southeast Asia would have looked to the United
States to take the lead, but it is increasingly clear that Japan is in a
better position to lend the necessary support in the 1990s.

In October 1986, the OECF, in collaboration with the Institute of
Developing Economies and the Japan External Trade Organization
(JETRO), issued a report urging the government to increase assistance to export-oriented industries in Indonesia, Malaysia, the Philippines, and Thailand. The report recommended that OECF yen loans
be channeled to domestic development financing agencies which would
in turn finance private firms, and that nonconcessional yen loans be
extended for government projects to improve their economic and
social infrastructures.[16] MITI acted on the report soon thereafter.

During a January 1987 visit to Indonesia, MITI Minister Tamura
Hajime announced the New Asian Industries Development Plan (New

AID Plan). He acknowledged, in meetings with Indonesian President
Suharto, that MITI was changing the emphasis of its aid program
toward more focus on assisting the development of export industries.[17] The announcement of this plan, however, caused concern in
the United States since Japan had not opened its markets sufficiently
to LDC manufactured goods. According to the General Agreement on
Tariffs and Trade (GATT), almost 62 percent of the total manufactured goods imported into the United States in 1984 came from less
developed countries, a greater than 4 percent increase over 1983 figures. On the other hand, LDC—manufactured goods comprised only
8 percent of Japan's total imports of manufactured goods in 1984, less
than 2 percent more than in 1983. Thus, if the New AID Plan were not
accompanied by measures to provide greater market access in Japan,
the increased volume of manufactured goods stimulated by the plan
would have to be sold elsewhere, which meant probably the United
States. This concern was echoed by ASEAN officials as well. In a
speech at the ninth annual ASEAN–Japan forum in June 1987, Director General Abdullah Zawawi Mohamed of the Malaysian ASEAN
secretariat pointed out that "there is growing feeling that Japan has
not adequately met ASEAN's request to dismantle its remaining trade
barriers."[18] An editorial in the *Yomiuri Shimbun* acknowledged that
Japan should not expect the United States to carry the burden due to
"its huge trade deficit" and that "Japan will have to replace the
United States in importing such products."[19]

Another Japanese government initiative in ASEAN has been spearheaded by MOFA. The Foreign Ministry created the $2 billion ASEAN–
Japan Development Fund for the purpose of extending low-interest
loans to foster joint-venture enterprises focusing on advanced technology. The idea was proposed at the ASEAN Foreign Ministerial Conference in June and formally submitted to the ASEAN Summit Conference in Manila in December 1987.[20] ASEAN members have criticized
what they view as the slow disbursement of funds allocated for the
program.

Japan's emphasis on yen loan assistance, particularly project lending, to the region has created the concern that Tokyo was producing
as much debt as development. Interest rates on Japanese loans have
almost doubled because of the yen's appreciation. Former Foreign
Minister Okita Saburo expressed concern over this issue in a *Japan
Times* interview on January 1, 1989.[21]

Having examined Japan's aid approach as it relates generally to
ASEAN, how may we interpret this policy on a country-by-country

basis? With the exception of Brunei, where the gross national product per capita of over $20,000 per annum precludes consideration as a potential aid recipient, every member nation receives Japanese ODA. Thailand has been a major recipient of Japanese aid since the 1950s and one of the top three aid recipients almost every year since 1980. Over two-thirds of Thailand's ODA, amounting to $360.62 million in 1988 disbursements, comes from Japan. This constituted more than 5½ percent of Japan's total aid disbursements that year. Well over half of this aid was in the form of yen loans, while the remainder was comprised of grants and technical aid.[22] Japanese loans to Thailand are greater than the concessional lending of the World Bank in Thailand. In the Japanese fiscal year 1988, they accounted for $222.2 million of all Japanese assistance to Thailand in comparison with the 44.2 million in grants and $94.3 million in technical aid. In 1988, the 14th yen loan package was diversified among several kinds of infrastructural projects. For example, over ¥4 billion was disbursed for the Chanburi-Pattaya Highway construction project while ¥6.1 billion went for a Provincial Power expansion program. Improving water facilities in Thailand was also targeted with loans as well as fishery projects.[23] After considerable bureaucratic conflict, particularly between the Finance and Foreign Ministries, over how to approach the financing of local costs, the Foreign Ministry's support for more flexibility won out. In Thailand, this was reflected in the $57.48 million in loan disbursements for local costs in 1987. Grants and technical aid disbursements have included funds for disaster relief, increased food production, and equipment for universities.

Thailand provided the first test case for extending aid under the comprehensive security rubric. Following the Vietnamese invasion of Cambodia in 1978, Thailand experienced a massive influx of refugees. In addition, its military engaged in periodic combat with Vietnamese troops attacking refugee base camps in pursuit of the Cambodian resistance. The refugee situation taxed the resources of what was already Thailand's poorest region, and Japan has directed much of its aid effort to this area.

Indonesia has been the largest recipient of Japanese aid since the inception of the program. In many ways, these flows of aid to Indonesia can be regarded as a barometer for the changing nature of Japanese aid policy since the 1960s. In the 1960s Japan's foreign aid policy focused exclusively on export promotion, whereas in the 1970s it began to address the development of natural resources. The latter policy was centered around large energy-related capital projects.

However, Japan has had occasional problems with Indonesia's capital absorption capacity, creating a pipeline of undisbursed funds that continues to plague OECF aid planners.[24] In the 1980s, some of Jakarta's difficulties were related to falling oil revenues which reduced Indonesia's budgetary resources and limited the country's ability to contribute to the implementation of aid projects.

A study under the direction of Bruce Koppel in 1988 of Indonesian attitudes to Japanese and U.S. foreign aid pointed out that at least one-third of Indonesia's debt, which stood at $42 billion in 1987, was denominated in yen. Because of this, Jakarta has been leery about receiving too many more project loans from Japan.[25] In 1988, Indonesian Finance Minister Johannes Sumarlin told a Japan–Indonesia conference that Japan should seriously consider allowing debtor nations to repay outstanding loans at the 1986 yen rate to the dollar, before the Japanese currency's dramatic appreciation. There have also been newspaper reports that Indonesian authorities requested dollar-denominated loans in 1988, something that Finance Ministry officials rejected out of hand.[26] The Foreign Ministry's answer to the Indonesian yen debt issue has been to lower the interest rates on loans, increase local cost financing and program lending. It is also hoped that these measures will reduce pressure on the pipeline. The experience of Indonesia most clearly suggests the danger that yen loan aid can be a debt creator rather than a generator of development.

The primary mechanism by which all donors attempt to coordinate aid policy to Indonesia is through the Intergovernmental Group for Indonesia (IGGI) established in 1966 and chaired by the Netherlands. Since 1986, Japan has played the lead role in the IGGI in addressing Indonesia's balance of payment and current account problems through rapidly disbursing commodity loans to relieve debt pressures, at least temporarily.

The staffing inadequacies that we have discussed elsewhere hamper efforts in Indonesia as well. The more than $700 million in assistance that was disbursed in 1987 was administered by twenty professionals from the OECF, JICA, and the Japanese Embassy. In contrast, the United States aid program in 1989 was a little more than $57 million and it was implemented by 110 US AID officers, including Indonesians hired locally.[27]

The Japanese method, in compliance with its centralized aid decisionmaking system in Tokyo, is to send "expert missions." In 1987, this amounted to 1,200 JICA missions from Tokyo alone. As a consequence, as Koppel relates, missions overlap, are redundant, and tend to focus on minutiae, which tends to frustrate Indonesian technocrats.[28]

Another major recipient of Japanese ODA is Malaysia. In 1984, Kuala Lumpur was the largest recipient of Japanese aid, but its share decreased in 1985 and tumbled in 1986. In 1987, Japanese aid disbursements to Malaysia leaped to $276.39 million.

Malaysia represents an unusual case because of the nation's relatively high GNP per capita ($1,800 in 1987). Kuala Lumpur has usually ranked among Japan's top ten recipients. Malaysia's strategic location on a vital sea route for Middle Eastern oil and its relatively conciliatory approach toward Vietnam as a means of countering Hanoi's dependence on the Soviet Union contribute to Tokyo's continued support. In addition, Malaysia is a source of essential natural resources and Tokyo has taken particular interest in the country as a result of Prime Minister Matahir's "Look East" policy. This policy designates Japan as the model for economic development to which Malaysia should aspire. All of this means that consensus among the ministries is more easily achieved. After Prime Minister Takeshita announced his resignation in the spring of 1989 on a swing through Southeast Asia, he committed Japan to a significant increase in aid to Malaysia.

Singapore receives mostly technical assistance, commodities, and training amounting to $11.2 million in 1988 and is therefore only a minor recipient of Japanese ODA because of its high GNP ($7,940 per capita in 1987). Singapore's position on the Straits of Malacca gives it strategic importance. Also, Japan views Prime Minister Lee Kuan Yew as an ASEAN leader who to a certain extent shares Malaysia's "Look East" philosophy in regard to modeling development after Japan.[29]

The Philippines is perhaps the most controversial and, arguably from a political perspective, the most important country on Japan's aid agenda in Southeast Asia. Although the nature of that "political importance" is unclear, I would argue that political stability leading to economic stability is buttressed by retention of the U.S. commitment to Manila. Or, as a Philippine official has suggested, "Japan's interests in the Philippines can be defined as the political in support of the economic. while American interests tend to be the economic in support of the political."[30]

Although ODA to Manila declined following the completion of reparation payments in 1976, the nation has ranked among Japan's major recipients throughout the 1980s. The Philippines is the only nation in the ASEAN group that has consistently posed a dilemma for Japanese policymakers. Although Tokyo was a steady contributor of ODA to the Marcos regime, this policy resulted in considerable criticism in Japan. The attacks on the government were on two levels. First, Japan was seen as contributing aid mainly to support American strategic objectives.[31] Second, there was concern in some circles that Japanese aid was merely lining the coffers of the Marcos family. The criticism substantially increased after Benigno Aquino was assassinated in August 1983. Although opposing views to aid for the Marcos regime had long been expressed in opposition quarters, dissenting voices began to be heard from within the ruling LDP as well, most notably from novelist-turned-politician Ishihara Shintaro.[32]

Following the fall of the Marcos regime in February 1986, evidence was revealed by the Subcommittee on Asia and Pacific Affairs of the U.S. House Foreign Affairs Committee concerning kickbacks from OECF yen loans. This scandal can at least partly be explained by the fact that Marcos acted as the final arbiter on all OECF loans. The resulting furor caused the Japanese Diet to establish a special committee to look into the affair and propose government audits of future Japanese aid contracts.[33] In order to sweep some of this under the carpet, it was reported that Prime Minister Nakasone had urged Philippine Vice President Salvatore Laurel to regard the affair as a domestic matter.[34]

While a peaceful solution to the political turmoil in the Philippines, essentially in order to protect base rights, had been a long-standing U.S. objective, the American hand in preserving order became especially apparent in easing Marcos out and Mrs. Aquino in. Because of the relatively peaceful transition of power to a more democratic order which basically was supportive of U.S. interests, Washington threw its full weight behind reinforcing the new Aquino government.

In spite of domestic criticism, Japan had been responsive to Washington on requests for increased aid to Manila while Marcos was in power. This was largely because aid to Manila very clearly served Japanese interests while simultaneously placating the United States. Since the formation of the Aquino government, aid to the Philippines has been a contentious subject between the United States and Japan. Initially, Japan was reluctant to make large-scale commitments until the political atmosphere settled. As a result, many officials in the State Department and USAID were critical of what was viewed as Japan's lethargy toward making new commitments.[35]

In November 1986, Mrs. Aquino made a state visit to Japan in which she was very warmly received. During her visit, the Japanese government made a ¥40.4 billion aid pledge, the first promise of assistance since Mrs. Aquino had assumed power. This low-interest loan is financing the construction of a thermal power plant in Batangas province in south Luzon.[36] Aquino requested that aid to the Philippines be extended at levels similar to those granted Thailand. But the Nakasone government made no further commitments indicating only that additional contributions would be considered. The pledge made during President Aquino's visit was classified as a "special loan" and was not to be included in the annual aid package.

Immediately after the Aquino visit, Mitsui executive Wakaoji Nobuyuki was kidnapped outside Manila. As the case dragged on, officials both in the Philippines and in Japan began to express concerns about the effect on cooperation between the two countries. Philippine Finance Minister Jaime Ongpin told reporters that the kidnapping had "created problems . . . in terms of expediting many of our pending aid requests with the Japanese government."[37] Some critics in Japan regarded the Philippine government's handling of the problem as incompetent and therefore suggested a review of Japan's aid pledge. As elsewhere in Asia, whereas U.S. ODA has been predominantly grant-oriented, Japan's assistance has been primarily through yen loans.

The Philippine government, according to the Koppel study, has difficulties with the Japanese aid program at several levels. First, Japan's complex bureaucratic decisionmaking process, especially the rivalry between the Foreign and Finance Ministries, impedes rapid responses to Philippine needs. Second, while Manila acknowledges Japan's movement toward the general untying of yen loans, there is still a feeling that Japan's aid efforts are often directed at enhancing its consultancy industry. Further, sourcing requirements in general are still too closely connected to Japan where prices are usually significantly higher. Finally, Japan's aid is not sufficiently concessional and contains too many rigidities. For example, each of the implementing agencies tends to administer aid that fits only its own institutional style.[38]

Here, too, the issue of staffing arises. JICA does not have any in-country Philippine experts, and personnel seem to be largely technicians incapable of dealing with wider issues relating to Philippine economic development. Also, criticism is heard concerning the numerous survey "missions" which are sent out from Tokyo to assess problems for a week to four weeks at a time.[39]

One of the largest issues confronting the Philippines is agrarian reform. It is a problem in which the United States, Japan, and the World Bank have been expected to play important roles. Both the United States and Japan have had unique experiences with agrarian reform during the American occupation. While serious consideration had been given to land reform in Japan, the "American interlude" provided the needed push to ensure acceptance in Japanese society.

Philippine land reform, although I would suggest that it is undoubtedly necessary for the long term, involves considerable short-term political risks that none of the donors are willing to face alone. In fact, approaches to handling these reform issues bear striking resemblances to the passing of a hot potato. While Japan seems to have more sympathy toward the problem than the United States, none of the donors is really willing to take responsibility. The issue has therefore led to some conflict among the contributors to the "Multilateral Assistance Initiative" to the Philippines which has also come to be called the "Mini-Marshall Plan."

MYANMAR (BURMA)

No country is as dependent on Japanese foreign aid as the former Burma, now called Myanmar. Japanese ODA accounts for over 20 percent of Myanmarese budget disbursements. In 1987, Japan provided 71.5 percent of all the economic assistance received by Rangoon. In 1988, Japan disbursed $259.6 million to Myanmar of which 168.3 million were yen loans.[40]

Japan's close relationship with Myanmar extends back at least to World War II. Initially, Burmese guerrillas supported the invasion by Japan as a means of expelling British colonialists. A puppet regime was quickly established and many of Burma's independence leaders were educated in Japan, a point which was brought home to me when I visited the Burmese Embassy in Washington several years ago and noticed a portrait of national hero Aung San wearing the uniform of the Japanese Imperial Army! The harshness of Japanese colonial administration was quickly realized and anti-Japanese resistance developed. Despite efforts by Britain to resume colonial administration after the war, Burma succeeded in gaining independence.

Many Japanese soldiers coming home from Burma at the end of war wrote admiringly of what they saw as the "purity" of the Burmese. This positive image was reinforced with the publication of the

popular melancholic novel *Harp of Burma,* which was a fictional
account of a Japanese soldier who remained in Burma to find and
bury the remains of his fallen comrades. A whole generation grew up
knowing the novel which has been required reading in many Japanese
schools since the end of the war. It was also made into two films.
Thus, the popular consciousness has remained rather positive toward
Burma/Myanmar.

On a more tangible level, although Myanmar, which is not an
ASEAN member, is the poorest country in Southeast Asia, it is also
regarded as a nation that has great economic potential. But since
1961 when Ne Win came to power, the nation has been racked with
insurgencies and economic mismanagement. Only Japan was allowed
to play a significant role in Myanmarese development and as a result,
Tokyo has maintained a special and subtle influence in Myanmar.
During the 1980s, Burma began to open and accept assistance from
other donors. Real changes, however, started to occur with the emergence of domestic political turbulence in 1988. Burmese military forces
battled protesting students, long tired of the oppressive hermetic
regime, in the streets.

The way in which the Japanese government handled the repercus-
sions of the political turmoil in Rangoon provides an interesting case
reflecting the domestic politics of foreign aid. In recognition of the
human rights violations being perpetrated by the government, Japan,
along with other donor countries, suspended aid in the fall of 1988.
The Japanese government's position was unequivocal when the action
was initiated. Japanese businessmen were discouraged from visiting
the country and the nineteen aid projects being funded by Japan
grounded to a halt. But suddenly, in March 1989, Japan unilaterally
resumed aid efforts in Burma.

There are two sides that emerge from this story. One has pressure
from some in the Japanese business community through several high-
ranking LDP members playing a pivotal role in breaking with the
other donors and starting Japan's aid efforts in Burma up again. This
included pressure from war veterans' associations closely linked with
important LDP leaders such as Watanabe Michio, one of the heirs
apparent in the Nakasone faction and a former MITI Minister, as well
as former Foreign Minister Abe Shintaro who was also the General
Secretary of the LDP under Takeshita's reign as party president. Both
are members of the Japan–Burma Parliamentary League. Normally,
the business community's lobby is effective only at the micro level,
since each firm tries to protect the projects with which it is associated,

or when there is a consensus to support or oppose a particular governmental policy through one of the associations. This scenario suggests that a consensus did emerge among those companies that were the most seriously affected by a cessation of aid.[41]

The American leverage vis-à-vis Japan or Burma in this case was limited since U.S. aid levels are negligible. High-level U.S. reaction to Japan's aid start-up was further hindered by the disorganization that usually afflicts the dawning days of a new American administration.

The Foreign Ministry's version of Japan's resumption of aid to Myanmar is that the new government had effectively regained control of the country and was observing international laws, and therefore normal government-to-government relations could commence anew.

The reality of the internal bickering over aid to Myanmar is more nearly related to the bureaucratic politics that dominates the system. Since the Foreign Ministry's decision temporarily to halt aid to Myanmar, largely because other donors were doing so and the ministry was worried about Japan's international image if it did not follow suit, both the Finance Ministry and MITI were equally concerned over issues falling under their bureaucratic purview. MOF was worried about terminating aid to a country that had received so much aid from Japan. While aid to other recipients had been halted in the past, none of them had been a recipient on the scale of Burma. The ministry officials contemplated the effects of confidence in Japan's aid program and considered whether stopping aid would result in financial chaos, forcing Rangoon to default on previous yen loans.[42]

This was no idle concern. At the end of 1988, Burma owed Japan some 8.2 billion yen. In mid-1988, Prime Minister Takeshita promised to cancel loan debt to all least developed countries before April 1988; for Burma the debt equaled 257 billion yen. But the Finance Ministry refused to go along insisting that all loans had to be repaid before the funds could be changed for grants.

The Ministry of Finance is adamant that such projects as the expansion of Rangoon airport, a sugar mill, and a power station will not be carried out unless it is sure that they will come to completion. MITI, like their private sector clients, was worried about the effects on future business in Burma. The combined effects of these bureaucratic interests in addition to those of the private sector were simply too much for MOFA to overcome, and the result was Japan's decision to proceed with aid disbursements.

REPUBLIC OF KOREA

Japan has always had to conduct relations with South Korea in a circumspect manner or risk igniting a heated exchange with its closest cousin. Hosup Kim has suggested that bureaucratic politics is an inadequate device to use in the analysis of Japan's aid policy with South Korea. Rather, because of a confluence of factors such as geopolitical security concerns and historic connections, unofficial and nongovernmental channels very often are more effective in smoothing aid relations. Kim also argues that this translates into greater private sector dominance over the process vis-à-vis Seoul as well as heightened interest on the part of Japanese politicians.[43]

While not disagreeing with these conclusions, I would argue that political actors have been more involved in the aid decisionmaking process to South Korea primarily because there has often been an element of crisis in the South Korea–Japan relationship. When bilateral issues are less contentious, bureaucratic actors have tended to be the dominant players and, as Kim also points out, the Foreign Ministry has usually won out over the Ministry of Finance.

Opposition parties have never been pleased with the succession of authoritarian governments in Seoul, but with the exception of the provisions of Japan's first aid package in 1965, assistance was extended with few hitches until 1981. In the summer of that year, the South Korean government requested $6 billion in limited project assistance. This money was requested in lump sum so that South Korea, which earmarks roughly 35 percent of its annual budget for defense, could determine how much of the remainder of their budget to allocate to its five-year economic plan.

The Japanese reaction was one of shock. Foreign Minister Sonoda Sunao was apparently irked because South Korea's short project list, partially handwritten, had seemingly been thrown together at the last minute. Also, the amount of the request, had it been accepted, would have equaled 60 percent of Japan's entire Asia aid budget over the proposed five-year period. Finally, the Japanese government found the not so subtle connection with Seoul's security needs to be totally unacceptable and probably in conflict with the spirit, if not the letter, of the Japanese Constitution. Furthermore, Japanese government officials were concerned that accepting a security rationale from the Republic of Korea would open a pandora's box among opposition parties in the Diet as well as create a precedent for similarly argued

requests from other countries.[44] Characteristically, conflict erupted
over the request within Japan's aid bureaucracy. While MITI played
virtually no role in the issue because details were insufficient to generate Japanese private sector interest, Foreign Ministry and Finance
Ministry positions were often in sharp contrast.

The Foreign Ministry took the position that extending the requested amount was important within the context of regional burden
sharing with the United States. MOFA believed that South Korea's
request for commodity loans was justified, but the Finance Ministry
did not want to make an exception of Korea. Normally, commodity
loans are provided only to recipient nations with balance of payment
problems. Also, Finance did not want to provide a special package for
South Korea but rather balance the requested portion against aid
designated within Japan's overall ODA doubling pledge. Finally, MOF
opposed extending more than $1 billion to South Korea in loans at
less than commercial rates.[45]

In the months subsequent to the initial request, several South
Korean parliamentarians and businessmen signaled to their Japanese
counterparts that they thought the request and rationale were inap-
propriate and suggested a softening in the South Korean demands. At
a December 1, 1981, press conference, Prime Minister Suzuki implied
that if South Korean officials accepted Japan's aid requirements, the
government would be willing to cooperate.

On April 28, 1982, Deputy Foreign Minister Yanagiya Kensuke flew
to Seoul in an effort to break the impasse. During meetings with
South Korean Foreign Minister Cho Shin Yongi, Yanagiya indicated
Japan's willingness to extend $4 billion in loans to aid Seoul's five-
year plan. South Korea did not immediately accept the offer.[46] It is
possible that this issue could have been settled earlier, but shortly
after the Japanese offer, South Korea's angry reaction to revised Japanese school textbooks depicting a more benevolent wartime role for
Tokyo placed all economic questions on the back burner until a solution was found to this sensitive historical and political issue.

The domestic bureaucratic and bilateral impasse was eventually
resolved by cabinet-level political intervention. In November 1982,
Nakasone became Prime Minister and made solution of the aid imbroglio with South Korea his top priority. His first act in office was to
telephone South Korean President Chun Doo Hwan, and in December,
he dispatched political confidant Sejima Ryozo with his personal
mandate to solve the issue. Representing a victory for MOFA, the final
terms of the settlement included $1.8 billion in concessional yen loans

and $2.15 billion in harder Export–Import Bank credits to be extended over a seven-year period. The package did not include commodity aid because of fear that the South Korean government would use these credits for defense-related purposes, but it did include financing for local costs.[47] Disbursement of the aid package has been carried out relatively smoothly.

OCEANIA

Other than through Japan's World War II experiences in the region, the Pacific Basin states were of little importance to Tokyo until the mid-1980s. One reason for the lack of historical interest in the area was that except for the Solomon Islands, Japan did not extend war reparations to the region. Another factor was the infrastructural nature of Japanese ODA itself which did not conform with the economic interests of the Basin since these countries would have difficulty absorbing large capital projects. Furthermore, the population and market were viewed as too small to warrant much interest on Japan's part. Japan was also reluctant to play a major role since the South Pacific, particularly Fiji and Papua New Guinea, was regarded as coming under Australia's purview.[48] In large part, most of Japanese aid to the Pacific comes under the heading of *otsukiai enjo* or, loosely translated, friendship aid, which is used to describe aid flows to smaller countries of little political or economic significance to Japan.[49] In 1985, Japanese disbursements to Pacific nations increased slightly to $19.68 million, and in the following year they jumped to $54.69 million. With the exception of the massive amounts of aid Australia extends to Papua New Guinea, which administered the nation as a UN trustee until 1974, and America's support for the Pacific trust territories, Japan's contribution had become the region's largest aid contribution. In 1988, Japan's aid sum reached $93.07 million.[50]

These increases reflected a basic change in policy toward the South Pacific. There are several factors that contributed to this heightened awareness of the importance of the South Pacific to Japanese interests. First was increased Soviet activity in the region. In 1985, Moscow provided $2 billion to Kiribati in exchange for fishing rights and in April 1987 also signed an agreement with Vanuatu allowing port calls for Soviet fishing vessels. The Japanese government was concerned over these Soviet inroads, and the United States advised Japan that increasing aid in the South Pacific would be a contribution to burden sharing. Secondly, the collapse of the ANZUS pact created concomitant concerns over the western security structure for the South Pacific.[51] A final factor was the difficulties that the Australian economy encountered, which caused a drop in Canberra's aid program to regional nations.

In January of 1987, during a visit to Canberra, Japanese Foreign Minister Kuranari Tadashi agreed with his Australian counterpart, Bill Hayden, to work together as a "South Pacific Axis" to ensure economic and political stability in the region. The Australians stressed that increased Japanese interest and aid in the South Pacific was welcome. Kuranari reportedly remarked at the close of the meetings that Japan would increase ODA in order to cope with the "growing Soviet presence in the region."[52] At the next stop on Kuranari's tour, New Zealand, the Foreign Minister reiterated his pledge to step up aid to Pacific nations and termed the plan the "Kuranari doctrine."[53]

Part of the significance of the changing approach toward the Pacific may reflect a more aggressive aid policy in which project proposals are actively put forward rather than waiting for a "request," which until 1986 had been the exclusive tenet of Japanese ODA. Also, in an effort to cut through sectionalism in the Foreign Ministry and create a comprehensive strategy for the South Pacific, a task force was created to coordinate regional aid policy. In order to follow up on the pledges made during the Canberra visit and identify feasible projects, the Foreign Ministry dispatched a team to the South Pacific at the end of March of that year. Secretary of State George Shultz signaled U.S. support for the Kuranari initiative in the South Pacific in a letter shortly after the Foreign Minister returned to Japan.[54]

While the Americans and Australians are pleased with Japan's increased interest in the South Pacific, at least one regional nation, Vanuatu, expressed concern over the prospects for big power rivalry.[55] As might be expected, a Radio Moscow broadcast criticized the Kuranari doctrine as "promoting realization of the U.S. strategic plans for the Asian and Pacific regions." The Soviets also argued that the doctrine was designed to "help Japanese capitalists advance in the region."[56] I suspect the latter Soviet assessment found agreement and concern in some Washington circles.

SOUTH ASIA

While the Japanese government granted its first yen loan to India in 1958, by 1986 Tokyo had become India's largest donor, financing foreign exchange costs of projects such as oil and gas exploration, telecommunications, fertilizer plants, thermal power plants, and heavy equipment for irrigation. Tokyo's ODA disbursements to India in 1988 amounted to $179.46 million. We again see staffing insufficiencies contrasted with large volumes of assistance. Japan's in-country staff consisted of three Embassy officials, one JICA official, and three OECF representatives. In 1989, USAID's committed program funds amounted to $105.56 million. Nonetheless, the 141 mission staff members, who include American as well as local employees, provide quite a comparison with Japan's smaller albeit less labor-intensive operation.[57]

In Koppel's survey of Indian attitudes toward Japanese aid, New Delhi officials expressed frustration with both the low grant ratio of Japanese assistance and the seeming conflicting priorities and criteria governing grant and loan allocations.[58] This is apparently how Japan's interbureaucratic battle translates in New Delhi.

Bangladesh has been the largest recipient of Japanese ODA in South Asia since 1984. In 1988, Tokyo's aid to Dacca totaled $341.96 million which was fifth overall among Japan's recipients. Bangladesh has been deemed worthy of Japanese ODA mainly on humanitarian grounds since the country's GNP per capita is $160 per annum (1987) making it among the lowest in the world. The United States was traditionally Bangladesh's largest donor and has also played a role in encouraging greater Japanese aid efforts to Dacca. Humanitarian interests aside, some peculiar projects can slip through, such as Dacca's largest luxury hotel built by OECF yen loans.

Nepal is another regional country with a very low GNP which qualifies it as a least developed country (LLDC). Japan is Katmandu's largest donor, disbursing $62.4 million in 1988 which made up roughly 40 percent of all the assistance received by Nepal. Both Pakistan and Sri Lanka have had strategic importance to Japan and the western alliance in recent years. Following the Soviet invasion of Afghanistan in 1979, Japan placed aid to Pakistan under its comprehensive security rationale.[59] In 1987, Japan was the largest donor to Islamabad, providing almost 30 percent of all ODA to Pakistan. In 1988, disbursements were $302.2 million. Japan is the largest donor to Sri Lanka providing $199.8 million in aid in 1988. While Colombo has consistently ranked among the top ten recipients of Japanese ODA, the political disturbances resulting from the strife between Tamil separatists and the Sinhalese-dominated government have heightened Tokyo's concern over the long-term stability of the island nation and the possibility that protracted conflict could invite unwanted external participation. This is a concern mirrored in Washington and has played a role in encouraging the United States and Japan to consult frequently on the uses of aid to abet economic stability.

THE MIDDLE EAST

The importance of the Middle East within the context of Japan's foreign aid relations emerged in full clarity during and following the oil embargo in 1973–1974. After years of relative neglect, Japan's dependence on oil from the region forced changes in Japanese policy after the embargo was initiated. Japan was particularly vulnerable to the oil weapon not only because it was more dependent than Western Europe or the United States but also because Middle Eastern oil had been the lubricant of the economic miracle. The changes in aid policy to the region, which have been discussed elsewhere in this book, set the tone for the current aid relationship.

Although Japan has desired to make significant contributions through ODA to Middle East states, efforts have been hindered by seemingly eternal political instability and by the fact that many oil-producing states have incomes too high to meet Japanese ODA requirements. Thus, although roughly 10 percent of ODA allocations have been earmarked for the region on an annual basis, the programs have been marked by inconsistent disbursement. In 1986, only two Middle Eastern countries, Turkey and Jordan, ranked within the top thirty recipients of Japanese ODA disbursements.

Turkey did not emerge as a major recipient of Japanese ODA until 1981. Observers have regarded the country as an example of foreign pressure's affecting Japanese aid decisionmaking. Other major recipients in the Middle East include Iraq, which has received mainly yen loans for medical equipment, and the Yemen Arab Republic, which receives largely grant assistance from Japan for a variety of projects. In 1981, the Suzuki cabinet pledged $100 million in OECF loans to Saudi Arabia for the construction of a petrochemical plant and by 1985 roughly 90 percent of those funds had been disbursed.[60] Oman, which is situated at the vital mouth of the Persian Gulf, has received technical assistance from Japan. The fact that OPEC nations provided 80 percent of Japan's petroleum needs in 1980 and that Saudi Arabia, the United Arab Emirates, and Iran were the primary suppliers also helps to explain Tokyo's attention to the region in respect to aid.

There are two countries where, in terms of economic assistance in the region, there appear to be some differences between Washington and Tokyo. The United States maintains no diplomatic relations with the Islamic fundamentalist regime in Tehran whereas Japan still does so and for a time had a rather viable and active aid program in the country focused on the Bandar-Khomenei petrochemical project largely funded by OECF loans along with private flows from Mitsui Trading Company. But Iraqi air strikes significantly disrupted operations at the plant and forced a partial closure and a withdrawal of the Japanese personnel. Since that time, Japanese government approaches to Iran have been very cautious despite Tokyo's considerable interest, lest Japan provoke Washington's wrath.

The case of Israel suggests practically no harmony of foreign aid interests between Japan and the United States. The United States is far and away Jerusalem's largest donor, contributing annually well over $1 billion plus almost $2 billion in outright military assistance. The ODA is nonprojectized, largely budgetary supplemental aid, Washington's only such program. Japan provides an insignificant amount of technical assistance and in general maintains a very low profile relationship with Israel. Tokyo obviously feels there is no need to create problems with regional oil producers.

AFRICA

Africa is representative in many ways of a region in which Japan has had difficulty in identifying its interests. Africa has experienced the world's greatest poverty but is also extremely diverse. Gross national product per capita ranges from $120 per annum in Ethiopia to $1,140 per annum in the People's Republic of Congo. In addition, Africa has been plagued with considerable political turbulence since the late 1950s when the yoke of colonialism was finally broken. Regional nations have also been used as strategic pawns in the East–West conflict, with the Soviets and the Americans each trying to maximize their advantage at the expense of the other.

As Inukai has argued, Africa is not well understood in Japan since there has been little historical contact. Japan, of course, was not a colonial participant in Africa. The Europeans gained a great deal of experience in the region at the expense of African independence. Consequently, Japan also viewed Africa as within the domain of the European powers.[61] This fact is apparently not lost on Africans. In 1987, Japan launched a $500 million nonproject grant program in subsaharan Africa. Because of Japan's lack of familiarity with the region and staffing shortages, the Japanese Foreign Ministry employed British Crown Agents to act as procurement officers in order to prevent wasting aid funds. To some Africans, however, "implicit in the act is that elusive Japanese perception that Africa still belongs to its former colonial powers."[62]

Japan has maintained a steady relationship with Egypt, which is regarded in the Ministry of Foreign Affairs as an African state. Aid to Egypt began to creep upward particularly following the signing of the Camp David accords in 1978. Between 1977 and 1980, Egypt received $441.64 million in Japanese ODA. Through the mid-1980s, Egypt enjoyed the highest amount of yen credit increases of any recipient, with over 40 percent of these funds going for projects in the Suez Canal.[63]

However, for the rest of Africa, Japan applies several criteria for candidates of ODA. First, aid often depends upon the extent to which a country provides natural resources to Japan. Second, countries that are important to western strategic concerns are potential recipients. Third, Japan extends aid to certain countries in order to deflect criticism from black Africa. And finally, countries may receive aid if they are important recipients of Japanese exports. Noticeably absent are criteria that include the need of African nations. Even during the most critical period of drought in Africa, Japan did not react until the other western donors had responded to the crisis.[64]

Nonetheless, in general terms, aid to Africa increased by 130 percent between 1973 and 1984. Despite these increases, Japan is not one of the principal bilateral donors in Africa ranking fifth in 1987. European donors and the United States continue to be the largest aid providers in the region, but particularly in subsaharan Africa. In 1987, while globally Japan was the largest donor in twenty-nine countries, only four of them were located in Africa.

Although virtually all African countries received some form of Japanese ODA between 1960 and 1981, just eight countries shared 70 percent of all ODA extended to the region. Two of these countries are not major sources of natural resources for Japan but are regarded as bellwethers for African public opinion. In addition, Japanese aid authorities find it easier to work with English-speaking Africa than with the Francophone regions.[65]

Public opinion in Japan was aroused significantly during the 1984–1985 period over the plight of drought-stricken countries.[66] A blanket donation campaign was initiated by voluntary groups and the Foreign Ministry established an extremely short-term "starvation lunch" program which was supposed to sensitize Foreign Ministry bureaucrats to the starving masses in Africa but largely succeeded in provoking amusement among other donors and contempt from many African countries. More substantively, in September 1985 Foreign Minister Abe Shintaro proposed a "Green Revolution for Africa" plan at a conference of Foreign Ministers from the seven major industrial countries.[67] A direct result of this proposal was the creation of a "Green Corps" under the direction of JICA. Members of this corps, which consists of young volunteers, plant trees near villages and cities in an attempt to aid the restoration of ecological balance to certain areas of Africa. Other "Green Aid" efforts include funding for international agricultural research institutes, efforts to improve agricultural technology, and increased aid for small landholders.[68]

Japan does provide food aid to Africa. Under the Food Aid Convention of 1980, Japan is obliged to provide each crop year (July–June) the dollar equivalent of 300,000 tons of wheat for food assistance to less developed countries in general.[69] This usually means that Japan ships surplus domestic rice, or Thai rice or purchases U.S. wheat for food aid.[70]

One of the main weaknesses of the Japanese aid program in Africa is the lack of trained specialists on regional affairs. This mirrors the dearth of trained scholars in African problems in the Japanese academic community. Thus, even should the government wish to contract with an African specialist, there are very few to choose from. There are perhaps two reservoirs of African expertise. First are the returning Japan Overseas Volunteer Cooperation (JOCV) members. Some of the JOCV members have developed a rudimentary knowledge of some African languages. However, their tours of duty rarely last more than two years, an insufficient period in which to develop bona fide experts. Besides, heretofore returning JOCV members have had difficulty gaining employment in Japan and only recently has the Foreign Ministry begun to give serious consideration to how the returnees can be, in a sense, recycled through the Japanese aid system. The second source of specialists on Africa is the private sector. Trading companies tend to station their employees abroad for a longer period and, although they do not often develop the linguistic skills that might be useful, the men of the *Sogo Shosha* do develop the kind of networks that often help to smooth the implementation process. Of course, there is rarely any trace of altruism involved. Thus, while project implementation may be relatively trouble free, there is nothing to assure that the project being promoted truly serves the recipient country's interests.

There are several other serious issues confronting Japan's aid program in Africa. First, there seem to be comparatively fewer Africans who desire to pursue technical training from Japan. While the overall acceptance rate in developing countries is 87 percent, according to Inukai, that ratio drops to 72 percent in Africa. Part of that can be attributed to language; applicants from French-speaking countries prefer to be trained in French, which Japan does not do. In the past, most training programs were conducted in English, and this accounts for the fact that over 70 percent of the trainees were from English-speaking countries. However, in the 1980s, many technical training courses were being increasingly taught in Japanese. Although training programs are often preceded by courses in Japanese, the difficulty of the language can prove discouraging for the trainees. Another impediment is that Japan simply does not maintain embassies in a number of French-speaking African capitals. Further, the only two offices that the OECF maintains in Africa are in Cairo and Nairobi.[71] As a consequence, there is sometimes a lack of knowledge about what Japan might be able to offer. And as a result, net disbursements to francophone Africa are noticeably lower than those to English-speaking Africa. The region also seems more impregnable because of the network of French companies that control many aspects of development in these countries.

One particularly delicate aspect of Japan's economic policy in Africa in general is Tokyo's relationship with the Republic of South Africa. Japan was the second largest trading partner with Pretoria in 1988. Japanese have been categorized as "honorary whites" by the apartheid government which seems to suit some Japanese companies as they continue to conduct business with little regard for the wishes of the "front line" African states.[72] Consequently, aid has sometimes been used in an effort to mollify some of Japan's sharpest critics over its relationship with Pretoria such as Zambia and Mozambique.[73]

LATIN AMERICA AND THE CARIBBEAN

Three main factors act as the underpinnings of Japan's foreign policy toward Central and South America. The first of these is Japan's long-standing emigration policy toward the region. More ethnic Japanese live in Latin America than in any other place in the world outside of the archipelago.

Second, Tokyo has always been interested in a continent possessing the abundant resources that Japan so woefully lacks. Finally, the role of the United States in influencing Japan's approach to Latin America cannot be understated. Japan has been hesitant to take too high a profile in the region since Latin America is seen as falling largely within the American sphere of influence, but aid extended to countries after U.S. requests is viewed in the Foreign Ministry as helpful to Tokyo's often contentious relationship with Washington. Consequently, the United States has had an important role in shaping and defining Japan's aid focus on the region. This has been especially the case in the Caribbean and Central America.[74]

The Latin American region has been the recipient of roughly 10 percent of Japanese aid per annum. The ODA totals for several countries in the region appear to demonstrate the extent to which Japan has been increasingly playing a more important aid role in Latin America. In 1986, seven of the top thirty countries receiving ODA disbursements from Japan were in Latin America. In 1987, Japan was Mexico's third largest foreign aid donor and the most generous aid provider to Ecuador and Paraguay. Japan is also the second largest donor in seven other nations of the region, including, in 1987 Honduras, a key country in America's strategic agenda for Central America, and Bolivia. Notably, the heart of the U.S. aid program in Latin America in the 1980s has been in the states of Central America, except for Nicaragua, and in the Caribbean Basin through the Reagan initiative of 1982.

Trade patterns also suggest a high correlation behind some of Japan's regional ODA recipients. As a matter of long-term interest, Japan is cognizant of the importance of the debt crisis. Japanese banks hold over 15 percent of the total regional debt. Japan has on several occasions extended yen loans to countries that have deferred debt repayments. However, the Japanese government has occasionally been at odds with the United States over the role that Tokyo is expected to play despite the fact that the government has urged Japanese banks to go along with the basic U.S. strategy for the region.

Japan stepped up its support for Latin America during the Reagan years. Following Prime Minister Suzuki's participation in the Cancun conference of developing and developed countries, a heightened awareness of the region encouraged other members of the cabinet to visit Latin America. In 1983 and 1985, Foreign Minister Abe visited Central and South America as well as the Caribbean equipped with aid *omiyage* or gifts for the countries he visited. The first overseas trip taken by Prime Minister Kaifu Toshiki included Mexico, where he made concessional and non-concessional lending pledges.

Perhaps the ground-breaking event in terms of increased Japanese aid to the Caribbean was the extension of an OECF loan to Jamaica in 1981 followed by larger loans in 1982. This represented Japan's first significant aid package for the Caribbean and marked the beginning of other efforts in the region. However, the principal motive in providing, or for that matter not providing, aid to the region was more nearly connected to Japan's relations with the United States than to those with the recipient countries.

Japan's recycling initiative is primarily directed at Latin America. In April 1987, during the visit of Prime Minister Nakasone to Washington, an unprecedented $20 billion recycling package was announced, which followed a $10 billion package announced the previous year. Although only $3 billion has been designated as ODA, in other words disbursements carried out by the OECF in the form of yen loans, the remainder is being disbursed in less concessional terms by institutions such as the Export–Import Bank. Again, the primary motive for creating the package seems to have been related less to Japan's relations with Latin America than to bilateral concerns with Washington.

MULTILATERAL DEVELOPMENT BANKS

Although the focus of this study is primarily on bilateral assistance, it is worthwhile to review several basic elements of Japan's aid policy to the multilateral development banks (MDBs). Many of the impediments to smooth policymaking that we have seen to affect bilateral assistance apply to international organizations as well.

As I have mentioned elsewhere, aid decisionmaking related to the banks rests principally in the Ministry of Finance. It is therefore not surprising that this ministry is often the strongest proponent of increasing aid to the MDBs. Although the Foreign Ministry has a say on this policy, it is generally not so decisive as Finance.

The private sector is also not a major supporter of aid to the banks since Japanese construction and trading companies usually win less than one percent of the projects let by institutions such as the World Bank. Of course, this rule does not apply to the Asian Development Bank, a creation of Tokyo in 1966, where Japanese companies play a major role in carrying out projects. Many in the U.S. government and throughout Southeast Asia have come to view the ADB as a Japanese bank. Even though capital subscriptions are divided among nations, the United States and Japan are by far the largest contributors to the bank, maintaining a rough equilibrium. The management of the bank, however, is almost entirely Japanese. The president of the ADB has always come from Japan just as the president of the World Bank has always been an American.[75]

Because of the chronic staff shortages which affect the Japanese aid system, it may seem natural for Japan to divert more aid toward the multilateral institutions since these organizations are better equipped to handle implementation. Actually as a total percentage of DAC contributions to multilateral organizations, Japan's was the highest for the 1986–1987 period at 21.6 percent, compared with the 21.1 percent of the United States.[76] Of the $30 billion recycling plan, at least 60 percent is devoted exclusively to multilateral aid. But multilateral assistance dilutes the potential foreign policy benefits of the direct approach, which helps to explain why MOFA supports bilateral aid. Nevertheless, multilateral aid could make Japanese financial contributions more immune from criticism since it mixes with other donors.

The Foreign Ministry is much more comfortable in promoting policy reform issues with recipients through multilateral organizations than on their own. While the United States pushed the "policy dialogue" with developing countries throughout the 1980s, Japan was very reluctant to follow suit, at least on a bilateral basis. The banks can undertake such a dialogue without exposing any particular donor to the international limelight.

Although Japan's overall financial resources are considerable, it should be remembered that they lie largely in the private sector. The government must operate under severe financial restraints and until 1984 had to manage a budget deficit greater on a GNP basis than that of the United States.[77] Consequently, one way in which the government has tried to aid the World Bank, for example, is to urge the Japanese private sector to cooperate through cofinancing new developing country loans.

One of the most contentious issues related to Tokyo's increasing role in the World Bank is Japan's lack of concomitant voting share. The size of a country's capital subscriptions is supposed to be reflected in this share.[78] Increases in one donor's share translates into proportional reductions in another donor's, usually meaning the United States. While Japan has received an increase in voting share, the U.S. Treasury Department has conceded, albeit reluctantly. In order to avoid a direct confrontation with the United States over this issue, a "special fund" has been created for Japan, but this is unlikely to satisfy over the long term. The issue of burden sharing versus power sharing thus appears to be not only a bilateral issue but a multilateral one as well.

Japan's role in all international institutions is plagued by the small staff contingents that Tokyo contributes. This largely relates to the lack of career incentives for Japanese bureaucrats to seek a secondment to a multilateral organization. Consequently, the cream of the bureaucratic crop prefers assignments more closely related to positions that will promote a steady advance in the career path.

The rhetoric from Tokyo concerning the United Nations has always been very supportive. In part, this rhetoric has been matched by Japan's generous contributions, which amount to the third largest behind the Soviet Union and the United States. Nevertheless, the share of grants to United Nations agencies as a total of Japan's ODA has generally been low. For example, during 1985–1986, 6.6 percent of aid, lower than the DAC average of 8.0 percent, was designated for these agencies.[79]

Even in multilateral banking fora, it is apparent that Japan's relationship with America is of special importance. Only the United States retains veto power in the World Bank and thus far Tokyo has been unwilling to challenge U.S. preeminence for voting shares too strongly. According to a study prepared by the Japan Economic Institute, some World Bank officials regard Japan's views toward multilateral organizations as an extension of its relationship with the United States. The study cites one official as observing, "If the World Bank president asked Tokyo to do something, the answer might be no. If the U.S. Treasury Secretary made a similar request the answer would be yes."[80]

This analysis of aid administration and policy suggests several constant themes that help to explain why an external actor, such as the United States, can influence Japan's foreign aid policy. While Japan has had several goals designed to increase the quantity of ODA, concrete quality efforts have been slower in coming about. This has been particularly noticeable in Japan's weak approach to project evaluation, a problem that the government has readily admitted in the past. Determining whether aid was effective or not was simply regarded as a lower priority to forming ever larger aid budgets in response to international pressure for Japan to "do more."

Thus, the underlying objective of Japan's aid program has always appeared to be designed more specifically to attempt to lessen some of Japan's vulnerabilities. These include natural resources, an unstable global economy, and, last but not least, foreign criticism. Therefore aid has traditionally been viewed as a means of making Japan more secure. This means that a rather reactive and protective aid program has emerged abetted by the system. Arguments within the bureaucracy are often aimed at domestic or foreign concerns that might affect the domestic situation. It is not that this note is absent in the aid debates of other donors; to be sure it is not. It is just that in Japan what is particularly apparent is that the needs of the recipient enter into the discussion less frequently. For example in the United States, a Country Development Strategy Statement (CDSS) must be formulated annually in order to analyze the recipient's changing development needs. Japan has no equivalent. The Japanese government would argue that this is because the recipient government must determine those needs on its own, but this hands-off approach appears disingenuous particularly when many of those "needs" have been determined by the Japanese private sector who have their own interests to secure. And as has been noted elsewhere, the primacy of the private sector in the implementation is directly linked to the lack of central authority in the decisionmaking process. Of course, this could change if the effect of aid untying allows Japan to diversify its implementation sourcing.

Clearly, there existed a few prewar roots for the aid program. However, these ante-bellum efforts were entirely connected to Japan's imperial policy in China. As Rix questions, was it an "accidental slip" that led to an export promotion program and then to a full-fledged aid policy?[81] Or is the Japanese aid program a result of pressure from the United States and other allies to play a greater role in sharing the burden of economic growth and strategic commitment to the West?

The above rationalizations hold a certain amount of currency. However, the use of aid as an element to respond to criticism in other spheres is fairly constant and the use of an outside actor as a bureaucratic ally for the Foreign Ministry strikes a rather persistent theme. The role of Japan's only strategic ally, the United States, has often been an identifiable feature in this policy formulation.

5

Foreign Pressure:
The Role of the United States

Since the end of the Pacific War, the United States has been without question the most important country within the context of Japanese foreign policy. Indeed, the relationship remains the cornerstone of that policy in spite of the frequent debates over trade issues.[1] As Japan increasingly emerged as an economic power in the 1970s, pressure on Tokyo to play a major role in regional defense and foreign aid questions mounted. This corresponded with a diminished American role in Asia and a desire by American policymakers to ensure that the vacuum was filled by a friendly power. Although, at least initially, Japan was reluctant to engage in the kind of military buildup sought by the United States, Tokyo's aid presence in Asia became conspicuous, surpassing Washington's in absolute volume in 1977. Many Japanese policymakers and planners argued that an expanded role in foreign aid was more appropriate for Japan because of constraints imposed on the nation's defense capacity by

This chapter is an expanded version of an article that appeared in *Asian Survey* (July 1988), 28(7):740–56.

the Constitution. Nonetheless, the aid factor in the relationship between Japan and the United States has not been without occasional
rancor, particularly when contentious issues arose stemming from the
more visible defense and trade disputes.[2] One source of mild disagreement in recent years has been the extent of Japan's aid role outside of
Asia. While the United States has considered itself the leader of the
free world and used foreign aid accordingly, Japan has been more
circumspect with aid, focusing most economic contributions on Asia.
Another consistent sore point with the United States has been the
view that aid was directed mainly at promoting Japan's own economic position. Despite Japan's protestations that this perspective is
a vestige of the past, many in Washington continue to doubt Japan's
sincerity on this question.

THE DEVELOPMENT OF THE
AMERICAN AID PROGRAM

From the origins of the Marshall Plan and the Truman Doctrine in the
late 1940s, aid was used as a strategic tool aimed at thwarting Soviet
foreign policy objectives. From 1952 until 1962, U.S. foreign aid was
extended under the Mutual Security Act, which stipulated that assistance could be extended only to strengthen the free world. Thus, in
the early 1950s, aid was virtually indistinguishable from strategic
policy.[3]

Specifically, there were two developments in the late 1950s that
significantly influenced the direction of America's aid program: first,
the emergence of the Soviet Union as a competitor in the developing
world and, second, the decolonization and independence of states in
Africa and Asia together with the growing economic needs of South
American nations.[4] In order to compete effectively with Soviet foreign
aid and appeal to developing countries, the United States began to
veer away from the explicit designation of aid as an instrument of the
cold war. In line with this new approach, nonaligned countries began
to be embraced and the rationale for extending ODA was increasingly
related to developmental purposes rather than just short-term foreign
policy objectives.

This was the outset of the Kennedy years and the period witnessed
a great deal of idealism in the American aid program. Under Kennedy's Administration, the Foreign Assistance Act was passed by Congress establishing the U.S. Agency for International Development.

With the creation of USAID, a largely centralized organization for aid policy formulation and implementation came into being. The Peace Corps was also established, designed to send young volunteers to provide technical skills to people in developing countries. The Congressional statute, now voluminous, sets out specific guidelines for the U.S. aid program and makes the executive branch answerable to the Congress for a wide range of foreign aid issues.

Following the assassination of President Kennedy and the increasing involvement of the United States in the Vietnam quagmire, a corresponding disillusionment with the effectiveness of foreign aid emerged. One reason was that the common aid effort by the DAC tended to obscure U.S. policy interests. But more importantly, the increasingly strident anti-American rhetoric heard in developing countries further eroded what public support had existed for U.S. foreign aid. In addition, the War between India and Pakistan in the early 1970s, both major U.S. aid recipients, raised questions about the usefulness of foreign aid since one rationale was to create an atmosphere of political stability.

During the late 1960s, there were approximately 16,000 USAID officials, of whom roughly half were stationed in Vietnam. Many of the USAID officers in Vietnam were not involved in development at all but rather in the public security program which was designed to train South Vietnamese law enforcement officers and counterintelligence operatives. These conditions were bound to cause a reaction and, as sentiment against the war rose in Congress, concomitant skepticism over America's foreign aid goals also developed. The first visible abrasion on the aid program was the inability of the Senate to pass an authorization bill in October 1971.[5] Gradually, Congress began to perceive that oversight of aid was insufficient and that the focus was not consistent with humanitarian aims. In 1973, the "New Directions" legislation passed in Congress changed the developmental emphasis from large capital projects, much like Japan's program today, to addressing the "poorest of the poor."[6] Under the Carter administration, this approach was particularly expanded along with concern over the human rights records of recipient countries. Nonetheless, there continued to be heated debate in Congress over the nature of aid. Foreign aid bills were frequently stalled and "aid fatigue" set in not only because of political squabbles but also because of diminished public support for aid as Congress and the President were unable to articulate effectively to the public how foreign aid benefited either the United States or poor countries. In short, the

American public came to view foreign aid as an ineffective international welfare program.

With the advent of the Reagan administration, there was a shift in
emphasis if not in basic policy. While "New Directions" was not
dismantled, efforts to aid the world's poorest began to concentrate on
stimulating the private sectors of third world countries as the most
efficient way of promoting development. This approach was based on
the premise of the "magic of the marketplace"[7] and was mirrored in
Reagan's domestic policy. Also, aid to strategically located countries
increased as part of the administration's effort to meet the perceived
Soviet military challenge. As a result, foreign aid again became focused more upon immediate U.S. foreign policy objectives. However,
because of fiscal imperatives which became more acute during the
latter part of the Reagan administration, aid faced further cuts and
remains today the most vulnerable account in the budget "pie."

The fact that American strategic interests have become increasingly focused on the Middle East is reflected in the ODA disbursement
chart in figure 5.1. Since the Camp David accords signed in 1978 by
the United States, Israel, and Egypt, Washington has become the
principal donor to both nations, contributing roughly 30 percent of
its aid budget.

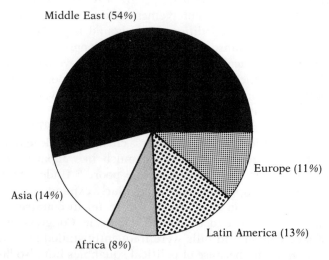

FIGURE 5.1. Regional Allocation of U.S. Aid (FY 1989 Appropriations)

Source: Larry Q. Nowels, *Foreign Aid: Budget, Policy, and Reform* (Washington, D.C.: Congressional Research Service, 1989).

FOREIGN PRESSURE: THE PROCESS

As I have shown, the Ministry of Foreign Affairs has tended to be the strongest advocate of DAC style ODA. Nonetheless, the Ministry also lacks a real domestic constituency and is therefore most likely to require bureaucratic backing from overseas. MOFA often uses international criticism and pressure as leverage to improve its bargaining position against the other ministries and particularly the Ministry of Finance. The United States and the DAC are the most likely coalition partners in the process.[8]

The United States frequently makes its aid policy positions known to the Foreign Ministry. It is only MOFA among the members of the four-ministry deliberation system that conducts regular consultations with the United States on foreign aid questions. The consultations take place between the USAID Administrator and the Director General of the Economic Cooperation Bureau and, since 1985, the Undersecretary of State for Political Affairs and the Deputy Minister of Foreign Affairs. In addition, there are opportunities for aid officials to exchange views more frequently at lower levels, and other fora such as regular DAC meetings and country-specific consortia exist.

Pressure from the United States on the Japanese government takes place at various times on various issues. For example, in the controversy over Japan's mixed credit policy, a spillover issue from trade conflict, both the United States and the DAC placed considerable pressure on Japan to agree to limit this practice. Tokyo, in the end, reluctantly acceded. Both countries, however, at least officially prefer to regard the role of the United States in the Japanese aid process as merely a series of "coincidences of interest."[9]

Because of the turbulent nature of trade relations, on occasion there have been efforts to use aid to attempt to placate Washington and, in a small way, to demonstrate cooperation by improving the bilateral climate. When this occurs, decisions along these lines usually are taken at political rather than bureaucratic levels. Thus, when the Secretary of State or the President requests Japan to increase aid to certain countries or regions, there is a much greater likelihood that Tokyo will agree since it is assumed that Washington places relatively high priority on the matter.

Officials in the Foreign Ministry are normally highly sensitized to U.S.-related issues, therefore, although the Economic Cooperation Bureau does not handle American relations on a daily basis, many of the senior personnel have served either in the United States or in the North America Bureau.[10] Nonetheless, in terms of intraministerial policymaking, the North America Bureau does make representations to the Economic Cooperation Bureau on precisely what the U.S. position may be on major aid questions and how it will effect bilateral relations.[11] As Japan has emerged as a major donor, the U.S. impact on Japanese aid has perhaps lessened somewhat, but American approaches remain fairly constant. MOFA, however, is still sensitive about how Japan's foreign aid is perceived overseas, and therefore the DAC and particularly the United States continue to play the role of unofficial member of the decisionmaking process.

One question that occurs is whether this is symptomatic of what Kent Calder calls the "reactive state." In other words, are policy institutions simply responding to external pressure without necessarily having a preconceived notion as to the optimum interests? Or is "reacting" more consistent with the state's interest than a "proactive" approach? Would proactivity in policymaking make the state vulnerable to hidden risks on the global stage? If so, a "follower" foreign policy would be very much within the perceived national interests.[12]

But perhaps there is another explanation as well. Rather than simply reacting to foreign pressure, state institutions may "interpret" pressure to suit their own policy objectives. In such a case, ministries such as MOFA would apply foreign pressure sometimes rather selectively in internal debate.[13]

Levels of Interaction. Levels of interaction between the United States and Japan on aid policy correspond with the concepts introduced in chapter 1 namely (1) bureaucratic coalition building, (2) "preemptive" aid packages, and (3) direct pressure from the United States on Japan. Furthermore, these levels can apply in either a negative sense, that is to cut aid or terminate a particular policy, or a positive sense, in which the United States encourages Japan to increase aid disbursements or adopt certain policies. They can be applied in analyzing broad-based aid policies and budget or country-specific programs.

The cases we will discuss in this chapter can be placed in these categories. The diagrams illustrate organizational actors involved in the transgovernmental process. The earlier examples discussed often fall under category three. This is because the United States enjoyed comparatively more preponderant power vis-à-vis Tokyo. As Japan gradually gained greater economic clout and trade friction ensued, aid has been increasingly used as a device designed either to forestall

U.S. action on the trade front or to demonstrate Tokyo's sincerity toward Washington. Thus, the descriptive *preemptive* is employed here. Category one is the most prevalent. It is also most directly linked with the bureaucratic style of decisionmaking largely because the bureaucracy has so dominated the aid process in Japan.

FOREIGN AID IN U.S.–JAPAN RELATIONS

The United States began to urge her major allies to assume a greater economic burden in the 1950s as postwar reconstruction of their economies progressed. In particular, West Germany and Japan were increasingly encouraged to share more defense and aid responsibilities.[14]

Japan's original aid disbursements to Southeast Asia, as we have noted, were part of her reparation policy in the region. One observer contends that Prime Minister Yoshida Shigeru's aid policy in Southeast Asia was conceived as part of a cooperative program with the United States. The concept was to combine "American funds with Japanese technology to develop Southeast Asia."[15] Since the Japanese aid program was basically in a prenatal condition, this cooperation must have been extremely limited. Under the Ikeda cabinet, the Yoshida emphasis on U.S.–Japan cooperation was strengthened. Ikeda had keen interest in the efforts of President John F. Kennedy and French President Charles DeGaulle to carve out what Ikeda viewed as regional spheres of influence in Latin America (through the Alliance for Progress program) and Africa, respectively. This encouraged him to consider a similar approach for Southeast Asia.[16] In March 1963, the Clay report to President Kennedy proposed, *inter alia*, that Japan be encouraged to provide yen loans at less than commercial rates to developing countries which would allow a reduction in U.S. assistance.[17] In 1965, both the DAC and the United States renewed pressure on Japan to increase aid to Asia. At the summit meeting between President Lyndon Johnson and Prime Minister Sato Eisaku which took place in January 1965, Johnson urged Sato to extend aid to Taiwan and South Korea. Shortly thereafter, Japan provided a yen loan package of 54 billion yen to the Chiang Kai-shek regime. In June of the same year, relations with the Republic of Korea were finally normalized and Japan provided $300 million in grant aid and yen loans amounting to $200 million to Seoul in 1967.[18] In April of the same year, Johnson proposed a $1 billion development program centered around developing the Mekong River basin and indicated support for the Asian Development Bank.[19] In July, the United States requested Japanese participation in the Mekong project. In addition to cooperating with the United States in Vietnam, the Sato government also extended aid to Indonesia, Malaysia, the Philippines, and Thailand. In November 1967, another summit was held between Sato and Johnson. Again, the United States pressed Japan to increase aid. In January 1968, a high-ranking American delegation followed up on the summit with a visit to Tokyo and requested an increase in aid to Indonesia in order to ease America's financial burden.[20]

From 1969 until 1972, a series of events occurred that cleared the way for an expansion of Japanese aid. These events included the successful conclusion of negotiations for the reversion of Okinawa, the articulation of the Nixon doctrine, detente with the Soviet Union, and de facto recognition of mainland China by the United States (de jure recognition would come in 1979). In addition, Japan's burgeoning balance of payment surplus was beginning to provide excess foreign exchange reserves. However, the reversion of Okinawa was the most immediate Japanese concern and aid played a role in this process as well. At the Nixon–Sato summit in November 1969, the Prime Minister promised to increase contributions to the economic stability of Southeast Asia as well as to South Korea and Taiwan. It was hoped that this cooperative spirit would help to demonstrate further Japan's willingness to share some of the economic burden in Asia.[21] As Japan's trade surplus continued to increase in the early 1970s, economic conflict with the United States began to boil to the surface. For the first time, Japan came under fire for overemphasizing Asia in terms of aid targeting. Also, the tied aid question became increasingly sensitive among the other donors but particularly for the United States. As a result of this pressure, and also because of the apparent instability of certain natural resource nations accompanied by the relative decline of U.S. power in Asia, Foreign Minister Fukuda Takeo argued that Japan should attempt to fill some of this void through economic assistance. When Fukuda became Prime Minister, he used this rationale to press for what became known as the first ODA doubling plan. Therefore, when Fukuda met President Jimmy Carter in March 1977, he was quite willing to be forthcoming to Carter's request to step up aid to ASEAN.[22] The following November during Tokyo meetings between Ambassador Mike Mansfield and Fukuda concerning trade, the United States urged Japan gradually to terminate the practice of tying aid to procurements.[23] The DAC had also exerted pressure on

Japan and therefore Tokyo began the process of untying loans, initially only for less developed countries and later in general terms.

By early 1978, foreign exchange reserves had reached a historic zenith. As a result, prior to Fukuda's meetings with Carter in May and the subsequent Bonn summit in July, the decision was made to shorten the period of doubling foreign aid from five to three years. This was a clear case of Japan's using aid to try to preempt the anticipated stern criticism at both meetings. This action, along with several other non-aid-related measures, was intended to be an important manifestation of Japan's increasing willingness to play a greater role in burden sharing. The plan was also viewed as a "trump card" in the Bonn summit to demonstrate to the leaders of industrializing countries that Japan was doing her best to reduce the trade surplus.[24] Apparently, Fukuda and Carter were in agreement as to the role aid should play in the relationship. Carter indicated that he understood the limitations on Japan's defense role and that expanded aid activities as a means of contributing to burden sharing were entirely appropriate.

In a limited sense, Japan began to follow the U.S. emphasis on basic human needs during the time of the Fukuda cabinet and it was continued under Prime Minister Ohira Masayoshi when he came into office in December 1978. The need to pursue a policy addressing the needs of the poor majority was frequently made clear to Japanese government officials during meetings with Carter Administration representatives. It was pointed out that emphasis on basic human needs could help to dispel persistent suspicions concerning tied aid.[25]

The Soviet invasion of Afghanistan succeeded in stimulating a move toward more strategic assistance in South Asia on the part of both Japan and the United States. The United States began to urge Japan to dramatically increase aid to Pakistan as a country bordering a conflict area *(funso shuhen koku)*. On January 25, 1980, Ohira indicated his support for more aid to Pakistan. In February, Pakistan made the request, and when special envoy Sonoda Sunao was dispatched to Islamabad, he promised to double assistance.[26] In April, Japan favorably responded to the urgings of both the United States and West Germany to extend a major aid package to Turkey. The geographically key NATO member had been suffering serious economic problems and Japan's pledge was well received in Washington.

Much of the credit for Japan's shift toward more "political" foreign aid must go to the Ministry of Foreign Affairs. Ever mindful of the importance of the U.S.–Japan relationship and also charged with the political aspect of foreign policy, MOFA was convinced that aid with more political objectives could serve both purposes. While taking this position, it frequently had to fend off criticism from the other ministries.[27] It was also at this point that the name "Comprehensive Security" came to be applied to Japan's three-faceted foreign policy which placed emphasis on defense, foreign aid, and diplomacy. This was the first time that aid had been articulated as an explicit and integral part of Japanese foreign policy.

With the untimely death of Ohira, the Prime Ministerial post was unexpectedly passed on to dark horse Suzuki Zenko. In November, Ronald Reagan was elected President of the United States and the shift toward more strategic and private sector concerns was intensified. Initially, the aid ministries were skeptical of the policies the Reagan administration wished to advance in the developing world. The "politicization of aid" was slowed down and there appeared genuine apprehension over Reagan's cold war rhetoric and what it could possibly portend for aid. It seemed to some Japanese aid planners that just as Japan had begun to move away from tied aid, the new American administration's avowed support for linking the private sector and aid could move the United States in the opposite direction. In the early days of the administration, Tokyo required repeated clarifications as to the nature of the private sector emphasis that would be pursued until it was satisfied that it was not an export promotion scheme hatched by the United States.[28] In May 1981 following the Suzuki–Reagan summit in Washington, the final communiqué characterized the U.S.–Japan relationship as an "alliance." In order to deflect domestic criticism, however, the nonmilitary aspects were subsequently highlighted, such as aid described as the pillar of comprehensive security policy.[29]

Suzuki announced a new ODA plan in January 1981. While the plan called for an increase of aid to "areas of importance for maintaining international peace and stability," Suzuki seemed to contradict other Reagan aid policy positions at the Ottawa and Cancun summits by emphasizing that ODA, rather than trade and investment, should be the preeminent factor in third world development.[30] Thus, in several key areas, Suzuki appeared to be pursuing an aid policy much more in tune with Carter's approach than Reagan's.

In the early days of the Reagan administration, specific guidelines for how Tokyo should be approached on aid were drafted by the National Security Council and circulated among the various departments and agencies along with other policy priorities relating to Japan. Through this process, a basic policy emerged that would set the tone of the aid relationship between the countries throughout the Reagan years. First, Japan would be urged to emphasize strategic targeting in its foreign aid program, in line with Japan's comprehensive security policy. It was also to be emphasized that increases in foreign aid or targeting would in no way be regarded as a substitute for defense spending. Secondly, the United States would encourage coordination of the two countries' aid policies, including the establishment of selected aid projects jointly financed. Finally, in addition to maintaining the aid levels Japan extended to Southeast Asia, Tokyo was to be urged to increase aid to other regions, in keeping with its efforts to shoulder a greater share of international economic and security burdens.[31]

There are a number of cases that illustrate the first and third applications of U.S. policy toward Japan. They involve Japanese aid to Jamaica, Sudan, Egypt, the Philippines, and Pacific Island countries as well as mixed credits. *Gaiatsu* or direct pressure is not evident in all these cases partly because, with the exception of the mixed credit issue, there is no implication of a quid pro quo threat. Actually, both the U.S. State Department and MOFA officials characterize aid extended to countries that are not *nenjikyoyokoku* in strikingly similar terms, that is, countries in which mutual interests are identifiable.[32] However, we must use caution in taking pronouncements by both governments on a prima facie basis. Diplomatic protocol clearly makes it difficult for either government to admit the extent to which one exercises influence over the other. There are obvious instances wherein the United States has requested Japan to extend aid to countries in which it is very difficult to identify either short-term or long-term Japanese foreign policy goals. Sometimes Japanese interest lies in simply placating Washington's requests.

Some observers have assumed that the $4 billion aid package that Japan eventually extended to South Korea in 1983 was a prime example of the United States' manipulating Tokyo into being forthcoming to South Korea for security reasons. This was certainly widely speculated upon in the Japanese press. After all, the first foreign leader to visit President Reagan upon assuming office was South Korean President Chun Do Hwan in February 1981. It is true that American officials suggested to South Korea that Japan might be responsive to an aid request just as Prime Minister Suzuki had told the Americans during the Ottawa summit. There were also members of the Reagan administration who felt that Japan could play more of a role in supplementing South Korea's defense efforts. However, the initial amount of the request and the explicit security-related rationale caused surprise in the U.S. government as well. At any rate, the Reagan administration wanted no part of the controversy and hoped it would be solved on mutually satisfactory terms. There was much sensitivity over the issue in Tokyo and there were a few occasions when the administration seemed to take the side of the South Korean government, completely unintentionally.[33] As discussed earlier, the matter was finally resolved when Prime Minister Nakasone made it a priority after entering office. Of course, the amicable resolution was consistent with U.S. interests as well.

The Jamaica case presents a somewhat different picture. Shortly after the Reagan administration came into office, it was decided that shoring up the enfeebled Jamaican economy would be the main element in the administration's Caribbean strategy. This decision was taken because the former Jamaican government had come close to allying itself with Cuba and in the new conservative government in Kingston Ronald Reagan had found an ideological cousin in terms of both leaders' aversion to Communism and support for a strong private sector role in the economy unencumbered by government. Consequently, there were immediate efforts to assist the Seaga government through increased U.S. aid, overtures to other DAC governments to expand assistance, and requests to Japan to introduce ODA programs in Jamaica. Indeed, there was no permanent diplomatic representation in Kingston. Japan pursued its governmental interest through annual visits by the Ambassador to the Dominican Republic who also had diplomatic accreditation in Kingston.

In early February 1981, Secretary of State Alexander Haig wrote Japanese Foreign Minister Ito Masayoshi urging that aid be extended to Jamaica, further heightening the Japanese government's awareness of the priority that Washington attached to the issue. The U.S. Embassy's Economic Minister-Counselor, William Baraclough, followed up the letter with a visit to Yanai Shinichi, who was the Director-General of the Foreign Ministry's Economic Cooperation Bureau. Yanai advised the Embassy that while there had been a general acceptance of an aid package for Jamaica within the bureaucracy, the size and type of aid was still the subject of debate. At that point in time, MOFA favored extending concessional loans, which was consistent with U.S. desires. On the other hand, the Finance Ministry supported providing Kingston with a nonconcessional export credit package.[34] One problem facing MOFA aid planners was that the Jamaican government had not made a concrete request for aid and therefore, under Japanese government guidelines, they could not go forward until a specific aid package had been requested. Without a request, Yanai informed Baraclough, the Ministry of Finance would block allocation of aid funds for that country.[35] Subsequent to this meeting, the U.S. Embassy in Kingston approached the Jamaican government and reminded officials of the importance of a formal aid request to the Japanese government. Specific proposals had already been in the planning stages. On February 18, the Jamaicans formally approached a Japanese delegation while at a World Bank meeting in Washington and requested economic assistance; they also invited Japanese government representatives to attend meetings concerning the proposed aid package in Kingston the following month.

With the request received, the Economic Cooperation Bureau along with the Second Latin American Division agreed to the position of supporting quickly disbursible soft loans not project-linked but tied for procurement, in the four-ministry deliberation system. The Finance Ministry stubbornly insisted that Export–Import Bank loans would be most suitable. MOFA's growing recognition of the wider implications of Jamaica's economic recovery was simply not echoed in the Ministry of Finance. In part, the intrabureaucratic struggle was related to the fact that Japan had never shown much interest in the Caribbean in the past. Thus, although MOFA had begun to change its view, in large because of U.S. pressure, it was difficult to bring the Ministry of Finance around to the same realization.

By mid-February, prior to the meeting in Kingston, the bureaucratic logjam over the exact nature of the aid package had still not been broken. Consequently, the urgency of the package was brought to the attention of Prime Minister Suzuki in order to apply political muscle to the problem. The importance of the issue in Washington was reinforced by former Foreign Minister Okita Saburo when he visited Suzuki following his trip to the U.S.[36]

The Foreign Ministry adopted the tactic within the bureaucracy and also in informal talks with members of the Diet that Jamaica was a country ideally suited for Japanese aid since it was democratic, seriously interested in economic reforms, committed to expanding the private sector, and important to U.S. interests. These arguments as well as cabinet-level intervention were successful in permitting MOFA to put forth the kind of aid package it had supported all along.[37] On March 11, Japan pledged 2.1 billion yen ($10 million) in soft loans to

Jamaica at the "Friends of Jamaica" meeting in Kingston. It was a nonproject OECF commodity loans, precisely what the United States and MOFA had preferred.

Further problems lay ahead in the Japan–Jamaica aid relationship. Following the aid pledge, the government spent months defending the aid from criticism by opposition party members in the Diet. These members criticized the linking of Japanese aid to what they viewed as U.S. strategic designs in the Caribbean basin.

In December of 1981, Prime Minister Seaga visited Japan. Although he did not make a request for further aid during his visit, many Japanese aid policymakers were nonetheless disappointed by what they viewed as Jamaica's slow absorption rate of the commodity loans being provided under the previous March agreement. MOFA advised U.S. Embassy officials that further economic assistance would not be forthcoming until Kingston had drawn down the funds allocated under the commodity loan agreement. Consequently, the United States again interceded and advised the Seaga government of MOFA's concerns. As the Jamaican government began to overcome its implementation problems, Japan again began to consider other kinds of economic aid. Subsequently in June 1983, Japan and Jamaica signed a $25 million loan for coffee plantation development (Japanese being large consumers of Jamaica-produced coffee) and $46 million for a barge-mounted diesel power plant in the same year.[38]

Jamaica

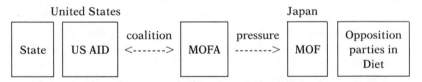

An important priority in the same region for the Reagan administration was the Caribbean Basin Initiative announced in February 1982 and approved by Congress in July 1983. The underlying philosophy consisted of a combination of "anticommunism, bilateralism, private investment, and the promotion of free markets." The first foreign aid component of the package was $350 million. Those eligible for assistance were not only the island states of the region but also the Central American nations of El Salvador, Costa Rica, Guatemala, Belize, and Honduras.[39]

The announcement of the CBI coincided with a particularly tense time in U.S.–Japan trade relations in which there were several amendments circulating in the Congress that would have required up to 90 percent domestically produced parts in American-made automobiles. The Ministry of Foreign Affairs was eager to demonstrate to the Congress that Japan was willing to cooperate with the United States in a critical strategic plan. Press reports indicated that project aid alone was being considered and that in addition to more aid for Jamaica, the Dominican Republic, Costa Rica, and Honduras were viewed as eligible for Japanese aid.[40]

Just prior to Foreign Minister Sakurauchi Yoshio's visit to the United States, MOFA authorities advised the State Department that Japan would favorably respond to requests for assistance to the CBI. The motivation of trade friction was clearly present in discussions between U.S. Embassy and MOFA officials when this topic was raised.[41] When MOFA Latin American Affairs Bureau Director General Edamura visited several countries in the Caribbean region in March, USAID officials were prepared with specific projects that were recommended to both the potential recipient government and to Japan.[42]

Caribbean Basin Initiative

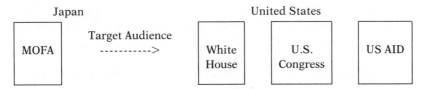

The cases of Sudan, Egypt, and Pakistan offer further evidence of the use of the National Security Directive toward Japan on foreign aid. As in the case of Jamaica, these approaches conformed with the first and third policy objectives vis-à-vis Japanese aid, that is, strategic targeting and increasing aid to countries outside of Southeast Asia. Increased aid to these countries did not, however, come about simply because of U.S. pressure. On the contrary, the Ministry of Foreign Affairs well understood the need to extend assistance to these countries and might have been able to do so without the U.S. request. American pressure clearly strengthened the hand of MOFA in its policy struggle with the Ministry of Finance.

In the spring of 1981, the government of Sudan indicated to the Japanese Embassy in Khartoum that it wanted an expansion of the Japanese aid presence in Sudan. Because of the fragile political order in and around the region, this was also supported by the United States. Japanese aid for the five years prior to 1981 had totaled $50 million. Initially, the Japanese government appeared to be reluctant to extend more aid since there were few identifiable intrinsic interests and Sudan had been slow in repaying outstanding amounts on prior credits. On June 11, 1981, the USAID Mission in Khartoum advised Washington that they would recommend that the government of Sudan make another approach to the Japanese. However, at the same time, the Mission informed Washington that they "doubted that Japan would make any meaningful response to anything short of a high-level approach by the U.S. government."[43]

Sudan

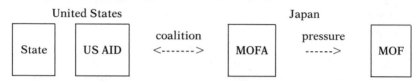

The assassination of President Anwar al Sadat of Egypt accentuated the strategic sensitivity of the region as a whole. Shortly thereafter, President Reagan sent Prime Minister Nakasone a letter specifically requesting an emergency aid package for Egypt. MOFA had wanted to increase aid to Egypt but had been stymied again by the Ministry of Finance. The Reagan letter managed to speed up the process.

This concern over regional instability triggered renewed aid interest in the Sudan. In an effort to speed along the process, the U.S. Embassy cabled Washington that it would be wise to share as much information concerning the Sudan as possible with MOFA in order to help the ministry justify to the Ministry of Finance a new aid package under the rubric of comprehensive security.

This came in the midst of a series of moves designed to encourage increased Japanese aid as a strategic device. On January 21, 1982, Assistant Secretary of State for East Asia and Pacific Affairs John Holderidge recommended to Secretary Haig a series of new high-level moves designed to signal the administration's keen interest in Japanese defense and foreign assistance efforts. Increasing aid to "areas in crisis" was the linchpin of this new policy approach. The objective was not only to spur Japan but also to soothe Congressional and public opinion concerning Tokyo's widely perceived limited security role or "free ride."

The high-level approaches aimed at urging Japan to increase aid to

Sudan recommended by the USAID Mission in Khartoum were finally taken in the form of a letter from Secretary Haig to Foreign Minister Sakurauchi on January 25, 1982. Sakurauchi responded indicating that Japan was "also much aware of Sudan's geopolitical importance and economic difficulties." He went on to say that "based on the recognition of these facts," Japan announced its intention at the donors meeting to provide 5.75 billion yen of which roughly 2.5 billion yen was quick disbursing commodity loans and 3.25 billion was in grant assistance. Knowing of U.S. concerns relating to Egypt and Pakistan, he also addressed those two countries. With regard to Egypt, characterized by the Sakurauchi letter as "Japan's most important and largest recipient in the Middle East," Japan pledged a 46 billion yen concessional loan on January 19, 1982. Sakurauchi indicated that Japan was "intensifying . . . aid to Pakistan, which is counted among the 'countries bordering conflict areas,' " and that further aid was currently being considered (and subsequently extended). The Foreign Minister noted that Japan's assistance to these three countries was part of Tokyo's policy of aiding countries "with geopolitical importance in the other regions of the world." Sakurauchi also noted that he firmly believed the policy he had described went "along with the basic line of U.S. foreign policy." He concluded by saying that the government of Japan would remain in close contact with the U.S. government and continue to strengthen ODA to developing countries.[44] Haig later responded by thanking Sakurauchi and saying that the Japanese efforts were "precisely the sort of action I had in mind."[45]

Egypt

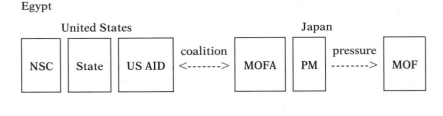

Pakistan

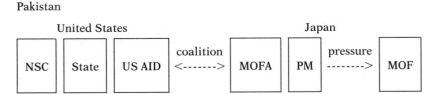

These cases demonstrate an aspect of U.S.–Japan aid cooperation outside of Southeast Asia. But what about the ASEAN states, the principal recipients of both Japanese and U.S. assistance in Asia? The Philippines presents an interesting case, that of a nation of great strategic importance to Japan and the United States which has had to contend with considerable political instability in recent years. The United States has all along encouraged Japan to increase aid to Manila both during the Marcos period and even more so under the Aquino government. Some have argued that the United States was the sole motivating factor behind the Nakasone government's provision of aid to the Marcos regime and that "emergency aid was given [to the Philippines] in response to President Ronald Reagan's request," mainly because of the presence of U.S. bases.[46] That strong U.S. interests are at stake in the Philippines is indisputable but this analysis appears to overshadow Japan's own interests in the nation's stability. Irrespective of U.S. pressure, there would have been a Japanese aid presence in the Philippines.

Since the beginning of the Aquino government in 1986, aid has remained a contentious subject between the United States and Japan. While Japan is willing to provide large amounts of ODA to Manila, many in the U.S. government were critical of what was initially viewed as the snail's pace at which aid implementation from Japan was proceeding.[47] During Undersecretary of State for Political Affairs Michael Armacost's consultations on aid with Vice Minister Yanai in March of 1987, he made it clear that the United States hoped Japan would expedite disbursement to Manila. Given the corruption of the Marcos regime, Yanai advised Armacost that Japan wanted to wait until the new Congress was instituted in the Philippines. Armacost also acted as a go-between with the Japanese on the Philippine government's request for a more active role in assisting land reform.[48] The principal role of the United States in this case is that of supporting MOFA in order to leverage funds from the Ministry of Finance.

The diagrams demonstrate how the change in the Philippine government caused a reconstruction of the transgovernmental coalition partners. For Japan, basically, opposition parties are no longer vocal critics of the Philippine government. Also, those opposed to aiding the Marcos government are not against assisting Philippine development under Mrs. Aquino. On the American side, Congress emerged as a strong supporter of the new regime in Manila.

Philippines (Marcos)

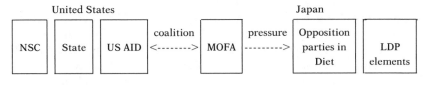

Philippines (Aquino)

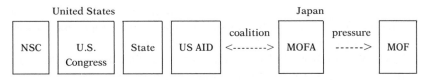

In the same vein, while some analysts have argued that Japan has been pressured by the United States to step up economic assistance to Pacific basin nations in order to counter a perceived expansion of Soviet influence in the region, strong pressure has not really been required. Again, it is easier for Japan to define its own interests in the region. It is more an encouragement process or a sending of positive signals from the United States than a case of *gaiatsu* per se.[49] This was amply demonstrated by the letter from Secretary George Shultz to the Foreign Minister after the Kuranari doctrine was announced in January 1987.

The foregoing cases all describe a positive role for the United States in the Japanese aid decisionmaking process. In other words, Japan has been requested to provide or increase aid to a given country. Occasionally, the United States also wields negative influence in Japan's aid program by discouraging Tokyo from extending aid to certain countries. In a sense, one of these countries, Cuba, perhaps should not be placed in this category simply because the United States has never requested Japan not to have an aid program in Havana. Washington has never had to do so, since Japanese officials are well aware of what American reaction would be if Japan established an aid program in a country long regarded as a Soviet proxy just ninety miles from the coast of Florida. The cases of the Socialist Republic of Vietnam and Sandinista Nicaragua are more clear-cut.

Following Hanoi's victory in Vietnam in 1975, Japan began to provide small but annually increasing technical assistance to Vietnam.

This ODA continued to flow until the Vietnamese invasion of Cambodia in February of 1978, ostensibly to overthrow the genocidal regime of Pol Pot but viewed among several ASEAN neighbors as the first step in Hanoi's expansionist policy. Washington, which was still licking its wounds from the Vietnam conflict, was also quick to condemn Hanoi's action. The People's Republic of China strongly contributed to this condemnatory chorus. In this atmosphere, Japan terminated its aid program to Hanoi.[50] Some officials in the Foreign Ministry and MITI, while criticizing Hanoi's military adventurism, believed that Japan should continue the program in order to maintain open channels. U.S. policymakers were aware of these sentiments and applied strong pressure on Japan to subdue them. There was suspicion in Washington and in ASEAN capitals that Japan wanted to maintain links primarily for commercial purposes. This issue faded into the background until December 3, 1981, when the Director of the First Southeast Asia Division in MOFA called in the U.S. Embassy Political Counselor to inform him that the Japanese government had decided to grant a 30 million yen package of medical supplies for use at the Cho Ray Hospital in Ho Chi Minh City. The decision had been reached after a Vietnamese parliamentarian delegation had broached the subject during a visit to Tokyo. The Ministry official insisted that this was not the first step in resuming an aid program in Vietnam, but Washington suspected that this might be a trial balloon and that it was best to shoot it down earlier rather than later. MOFA informed ASEAN and the PRC, which all expressed similar misgivings.[51]

U.S. suspicions concerning Japan's motives heightened when it was recalled that Foreign Minister Sakurauchi, who had assumed office following a cabinet reshuffle only days before, was also chairman of the Japan–Vietnam Parliamentarian Friendship Association and that during the visit of the Vietnamese parliamentarians, Sakurauchi had reportedly urged the resumption of economic assistance to Vietnam. Nonetheless, the fact that MOFA had called in U.S. Embassy officials to explain in detail what was a minor humanitarian gesture reflected the deep concern that it not be misinterpreted by the United States as a sudden switch in Japan's policy toward Vietnam. Japan also assured Washington that the humanitarian aid package would not develop into the substance of policy.[52] During aid consultations between USAID Administrator M. Peter McPherson and the Director of MOFA's Economic Cooperation Bureau Yanagi Kenichi, McPherson also cautioned against extending any food assistance to Vietnam.

Vietnam

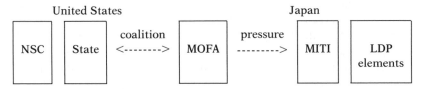

The United States also discouraged Japan from maintaining a serious aid program in Sandinista Nicaragua. Following the overthrow of the Somoza government in 1979, the Carter administration began an attempt to cultivate the new regime. This included extending token economic assistance which was expected to grow if relations developed normally. Japan had been encouraged to contribute aid to the fledgling government by the United States as well. However, concerns remained over an increasing tilt by Marxist members of the new junta toward the Soviet Union and Cuba. The closing of the liberal Managua daily *La Prensa* sent ominous signals to Washington even before Ronald Reagan's victory in the 1980 Presidential race.

Upon Reagan's assumption of power, a tougher stand toward Nicaragua became increasingly apparent as administration figures called for a "tightening of the screws on the Marxists in Managua."[53] In addition to such direct measures as funding a counterrevolutionary force known as the "Contras," Washington ended its meager technical aid program in the country and strongly urged other DAC members to act accordingly. Prior to the February 1982 meetings between McPherson and Yanagi, staff-level MOFA officials had informed USAID staff members that Japan was seriously considering providing technical assistance to the Sandinista government, in part in order to discourage too much dependence on the Soviet Union. McPherson advised Yanagi in no uncertain terms that this would not be well received in official Washington.[54] In subsequent consultations, the United States reiterated this position and through 1989 Japan never provided any substantial assistance to Nicaragua.

Nicaragua (cut ODA)

Influence wielding is not one way with U.S. interests relentlessly being articulated to an obedient Japan. In fact, at times the influence has been reversed and used by the State Department in much the same way that the Foreign Ministry uses American pressure against competing aid decisionmaking actors. One area of Japanese concern has been decreases in America's aid budget, particularly during the Reagan years. In late January 1981, the cuts in the aid budget proposed by Office of Management and Budget (OMB) Director David A. Stockman were leaked to the press from the State Department. Indeed, the supposed secret proposals were also sent to foreign embassies in Washington and U.S. Ambassadors abroad were reportedly instructed to "generate a reaction" from their host governments. Stockman, who felt aid institutions were "infested with socialist error," proposed a 45 percent reduction in U.S. aid over a four-year period.[55] The leaks had their desired effect as the U.S. government was inundated with a storm of protest.[56] In Japan, the then Director of the Aid Policy Division in MOFA, Matsuura Koichiro, called in the acting Deputy Chief of Mission of the U.S. Embassy and, on behalf of Foreign Minister Ito, voiced strong concern over the prospects of U.S. aid reductions. The Embassy was informed that MOFA had been very encouraged by the increased foreign aid request in the U.S. draft budget that had been submitted to Congress early in January. This budget draft had helped convince the Finance Ministry to agree to the new increases that were needed to attain the medium term target. The Foreign Ministry was concerned over the impact on its negotiating position with other ministries and in the Diet over aid in the future if the proposed Stockman cuts were accepted. MOFA also worried that the reductions signaled neo-isolationism on the part of the United States.[57] The Foreign Ministry, in the eyes of the Embassy, was clearly trying to weigh in before the Secretary of State met with Stockman. From this time on, USAID and State Department officials had to reassure MOFA representatives constantly that the United States still maintained a commitment to a viable aid program. The Foreign Ministry's reaction to their subsequent demarches over the effects of the Gramm–Rudman budget-cutting measures on the U.S. aid program suggests more concern over the Ministry's internal negotiating position than over the effects of the reductions. At a time when the United States seemed to be instituting draconian aid reductions, Japan was going in the opposite direction.

1981 Proposed Aid Budget Cuts

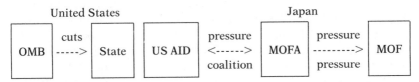

By the beginning of 1983, both the United States and Japan were clearly placing more importance on the foreign aid linkage in the relationship. This was partly because bilateral friction was taking place at so many other levels. In addition to defense and the ever present trade conflict, Tokyo and Washington were also engaged in contentious rounds of negotiations on fishing rights, whaling, and aviation. In short, there were very few bright spots in the relationship. Foreign Ministry and State Department officials wanted to point to some concrete areas of cooperation. During the first visits of Foreign Minister Abe Shintaro and Prime Minister Nakasone in January 1983, both Secretary Shultz and President Reagan raised foreign aid coordination during their respective discussions.[58]

However, one serious source of debate between the two countries has been tied aid and mixed credits. Both these issues represent cases in which *gaiatsu* or influence implying threat has been used by the United States. The United States has assailed Japan's use of foreign aid for "predatory commercial purposes" since the late 1970s, but sensitivity over the issue heightened in direct proportion with America's spiraling bilateral balance of payments deficit. In this sense, aid became very much part of trade conflict.[59] Negotiations conducted within the DAC designed to reach a compromise over mixed credits began in 1984. At the heart of the controversy was a proposal to revise the way in which ODA loans were defined and calculated by the DAC. Japan argued that the proposed changes would penalize it for having low domestic interests rates. The United States and other DAC members countered that the "easy money" environment in Tokyo gave Japanese exporters and contractors unfair advantage in developing world markets. Because Japan's official discount rate is low, the government was able to obtain funds at lower interest rates and therefore it cost less to dispense loans. To rectify this situation, the United States and the European Community proposed calculating the cost of loans using a "differentiated discount rate (DDR)" pegged to prevailing interest rates in each donor country.

In applying direct pressure in which there was an implied or real threat, the United States used several "weapons" designed to coerce Japan into signing the DAC-sponsored agreement over the strong objections of all the ministries involved in the aid process. In 1985, when negotiations seemingly stalled, the Reagan administration proposed and the Congress enacted "war chest" legislation which was a fund used by the U.S. Export–Import Bank in cooperation with the Department of Treasury designed to offer nonconcessional credits targeted mainly at Japanese competitors in developing countries. Part of the rationale for the war chest was to use it as a negotiating lever in the discussions on mixed credits.[60]

The United States took another step against Japan in October 1986 when the administration opposed Tokyo's bid to increase its contribution to the International Development Agency (IDA), known as the soft loan window of the World Bank. The United States clearly stated that it was against giving Japan more authority and voting rights in IDA as long as the Japanese government proved "unwilling to improve restrictions on tied yen loans." A Finance Ministry official was perplexed by the U.S. decision and was quoted as saying, "We cannot understand why the U.S. came to connect [a fund increase] with the mixed credit problem" and that "Japan cannot avoid a compromise on ODA because of the U.S. hard-line posture."[61]

U.S. frustration continued to grow and the issue was at the top of the agenda for the ODA consultations held in Paris between USAID Administrator McPherson and new Director General of MOFA's Economic Cooperation Bureau Hanabusa Masamichi in early December 1986. The issue was raised again during the annual DAC review in January 1987.

In the United States, the issue was comanaged by USAID with the Department of Treasury as the lead agency. In Japan, the Finance and Foreign Ministries contended for control over the mixed credit problem. The final push from the American side came on March 5, 1987, just ten days before the DAC-determined deadline for settling the issue. In letters addressed to Vice Minister of Finance, Gyohten Toyoo and to Hanabusa, Treasury Assistant Secretary for International Affairs David C. Mulford strongly urged Japan to endorse the differentiated discount rate proposal. The carrot-and-stick approach was clear in the language of the letter. "The European Community has already reached the limit of its flexibility, and the agreement represents the bottom line for the United States," emphasized Mulford. At the same time, the Assistant Secretary indicated understanding for Japan's concern that "the DDR formula in the agreement might be generally applied to all aid by the DAC." Mulford assured Gyohten and Hanabusa that if Japan accepted the tied aid credit package by March 15, "the U.S. approach would be that the DDR formula should not be adopted as a general DAC procedure . . . nor should the new rules affect the definition of ODA."[62]

On March 17, the DAC announced that "all participants . . . have accepted a package of measures to strengthen rules on tied aid and partially untied aid on commercial credits." The specifics of the agreement included two major points: the minimal permissible grant element on tied and partially untied aid credits was raised and, more important from Japan's perspective, the calculation of the grant element or the application of the DDR was changed.

In a statement issued by Secretary of the Treasury James A. Baker after signing the agreement, he acknowledged that the accord "imposes particular sacrifices on Japan." As an indirect message to the U.S. Congress, he praised Japan's decision to accept the agreement as a "welcome demonstration of Japan's willingness to take concrete steps to resolve important trade issues."[63]

Baker also maintained that the arrangement "culminates a long-standing effort by the Reagan administration to negotiate the virtual elimination of U.S. export credit subsidies" and that the agreement "achieved a major goal of President Reagan's attack on foreign unfair trade practices." He added that the mixed credit practice had "resulted in lost exports and lost jobs in the United States." The United States had initiated negotiation to raise the concessionality of tied aid with the view that increased costs would deter the use of such credits as trade promotion tools and sharpen the distinction between legitimate development assistance and export financing.[64]

Eliminate Mixed Credits (DDR formula)

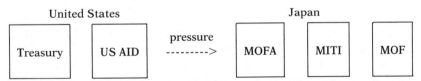

Efforts to use aid as a tool to mollify Congress in order to delay or prevent enactment of trade legislation was clearly the intention of Japanese decisionmakers when Prime Minister Nakasone announced his major "recycling package" proposal in April 1987. In addition to Japanese concern over a pending major trade bill in the Congress, the

United States had placed strict import duties on semiconductors in March. This action surprised many in the Japanese government. Nakasone's trip to the United States, although previously scheduled, was also designed to cool emotions in Washington as well as to seek elimination of the tariffs. The aid package as it was announced was drafted, in general terms, in the Economic Bureau of MOFA with input from the Second North American Division and the Economic Cooperation Bureau. The proposals that the Prime Minister brought to Washington were very vague. Initially, it was thought that the package was to be earmarked mainly for debtor nations in South America. Also, the $20 billion proposal was said at first to be ODA, but when it was learned that nonconcessional Japan Export–Import Bank loans would make up most of the programs, the measure was greeted with a great deal of skepticism.

During the difficult negotiating sessions with the Ministry of Finance, MOFA regularly employed the threat of protectionist legislation in the Congress as a reason for going forward with the recycling plan in order to demonstrate Japan's sincerity in handling the country's tremendous balance of payment surplus.[65]

The aid–recycling package represents another case in which MOFA used the "America card" as a means of achieving a policy victory. Moreover, the basic rationale for MOFA's policy position appears to have been dictated more by Japan's interest vis-à-vis the United States than by the needs of developing countries.

Recycling

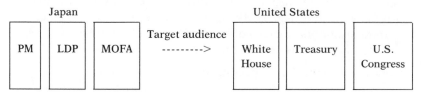

Japan				United States		
PM	LDP	MOFA	Target audience -------->	White House	Treasury	U.S. Congress

Another device whereby Washington has attempted to influence Japanese ODA policy is the consultative mechanism. In 1978, at the request of the Japanese government, the United States sent a high-level delegation consisting of the USAID Administrator and several high-ranking State Department officials to conduct the first aid consultations. The Japanese side was led by the Director General of the Economic Cooperation Bureau of MOFA. The next high-level consultations were held in Washington in 1979. In 1980 and 1981, because it was a presidential election year and because of governmental reorganization in the first year of the Reagan administration, only staff consultations took place. High-level consultations were postponed several times causing some concern in the Japanese government that the discussions might not continue. But as the new administration in USAID became untracked, planning proceeded for the first high-level discussions in almost three years. In early February 1982, delegations led by USAID Administrator McPherson and MOFA Director General of Economic Cooperation Yanagi met and produced agreements for the first time to pursue several jointly funded aid projects.[66] Both sides compared regional aid programs as well. The United States expressed support for Japan's efforts in the PRC while opposing any Japanese aid to Nicaragua.

The U.S. delegation had come equipped with a list of countries to which Washington urged Japan to extend ODA. This approach was characteristic of the problem of establishing clear priorities for requests that plagued policymakers. Cables come in from many American embassies throughout the developing world for requests for increased aid. These embassies are well aware of the aid budget shortfall faced by the U.S. government and, as a consequence, many of these requests are passed on to Japan either during consultations or through demarches issued by the U.S. Embassy in Tokyo or during high-level meetings. Sometimes these aid requests are passed on to Japan when they are not consistent with U.S. aid expertise. Often, the routing patterns for cables in the State Department are such that those who need to know about Japanese aid initiatives never receive notification.

The next bilateral meeting was held in June 1983 in Washington. The United States pressed Japan not to "limit its aid to Asia" and to increase it to other regions in line with its policy of comprehensive security. Japan made it clear that Asia would remain its most important priority.[67] After a one-year hiatus, again at least tangentially connected with the 1984 elections, the aid dialogue was reinvigorated. In January 1985 at a summit meeting in California, both President Reagan and Prime Minister Nakasone agreed to add another dimension to aid consultations. Following up on this agreement and focusing only on the strategic aspects of aid, Undersecretary Armacost and MOFA Vice Minister Yanai met in March in Tokyo. Armacost continued to urge Japan to think strategically in a larger context outside of Asia. In April, USAID Administrator McPherson continued the dialogue with Economic Cooperation Bureau Director General Fujita Kimio.

The next meeting between McPherson and his new counterpart,

Hanabusa, in Paris focused primarily on the mixed credit issue. McPherson, echoing the DAC in general, also urged Japan to make more aid resources available for Africa. The increasing pressure on MOFA to expand ODA to the region does not face much opposition but rather simply lack of enthusiasm because of the difficulty in identifying Japanese interests. Some MOFA officials, chafing under the persistent pressure from the DAC and the United States on Africa have come to refer to the organization as "Afridac."[68]

In April 1987, Armacost again visited Japan in order to discuss the strategic aspects of aid issues with his new counterpart, Vice Minister Murata Ryohei. Armacost brought a long list of countries where Japanese ODA would be viewed as contributing to western security interests and suggested to Murata that responsiveness to some of these nations could be useful on Capitol Hill in terms of demonstrating a cooperative Japanese attitude. In reality, I would argue that this overrates the value attached to Japanese foreign aid efforts in the Congress and is therefore somewhat disingenuous. Most members of Congress have little awareness of Japan's aid program, and, when there is cognizance, ODA is usually associated with the Japanese private sector's commercial objectives. Nonetheless, as we have seen in several other cases, some officials in the Japanese government persist in seeing the utility of aid as a tool to deflect criticism from Congress.[69]

The consultative channels with Japan concerning aid rapidly expanded. In addition to the formal conferences focusing only on aid, the subcabinet-level meetings on trade also occasionally introduce aid questions. The utility of the aid dialogue has received mixed reviews. Some high-ranking USAID officials are clearly dissatisfied with discussions they feel have "produced very little." This criticism is particularly directed at Japan's continued regional emphasis and the mixed credit–tied aid issues.[70] But in reality, the consultative mechanism and the manner in which the United States attempts to influence Japan have been much more successful than either side is willing to admit. Japanese aid decisionmakers understandably do not wish to admit that they take the views of another donor as seriously as they do and that such views have significant influence in several areas. The United States wants Japan to be even more responsive and therefore is reluctant to acknowledge the extent to which Japan receives American aid requests favorably even though this is often for domestic bureaucratic purposes.

Experience has shown that the best way for the United States to attain results in exercising influence in Japan's aid process is through high-level representation of U.S. priorities followed by consistent prodding at the lower levels through the consultative mechanisms as well as at the mission level. The U.S.–Japan high-level aid consultations have also spawned other bilateral dialogues between Japan and several donors. In this sense, the bilateral consultation process has become an added feature to the regular DAC channels among the donors.[71]

JOINT PROJECTS AND MISSION CONSULTATIONS

One approach that both the United States and Japan have tried to promote since 1978 is jointly financed aid projects. This has been a major feature of all aid consultative meetings.

Substantive cooperative aid undertakings have been recorded as far back as 1954. Although Japan had no aid program of its own, the Yoshida government agreed to accept trainees of the U.S. aid program (a forerunner of USAID). These were largely middle- and senior-level officials of developing countries receiving U.S. aid for whom training in Japan was judged to be more relevant because of Japan's intermediate level of economic development in the 1950s. The United States bore the local costs of this program until 1960.[72]

During the first aid consultatives at Shimoda, the United States raised the prospect of joint projects, but the proposal was not very warmly received by Japan. At the next consultative meetings, the roles were reversed, with Japan suggesting and the United States digressing in response to the possibility of joint projects. During the course of staff-level consultations, the idea was revived. Japan proposed joint funding for a tropical medicine institute in the Philippines in early January 1980 meetings. However, at the initial planning stages the concept encountered the same types of problems that would later confront all such ventures, namely, two very different aid systems at work. USAID's planning and implementation are virtually fully decentralized with the missions exercising a certain degree of autonomy, whereas the locus of authority in the Japanese development program remains in Tokyo. Japanese field representatives have little if any input into their development assistance portfolio. In addition, U.S. aid efforts in developing countries must be careful not to violate Congressional guidelines set by the Foreign Assistance Act. Finally, the budget cycle in the United States is different, with both countries having different fiscal years. The Japanese delegation advised USAID that they would nonetheless suggest to the Philippines that USAID/Manila be invited to participate in these discussions in order to learn more about the project and ascertain possibilities for cooperation.

From early on, Japanese aid planners were mainly interested in the Asia–Pacific region as the venue for undertaking joint projects. Further, Japan's interest in pursuing these joint undertakings was to cooperate with the United States. On January 28, 1980, a U.S. and Japanese delegation signed a statement outlining steps toward cooperation on aid projects. The Japanese side made several proposals for possible consideration as jointly funded projects.

Japan suggested joint cooperation in the area of provincial health services in Chanthaburi in Thailand; the United States suggested joint cooperation in a biomedical research facility in Indonesia. Specifically, USAID/Jakarta was involved in a "community immunization project" to distribute diphtheria vaccines. The area wherein the United States felt that Japan might play a role was in providing refrigerators on a grant basis. This joint project never materialized because planners felt it was of too small a scale. Other projects were suggested as well. The United States suggested the possibility of Japanese–U.S. cooperation in marine resource research at the University of the South Pacific; Japan suggested joint assistance in elementary education in Western Samoa and Tonga. These were among the more prominent joint project ideas that emerged during staff-level discussions. Further discussions were to be carried out at the mission level.[73]

Finally, at the high-level talks in 1982, agreements were made on several projects, most prominent among them a dry land agricultural center in northeast Thailand. The basic rationale for such projects on the U.S. side was to try to stretch USAID's developmental impact financially in a time of fiscal frugality. Also from the perspective of USAID professionals, cooperation could act as a shortcut to obtaining Japanese products, especially vehicles, without going through the lengthy applications to waive a law requiring the use of American-made equipment on USAID development projects.[74] Another reason, at least on the State Department's Japan Desk which was shared in the Foreign Ministry, was that joint aid cooperation could be a bright spot in a bilateral relationship already hampered by contentious trade and defense issues.

The jointly funded dry land institute in Thailand was seemingly plagued by confusion from the outset with each participant, the United States, Japan, and Thailand, going their own separate ways, each not exactly clear what the other was doing. Furthermore, the technical experts from the U.S. and Japanese aid agencies, while interested in the project, had little concern for the "high-level politics" of U.S.–Japan relations.[75] It was a case in which too many political expectations seemed to outrun developmental realities. U.S. Ambassador to Thailand John Gunther Dean and his Japanese counterpart Ogiso Motoo met on several occasions, giving their blessings to the undertaking, and were at the formal ribbon-cutting ceremonies that inaugurated the project. As Vice President, George Bush was reported to have pointed to the joint project in Thailand as a glittering example of cooperation at a National Security Council meeting.[76] In the Congress, Senator Charles Percy, then the Chairman of the Foreign Relations Committee, made reference to it in a speech on the floor of the Senate.[77] The joint project scheme was also thought to be of sufficient importance to be raised by President Reagan during Prime Minister Nakasone's first visit to the United States in January 1983. It was also on the agenda for the meeting between Secretary Shultz and Foreign Minister Abe.

Other joint projects have been initiated but with much less fanfare. One of the most noteworthy was the refugee training center on Bataan in the Philippines. This project began in 1983 and involved Japanese ODA funding for a job training facility for refugees prior to resettlement in the United States. The concept was introduced by U.S. Ambassador for Refugee Affairs William Douglas during meetings with MOFA officials in March 1982. Training refugees in the Philippines meant fewer costs for the states where the refugees eventually were to be relocated. For Japan, the venture was a means of deflecting criticism of Tokyo's unwillingness to resettle refugees on the same scale that other western nations have attempted.

Following bilateral discussions on joint cooperation, exchanges on the mission level have been critical. After the signing of the joint projects in February 1982, USAID Administrator McPherson enunciated a policy that was cabled to all USAID missions worldwide. This policy instructed missions to cooperate with Japanese government officials in project identification.[78]

Joint Projects

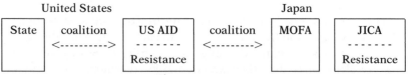

    Cooperation between USAID missions and Japanese aid representatives in the field goes beyond joint projects, however. Both sides have attempted to influence policy at the implementation level given the appropriate opportunities. For example, Japan has by far the largest aid program in Burma. Nonetheless, Japanese representatives in Rangoon in the early 1980s often advised their American counterparts that they viewed the relatively meager aid effort in Burma as an important supporting justification of their own. Japanese Embassy officials in Rangoon actively sought to encourage both the initiation and growth of the U.S. bilateral program and to keep close track of it through regular meetings at which information on both programs was exchanged. On one occasion, in 1980, the Japanese government even tried to persuade the Burmese government to bring USAID into a large irrigation project to which Japan was also planning to contribute.[79] Although this attempt was unsuccessful, mainly because Burma does not generally encourage donor cooperation since it likes to play one off the other, it did demonstrate an interesting aspect of Japan–U.S. aid relations at the recipient level. It also points to a fear that lies just under the surface with other Southeast Asian recipients of aid extended under the veneer of U.S.–Japan aid cooperation, namely, the imposition of an economic condominium. Therefore, most cooperative efforts between Japan and the United States have been careful to include the recipient country at the early stages of project or policy discussions.

    Many of the missions, particularly in Asia, have regular meetings with counterparts in the OECF, JICA, and the Japanese Embassy, sometimes at monthly donors meetings or on a one-on-one basis as in the case of Burma. One of the problems in cooperation at this level is that the USAID missions can interpret U.S. policy somewhat more independently in terms of decisionmaking. The Japanese aid program may be hydra-headed in Tokyo, but it is centralized in the sense that decisions are never made in the field.

    The United States has, on an annual basis since 1981, solicited mission views on U.S.–Japan aid cooperation, and Japan has the distinction of being the only donor that receives such global attention.

In 1987, the U.S.–Japan aid dialogue was further intensified when the Assistant Administrator for Asia and the Near East, Julia Bloch, made increasing regional aid management coordination a priority with her bureau. A special unit within the bureau was created to coordinate this effort. In May 1988 at the East–West Center in Honolulu, Bloch led USAID delegation to discuss aid cooperation with counterparts from the Japanese aid program. The Japanese delegation was led by Minoru Kubota, Deputy Director General of MOFA's Economic Cooperation Bureau, and consisted of representatives of JICA, OECF. This first bilateral meeting at the implementation level of both programs lasted three days and involved a comprehensive review of both countries' aid efforts in Indonesia, India, and the Philippines.[80]

The East–West Center meetings generated follow-up at the mission level to step up coordination. In both India and Indonesia, American and Japanese officials quietly began working out details for pursuing joint projects in consultation with the recipient governments. There was spillover as well to better coordination strategies in Bangladesh and in South Pacific nations in order to prevent waste of aid resources. Both Japanese and American officials regarded this collaboration as "a promising avenue for building a relationship between the United States and Japan in Asia that is based on a more equal sharing of the burdens and benefits of regional power."[81]

These efforts to strengthen coordination received the support of Congress as well. In the fall of 1988, Concurrent Resolutions passed in both the House and Senate urging further collaboration.[82] Additionally, language was inserted into a Senate Appropriations report commending the East–West Center meetings and encouraging further dialogue.

In October 1989, the second bilateral conference took place. This time at least part of the agenda included an exchange of views on future foreign aid related challenges for both countries centered around planning for an eventual resumption of economic assistance to the nations of Indochina, where Japan will no doubt play the lead role.

Japan has acknowledged its weaknesses in terms of developmental experience and therefore has welcomed the strengthened dialogue as an opportunity to learn more about USAID's approach to problems in poorer countries. Plans were put in motion to invite Japanese representatives to a Country Development Strategy Statement (CDSS) review to demonstrate how the United States, along with recipient nations, created a vision for long-term development. Also, JICA invited two USAID officers to Japan to learn more about evaluation techniques. Despite the success of the East–West Center meetings, these approaches were less enthusiastically received by USAID.

How could things change in USAID so suddenly? The answer lies more in the politics of Washington than in any aspect of U.S.–Japan relations. Several key officials in USAID departed and their replacements were reluctant to take up a policy approach created by their predecessors. Thus, the aid relationship fell victim to that old Washington affliction of wanting to put a new stamp on policy irrespective of the merits of the previous policy. The irony is that this appears to be in direct conflict with Congressional sentiments and at least the implied policy of the Bush administration.

Nevertheless, the aid relationship is bound to become an increasingly important element in the U.S.–Japan relationship, in part because larger forces in the U.S. government view it as important. This is reflected by the cooperation that will have to continue in the Philippines and by persistent debate over the nature of burden sharing in Washington.

Some of the discussion concerning burden sharing and the volumes Japan should be spending on overseas assistance is unreasonable. As we have seen in this study, Japan's administrative structure, in addition to personnel and training problems, makes spending the aid budgets Tokyo currently allocates difficult. Larger aid budgets without reform would continue to force Japanese planners to worry more about spending these huge sums than about the quality of assistance.

The United States has also apparently backed away from the idea first explicitly stated in the 1981 National Security Council directive that aid and defense spending should not be combined to help define Tokyo's regional security role. During Prime Minister Takeshita's February 1989 visit to the United States, both he and President Bush highlighted Japan's aid efforts and agreed that Japan could best support security burdens through ODA. Takeshita also said that Japan would increasingly extend aid to countries outside of the Asia region in cooperation with other western countries.[83]

The U.S.–Japan foreign aid connection has expanded in rough synchronization with the full blossoming of Japan's global economic power. There have been pitfalls along the way and there will doubtless be more in the future. But Japan's preeminent role in global economic development cannot be ignored and it ensures that the aid factor in U.S.–Japan relations is here to stay.

6

Conclusions:
The Meaning of the Process

The 1988 Annual Official Development Assistance white paper published by the Foreign Ministry of Japan included the very frank admission that one of the driving forces behind the expansion of foreign aid was to catch other donors. This logic was reminiscent of the desire by the Meiji leaders to "catch the west" in the last century and the early part of this century.[1] It is also consistent with Sato's description of Japan's fear of isolation.[2] Fukui suggests that this conformance mentality is particularly evident in the Foreign Ministry: "Virtually all MOFA officials [interviewed] agree that Japan should promptly accept the full economic, political and possibly military burdens as an equal ally, pretty much as defined by American and European leaders."[3]

But as we have seen, MOFA by no means carries the water on its own. The essence of the system relates to the web of competing bureaucratic interests over aid policy. While the locus of decisionmaking still resides in MITI, the Foreign Ministry and Finance Ministry which exercise authority over yen loans, they do not have a monopoly of power. Other ministries can have influence over the technical aspects of policy and, as grants expand, the four-ministry system itself is in danger of losing clout over aid policy.

The system is both highly fluid and often subtle. Securing one's own organizational interest vis-à-vis other ministries is paramount. These interests are frequently dictated by the interests that make up the constituent bodies of each ministry. The main problem confronting the Foreign Ministry is that it lacks a significant domestic power base on which to gain support from outside the bureaucracy and often must compensate for this weakness by other means.

The notion that Japan has hegemonic intentions in its overseas economic aid program derives from the assumption that a consensus exists within the government and the private sector on the use of aid to this end. This study shows that there exists no consensus on objectives and that this lack in itself causes confusion over Japanese intentions among aid recipients and donors alike. I am also suggesting that the image of Japan as a harmonious state always striving for and usually achieving consensus fails to take into account the very strong sense of institutional loyalties that exists in Japan. Nevertheless, a rough consensus has been achieved in one significant respect, that is, the essential virtue of making large foreign aid expenditures, although the exact amount every year is still subject to interministerial debate. Internal agreement on the definition of *quality* of assistance has lagged behind, in large part because it involves difficult policy choices inimical to the conflicting interests of the ministries. The very complexity of the Japanese foreign aid decisionmaking process establishes an opening for an external actor's role in making policy. This factor, combined with an estimation by policymakers in the Foreign Ministry of what constitutes the most important aspects of Japanese foreign policy interests, influences to a significant degree the large-scale as well as the regional emphases of aid policy.

But because of the mixture of policy voices speaking to the objectives of Japanese ODA, the government has apparently been unable to articulate the program effectively. Thus, in spite of the great expansion in the volume of Japanese ODA, it is a profound irony that it has not been generally matched by public acknowledgement in the less developed countries. A survey commissioned by USAID in the mid-1980s showed a widespread belief throughout Asia, the region of Japan's principal aid focus, that the United States remained the predominant donor despite the fact the Washington had relinquished that position in 1977.[4] Another possible explanation for the inability of Japan to reap publicity rewards for its aid program may be rooted in history. Among all the members of DAC, Japan is the only donor to lack the "missionary" experience. Western nations have for generations promoted Christianity in developing countries and are therefore quite used to "selling" an idea in the poorer regions of the world. As has been suggested, the very basic ideas of aiding developing countries stem from the private activities of Christian organizations reaching back to the turn of the century. Indeed, the impact of these missionaries on U.S. foreign policy has been at times rather significant.[5] Japan has had no similar experience.

The seeming inattention to DAC-defined aid quality may be explained by several factors.[6] First, while the request basis of Japanese ODA is theoretically designed to maximize the input of the recipient government in the development process, the fact that implementation has usually been guided by Japanese private sector interests is not lost on many analysts of the program. Coupled with this drawback has been the fact that the government has tended to place less emphasis on project evaluation except in terms of cost effectiveness. Thus, critical questions concerning the social impact of aid in a given area are inevitably skirted.

Consequently, this study concludes that aid policy very often is not limited to economic development but that indeed policymakers, particularly in the Foreign Ministry, have other objectives as well. The Foreign Ministry acknowledges that the U.S.–Japan relationship is the bedrock of foreign policy. Using aid as a device to mollify critics on other fronts is therefore not inconsistent with the basic goals of this policy.

The implementation agencies, namely OECF and JICA, appear to be almost totally powerless. But are they? During the four-ministry decisionmaking process for yen loans, the OECF can be influential in that it has virtual veto power over the technical aspects of aid. If the OECF indicates that a project is infeasible, it is simply not undertaken, no matter how urgently any of the ministries wants to pursue it. This could easily be construed as policy power, but the OECF has been careful not to exceed the realm of its mandate in the deliberation process. Thus, the Fund stays away from broad-based policy pronouncements. Nonetheless, when administering a program that receives widespread bureaucratic support such as in China, the only real issues are related to feasibility, and consequently the OECF can play a significant role by shaping the content of the aid relationship at the project level. JICA appears to have no similar impact on the program since there are fewer multiministerial discussions involved in grant aid and it has a smaller program to implement.

The Diet's role is of particular interest, not only because it contrasts with the extreme activism in foreign aid of the U.S. Congress, but also because Japan's legislative body sets no broad guidelines for the program, guaranteeing that policy is for all practical purposes a child of the bureaucracy and the private sector. High-level political activity in aid occasionally takes place, but more often than not only to address highly political problems such as trade. Except during a scandal when Dietmen can help generate press and attempt to influence aid policy, parliamentarians can be characterized more as lobbyists than policymakers, lobbyists in the sense that they can apply pressure to the bureaucracy to be responsive to their pet aid projects —a kind of international pork barrel. Occasionally this works, especially if the pressure is sufficiently concentrated and the bureaucracy can find no reason *not* to acquiesce. But usually bureaucrats merely pay lip service to the parliamentarians and the issue is often forgotten.

In the past, the private sector could depend upon foreign aid as a source for noncompetitive profits because there was no competition with companies from other countries. By 1989, this arrangement was being eroded as foreign pressure became more effective in reducing the explicit tied nature of Japanese aid. Of course, Japan is the ultimate "old boys" network, and that in itself helps Japanese companies during the aid contract bidding process. While Japanese weaknesses in staffing and training will remain for the foreseeable future, the move toward untying may mean that aid implementation could become increasingly internationalized. Since grant assistance comes directly from the General Account Budget and is therefore taxpayers' money which is not expected to be paid back, it will be harder to justify totally untying this form of aid. On the other hand, yen loans, especially in the area of procurement, are increasingly open to outside bidders. Ironically, with the DAC and the United States both pushing Japan to continue untying while increasing grants, they could be working at cross purposes. In a sense, other donors are asking Japan to do something that no other major donor does—have an untied grant assistance program. It is unrealistic to imagine that Japan's critics will be able to have it both ways.

Regionally, Japan will continue to focus largely on Asia, but because of U.S. encouragement along with that of the DAC, we can expect to see a somewhat wider globalization of Japanese aid recipients. It bears repeating that by 1987 Japan was the largest donor in twenty-nine countries in contrast with 1980 when Japan was the preeminent aid giver in sixteen countries and in 1970 the leader in only six.[7]

At the outset of this study, five basic psychological elements underlying Japanese foreign policy were introduced. To what extent can we identify their impact on the foreign aid program? The points in many ways are mutually supportable. Sato argued that Japan has a strong sense of self-identity coupled with "deep rooted feelings of inferiority." At the beginning of this chapter, we saw how important keeping apace of industrialized countries was to Japanese aid planners. Connected with this desire is the intense concern over Japan's image in the world and fear over being internationally isolated. As a result, there exists a desire to conform to global trends. If we assume that these factors are indeed preeminent in the Japanese consciousness, then they go far in explaining the true motivating forces in the Japanese foreign aid program, at least from the perspective of the Ministry of Foreign Affairs. Thus, aid can be viewed as a tool to insure Japan's international status relative to that of the members of the DAC and, in particular, the United States. As a consequence, in the eyes of the Foreign Ministry, using aid as a foreign policy instrument often means satisfying this audience. Therefore, the Foreign Ministry sees U.S. influence in the system to win bureaucratic turf battles in order to advance this important aspect of Japanese foreign policy. The final psychological factor, emotional commitment to Asia, helps to explain the overwhelming attention that Japan pays to that region in its ODA disbursements.

The cases that have been presented herein illustrate the three approaches to understanding how foreign pressure is digested in the Japanese aid system. The Ministry of Foreign Affairs basically supported extending aid to Jamaica and Sudan but needed U.S. pressure to convince the Finance Ministry. The only difference between the two countries was that opposition parties in the Diet raised few concerns over expanding ODA to Khartoum, in large part because U.S. strategic interests, although present, did not appear to be the exclusive rationale for maintaining an aid program there in contrast with Kingston.

The cases of Egypt and Pakistan involved basically the same cast of bureaucratic actors. National Security Council interest on the U.S. side was triggered by the high profile of the strategic concerns. The involvement of the Prime Minister of the Japanese side was for much the same reason. In both cases, the Finance Ministry raised concerns over the extent of Japan's financial commitment.

The Philippines under Marcos and then under Aquino is of interest because of the change of actors with Mrs. Aquino's entry into Malacañang Palace. On the part of the United States, Congressional support appears absent under Marcos but emerges under Aquino. This is not to say that no Congressional support existed but to suggest that it was divided and as a consequence often cancelled itself out. Inconsistent Congressional support for the Philippines aid program under Marcos meant that Capitol Hill had very little to say about Japan's aid efforts in the country until the House Foreign Affairs Committee uncovered evidence of OECF kickbacks after the fall of Marcos. Divided Congressional support for the Philippine aid program was particularly apparent during the final years of the Marcos regime. After Aquino came to power, Congressional support for her government became almost universal and, with the atmosphere of fiscal frugality in Washington, Congressional interest in greater Japanese aid activities to support her fledgling government expanded.

In Tokyo, the principal opponents to Philippine aid migrated from political elements to the bureaucracy. Under Marcos, these opponents consisted mainly of political parties on the left in the Diet, who criticized aid to Manila as a guise to cover U.S. strategic designs, and several members of the LDP's special aid committee led by Ishihara Shintaro. Opposition from those quarters vanished under the Aquino regime. Rather, the Ministry of Finance, concerned over the stability of the government and consequently of the country's financial standing, dragged its feet over going forward with the aid program. This was mirrored to a much lesser degree in the Foreign Ministry by those who favored a more cautious approach to the new government.

The case of Vietnam is more complex and continues to reemerge occasionally as a bone of bilateral contention. The Foreign Ministry essentially favored termination of the program since it feared destabilization of relations with ASEAN, which in turn was worried over the implications of regional Vietnamese adventurism. Nonetheless, MITI and members of the Diet's Japan–Vietnam Friendship League *(Giin Renmei)* headed by Sakurauchi Yoshio supported a more flexible policy.

In the United States, the 1981 aid budget cut proposal was also complicated mainly because it involved cross-coalition partners. The State Department and USAID used Japanese concern over the proposal in internal deliberation with the Office of Management and

Budget. MOFA, worried that drastic U.S. aid cuts would weaken its bargaining position with the Ministry of Finance in sustaining Japan's aid increases, made sure the United States understood the potential impact that the cuts would have in Tokyo.

Coalitions on joint projects among the top decisionmakers in Japan and the United States were relatively straightforward. However, stumbling blocks occurred at the implementation level in both governments. In a sense, political expectations exceeded the ability and the desire of the implementors to pursue joint projects. Nonetheless, both sides intermittently continue to explore ways in which to cooperate.

The second category which has been termed preemptive, involves Japanese government decisions to formulate aid initiatives without a prior request by the United States, ostensibly to deflect Washington's pressure in other areas such as trade. Japan's aid proposals for the Caribbean Basin Initiative (CBI) were brought as an *omiyage* or souvenir to the United States during a time when the Reagan Administration was attempting to deflate pressures from the Congress on domestic content trade legislation. USAID was part of the target audience since it was the agency designated by the President to handle the aid aspects of the CBI on Capitol Hill.

The recycling package announced by the Japanese government in the spring of 1987 offers a classic example of aid used to mollify Washington on the semiconductor issue. While discussions had been progressing in the Japanese bureaucracy prior to the announcement of import quotas on semiconductors, Japanese decisionmakers were seriously concerned that the Administration's action would serve to fuel an already contentious trade climate. The Foreign Ministry, in pushing for the adoption of the program, frequently referred to the recycling packages' utility as at least a partial means of making sure that cooler heads prevailed in Washington. The plan was announced during Prime Minister Nakasone's April 1987 visit to Washington before it had successfully threaded itself through the system in Tokyo. The target audience included the White House, whence the quotas had emerged; the Congress, which was considering the omnibus trade legislation; and the Department of Treasury, which through the leadership of Secretary Baker was generally acknowledged to have assumed the ultimate stewardship of trade policy formulation.

The final category addresses pressure that meets resistance throughout the aid policymaking mechanisms of the Japanese government. The first case involved Nicaragua. With the election of the

Reagan administration, U.S. policy toward the Sandinista regime in Managua stiffened considerably. Although the Carter administration had reinitiated an aid program to Nicaragua, the Reagan administration reversed this policy and also placed pressure on all the DAC donors to follow suit. Nonetheless, the United States was unsuccessful in persuading the other donors to desist from providing ODA. However, Tokyo acceded to Washington's request and did not proceed with an increased aid program. No branch of the Japanese government was enthusiastic about this, but neither was there strong resistance to the U.S. position.

The case of mixed credits was more contentious. None of the decisionmaking principals of the Japanese government supported the policy position being advocated by the DAC and the United States. Indeed, U.S. pressure received strong resistance which lasted over a two-year period. In addition, Washington responded to Tokyo's reluctance with threats: the adoption by the Reagan administration of the $300 million "war chest" plus the sharp language exchanged by both sides in the deliberation. In essence, the mixed credit problem became intrinsically linked to bilateral trade friction. Thus, policymakers handled the issue with the same "hard bargaining" approach which has come to characterize the way in which trade issues are addressed. This was a clear case in which the United States employed the *kurofune* or black ships in order to achieve changes in Japanese policy.

I would note that the United States has not always been successful in pressuring the Japanese government. "Policy dialogue" is an approach, adopted by the Reagan administration, designed to increase the conditionality of foreign aid. In other words, from its inception the administration has attempted to link the extension of U.S. aid to changes in recipients' economic policies toward a free market orientation. In this sense, USAID would become more of a "tough banker," to use the words of Administrator McPherson. Thus, USAID began to attempt to pursue a policy somewhat more akin to that of the International Monetary Fund. In order to strengthen the chances of effectiveness, a pivotal aspect of this approach was to encourage other donors to undertake similar efforts. The United States repeatedly attempted to encourage MOFA to adopt more stringent conditionality connected to policy change but to very little avail.

One problem is that MOFA fears that policy dialogue would sharply conflict with the request basis foundation of the aid system and would also place Japan in a sensitive position vis-à-vis many of the same countries that suffered under the yoke of Japanese imperial dictates during World War II. Naturally, the Ministry of Finance is much more sympathetic to the policy dialogue argument, but since MOFA is the window for U.S.–Japan aid dialogues, neither USAID nor the State Department has ever teamed up with Finance to pressure Foreign Affairs. Thus, although MOFA is the most likely coalition partner for U.S. interests in the aid process because of the Ministry's role, it is apparent that it does not have to monopolize that position. If U.S. understanding of the process advances, other ministries could become coalition partners on different issues.

The principal channel through which the United States exercises influence in the aid process is MOFA, but this link occurs primarily on goals upon which there already appears to be agreement anyway. Pempel has correctly ascertained that "the Ministry of Foreign Affairs seems particularly ready to use the United States generally as an ally in advancing its interests against those of other agencies."[8]

But it would be a mistake to conclude from this analysis that pressure as applied by the United States is the sole determining factor in sculpting Japanese foreign aid policy. This is not the argument that is posed here. Rather, understanding how and why the United States is able to exercise influence is important in coming to terms with an expanding aspect of Japanese foreign policy.

What do "transnational politics" tell us about the policy process? First of all, the focus of previous generic studies on transnational politics have not addressed the government-to-government angle of analysis. This approach shows that bureaucratic politics, which is very much the dominant characteristic of Japanese foreign aid deci-sionmaking, can and often does involve actors beyond the system. The Japanese state is simply not monolithic as the term "Japan, Inc.," popularly used for many years in the United States to characterize Japan's policy process, would lead us to believe. The plethora of actors involved in the aid system attests to its being diverse almost to a fault.

As noted before, post–World War II Japanese policy toward the United States can be described as one of dependence. The fabric of the relationship, with the U.S.–Japan Security Treaty as the corner-stone, allows the United States more opportunities to exercise influ-ence in Japan than any other country. This aspect of the relationship is further enhanced by the fact that roughly 40 percent of Japan's trade is conducted with the United States. These conditions make Japan more susceptible to pressure and the wielding of influence from the United States on a variety of fronts.

Thus, it is the combination of factors—concern over international status, fear of isolation, desire to conform to world trends, and the need for the Ministry of Foreign Affairs to strengthen its bargaining position by using outside pressure in an often highly contentious bureaucratic atmosphere—that helps to explain the meaning of Japan's foreign aid policymaking process and emergence as an aid power.

NOTES

1. Approaches to Policymaking

1. Paul Mosley, *Foreign Aid;* p. 21.
2. Ibid., p. 3.
3. Charles L. Mees, Jr., *The Marshall Plan,* p. 79.
4. Japan was actually a member of the DAC three years before joining the OECD in 1964.
5. Seizaburo Sato, "The Foundations of Modern Japanese Foreign Policy," in Robert A. Scalapino, ed., *The Foreign Policy of Modern Japan,* p. 375.
6. See Takeo Doi, *The Anatomy of Dependence,* for a complete discussion of *amae.*
7. John W. Dower, *War Without Mercy,* pp. 236 and 305. Dower describes the image of the United States during the occupation as "large, powerful, human, protective, awkward, vaguely forbidding, generally but not entirely trustworthy."
8. Sadao Higuchi, *Seifu Kaihatsu Enjo.*
9. Dennis T. Yasutomo, *The Manner of Giving.*
10. Alan Rix, *Japan's Economic Aid.*
11. Stephen D. Krasner, *Defending the National Interest,* p. 26.
12. Peter Self, *Political Theories of Modern Government,* pp. 79, 80.
13. Ibid., pp. 95–97.
14. Graham T. Allison, *Essence of Decision,* pp. 144–45.

15. Barry Rubin, *Secrets of State*, p. 112.

16. Ibid., p. 258.

17. Two notable studies are Stephen D. Cohen's *The Making of United States International Economic Policy* and I. M. Destler's *Making Foreign Economic Policy*.

18. Interview with high-ranking official in the Aid Policy Division of the Economic Cooperation Bureau, Ministry of Foreign Affairs, June 23, 1987. According to this official, the massive recycling package for Latin American debt relief made public in April 1987 was a case of the Foreign Ministry's maneuvering, through a special assistant, around the Finance Ministry's tentative reluctance to the plan.

19. Haruhiro Fukui, "Bureaucratic Power in Japan," in Peter Drysdale and Hironobu Kitaoji, eds., *Japan and Australia: Two Societies and their Interaction*, p. 286.

20. I. M. Destler, Haruhiro Fukui, and Hideo Sato, *The Textile Wrangle*, p. 57. With respect to issuing resolutions on foreign policy, even in this sphere the approval of the bureaucracy has usually been received in advance.

21. As for the Parliamentary Vice Minister (Seimu Jikan), he has little influence on policy, particularly should he choose to buck the system. The same can be said for most ministers except to a lesser degree.

22. Fukui, pp. 290, 291.

23. Allison, p. 275. Allison acknowledged this weakness.

24. The framework for transnational and governmental relations was laid out in Robert O. Keohane and Joseph S. Nye, Jr., *Transnational Relations and World Politics*, p. xi and Robert O. Keohane and Joseph S. Nye, Jr., "Transgovernmental Relations and International Organizations," *World Politics*, pp. 39–62.

25. U.S. Congress, House Committee on Foreign Affairs, *Government Decision-making in Japan*, p. 167.

26. Chikara Higashi, *Japanese Trade Policy Formulation*, p. 77.

27. T. J. Pempel, "Unbundling 'Japan, Inc.': The Changing Dynamics of Japanese Policy Formation," *Journal of Japanese Studies*, p. 303. Also, see Robert C. Angel, "Explaining Policy Failure: Japan and the International Economy, 1969–71," *Journal of Public Policy*. Angel sees what he calls "bureaucratic compartmentalization" as making the Japanese system dependent on foreign pressure to make policy changes.

28. U.S. Congress, p. ix. The January 20, 1987 issue of *Tokyo Insider* reported with respect to the government's breaching of the 1 percent of GNP defense budget ceiling that "bureaucrats from the Defense Agency and the Foreign Ministry are privately pleased to have the Americans appear to be pressing Japan in this direction (exceeding the 1 % ceiling). They hope to use American 'demands' as a weapon against LDP politicians who are intent on adopting the 'about 1 percent' option."

29. Higashi, p. 76.

30. Pempel, "Unbundling 'Japan Inc.',", p. 303.

31. Destler et al., *Textile Wrangle*, p. 212.

32. I. M. Destler, Priscilla Clapp, Hideo Sato, and Haruhiro Fukui, *Managing an Alliance*, p. 140.

33. Destler et al., *Managing an Alliance*, p. 141.

34. U.S. Congress, p. 6; statement by Dr. Timothy Curran.

35. Ibid.

36. Ibid., p. 25; statement by Professor Hugh Patrick.

2. Aid Politics and the Decisionmaking Structure

1. Michael Blaker, *Japanese Negotiating Style*, p. 84.

2. Michael Blaker, "Probe, Push, and Panic: The Japanese Tactical Style in International Negotiations," in Scalapino, ed., *The Foreign Policy of Modern Japan*, p. 99.

3. Rix, *Japan's Economic Aid*, p. 84.

4. See Mosley, *Foreign Aid*, p. 14.

5. Kazumi Goto, "Aratana Enjo Gyosei o Motomete," p. 53.

6. Interview, Economic Cooperation Bureau, Ministry of Foreign Affairs, December 17, 1986.

7. See Seizaburo Sato and Tetsuhisa Matsuzaki, *Jiminto Seiken* for a detailed discussion of the process of LDP institutionalization.

8. McNeill, *The Contradictions of Foreign Aid*, p. 49. U.S. Congressional activism is seemingly an exception to this rule. This can be at least partly explained by the dynamic tension that is inherent in the American system of separation of powers.

9. Interview with LDP Diet member who is a member of the LDP Special Committee on External Economic Assistance (Taigai Keizai Kyoryoku Tokubetsu Iinkai), February 17, 1987. Interviews with other LDP members have confirmed this assessment.

10. Rix, p. 87.

11. Yuji Suzuki, "Rethinking Japanese Foreign Aid," *Japan Times*, June 30, 1986, p. 8.

12. Brooks and Orr, "Japan's Foreign Economic Assistance," p. 335. The resolution which passed was a compromise measure. The original Japan Socialist Party (JSP) resolution would have prohibited aid to all countries in conflict. The language in the resolution, based on chapter six of the UN Charter, is extremely vague and has almost no effect on Japanese aid policy. Point three has been applied at the government's discretion.

13. Rix, p. 108.

14. "ODA no Kanryo Kaigi" (ODA Bureaucratic Conference), *Nihon Keizai Shimbun*, November 12, 1988, p. 1.

15. Interview, Ministry of Foreign Affairs official, January 25, 1989.

16. Brooks and Orr, "Japan's Foreign Economic Assistance," p. 335.

17. Rix, "The Future of Japanese Foreign Aid," p. 424. Also documents supplied by the Japanese Ministry of Foreign Affairs and interview with LDP Dietman who is a member of the committee.

18. Interview, Economic Cooperation Department, Ministry of International Trade and Industry, February 13, 1987.

19. Interviews with LDP Dietman who is a member of the committee, September 30, 1986, and March 3, 1987.

20. Interview cited LDP Dietman, February 17, 1987.

21. See Kent E. Calder, "Elites in an Equalizing Role," for a discussion of how Dietmen who are former bureaucrats have built-in networks in the bureaucracy.

22. Isami Takeda, "New Factors in Japan's ODA Policy," p. 12.

23. Kasumigaseki is the area of Tokyo where most national government bureaucracies are located.

24. See Dennis T. Yasutomo, *The Manner of Giving*, pp. 34–38.

25. Interview with Professor Seizaburo Sato who was a member of the council at its inception.

26. Brooks and Orr, p. 336. Also, interview with Dietmember who is a former official in the Ministry of Finance, February 17, 1987.

27. Interview with MITI official.

28. "Gov't Snubs Call for Aid Money Audit," *Japan Times*, April 24, 1986, p. 1.

29. Interview with Dietman, September 20, 1986.

30. McNeill, p. 50. Quotation from John White, *The Politics of Foreign Aid* (London: Bodley Head, 1974).

31. Akio Watanabe, "Japanese Public Opinion and Foreign Affairs: 1964–73," in Scalapino, ed., *The Foreign Policy of Modern Japan*, p. 106.

32. "Distribution of Aid Questioned in Poll," *Japan Times*, April 3, 1989, p. 1.

33. Brooks and Orr, p. 335.

34. For example, the *Asahi Shimbun* ran a several week series in January 1985 called "Enjo Toho Koku" (Aid Country).

35. Annual Report provided by the Japan Engineering Consulting Firms Association (ECFA), 1987.

36. Interview with Senior Economist of ECFA, July 13, 1987.

37. Ibid.

38. Interviews with Dietman, February 17, 1987, as well as Foreign Ministry official, December 17, 1986.

39. While many other donors provide surplus crops of their own, Japan provides funds for the purchase of crops from other countries.

40. Interview with Dietman, February 17, 1987.

41. Interview, Budget Examiner for MOFA, MITI, and EPA, Ministry of Finance, March 19, 1987.

42. Ibid.

43. Interview with MOFA official, June 23, 1987.

44. Interview with Ministry of Finance official, March 14, 1986.

45. Ibid. Also interview with Ministry of Finance officials, March 1985.

46. Ibid. Also see Makoto Sumita "Politics of Foreign Aid: Japanese Bureaucratic Politics," p. 101.

47. Brooks and Orr, pp. 335, 336.

48. Stephen W. Pollock, "Cohesion and Competition: A Study of Japan's Foreign Aid," p. 103.

49. Tsuyoshi Yamamoto, *Nihon no Keizai Enjo*, pp. 21–22.

50. "MITI Minister Tamura Pledges Increased Aid to Indonesia," *Asahi Evening News*, January 1987, p. 1.

51. MITI 1986 While Paper, "Keizai Kyoryoku no Genjo to Mondai ten." See p. 146 for a discussion of this plan.

52. Interview, Economic Cooperation Bureau, Ministry of Foreign Affairs, February 20, 1987.

53. *Daily Yomiuri*, November 28, 1988.

54. Rix, *Japan's Economic Aid*, p. 57.

55. Interview, Economic Cooperation Bureau of MOFA, February 20, 1987.

56. "Kasumigaseki Confidential," *Bungei Shunju*, January 1986.

57. Kikuchi Kiyoaki became Japan's Ambassador to the United Nations. Yanai Shinichi was Deputy Minister from 1985 until March 1987 and became Ambassador to South Korea. Yanagi Kenichi became Ambassador to Pakistan, Fujita Kimio

became Director General of the Asian Affairs Bureau, and Hanabusa Masamichi
was appointed Consul General in New York.

58. See ODA jisshi koritsuka kenkyukai "Seifu Kaihatsu Enjo no kokateki koritsuteki jisshi ni tsuite" published by the ODA Kenkyukai, December 1985.

59. Isami Takeda, "South Pacific as Testing Ground," *Japan Times*, January 18,
1987, p. 6.

60. Hiroshi Matsumoto, "Japanese ODA to ASEAN Countries," p. 12.

61. "Biyajima, Shusha karo Wairo," *Yomiuri Shimbun* (evening edition), September 3, 1986.

62. "Gaimusho, Taishitsu toware Konwaku," *Asahi Shimbun*, October 8, 1987,
p. 2.

63. "Giwaku wo Manekanai Kaigai Enjo wo!" (editorial), *Yomiuri Shimbun*,
November 5, 1986, p. 3.

64. Several interviews in MOFA over dates cited above.

65. Interview, Economic Planning Agency official, April 25, 1984.

66. Rix, *Japan's Economic Aid*, p. 258.

67. OECF Annual Report, 1988.

68. Rix, *Quantity versus Quality: Trends and Issues in the Japanese Aid Program*,
Also see *Kikin chosa Kiho* No. 60 (July 1988), p. 142.

69. Rix, *Japan's Economic Aid*; see his chapter "Scrap and Build: The Origins
of JICA," pp. 49–77.

70. Joseph C. Wheeler, *Development Cooperation*, p. 196.

71. JICA Annual Report for 1987.

72. Interview with OECF official, October 3, 1987.

73. Interview with JICA official, July 10, 1984, in Bangkok, Thailand.

74. Haruhiro Fukui, "Bureaucratic Power in Japan," in Peter Drysdale and
Hironobu Kitaoji, eds., *Japan and Australia: Two Societies and their Interaction*, p.
290.

75. John Creighton Campbell, "Policy Conflict and Its Resolution within the
Governmental system," in Ellis S. Krauss, Thomas P. Rohlen and Patricia G.
Steinhoff, eds., *Conflict in Japan*, p. 324.

3. Aid Policy Evolution, Philosophy, and the Role of the Private Sector

1. See the DAC Aid Review of Japan, January 20, 1987, points 5, 6, and 7.

2. Brooks and Orr, "Japan's Foreign Economic Assistance," p. 324.

3. Rix, "The Philosophy of Japanese Foreign Aid," in Susan J. Pharr, ed. *Japan
and the United States in the Third World*, forthcoming.

4. Ministry of International Trade and Industry, White paper on Economic
Cooperation, 1960.

5. Michael Yoshitsu, *Caught in the Middle East: Japan's Diplomacy in Transition*,
p. 7.

6. Brooks and Orr, p. 327.

7. Rix, "The Philosophy of Japanese Foreign Aid."

8. Ministry of Foreign Affairs, *Wagakuni no Seifu Kaihatsu Enjo* (Our Country's
Official Development Assistance).

9. Rix, "The Philosophy of Japanese Foreign Aid."

10. This is not new. President Eisenhower encouraged Congress to support the American foreign aid program not for purposes of altruism. He once reminded several Congressmen of the importance of foreign aid by saying, "We're talking about the security of our country—nothing less." See Stephen E. Ambrose, *Eisenhower: The President*, vol. 2 (New York: Simon and Shuster, 1988), p. 119.

11. Interview, Overseas Economic Cooperation Fund (OECF) official, November 8, 1986.

12. Steve Pollock, "The Role of the Private Sector in Japan's Foreign Aid Program," in Susan J. Pharr, ed., *Japan and the United States in the Third World*, forthcoming.

13. Norio Ozawa, "Opportunities for U.S. Business," May 1989.

14. Ibid.

15. Interviews with official in the Overseas Construction Association of Japan, November 18, 1988, as well as an LDP Dietmember who is a member of the construction caucus (Kensetsu Zoku), June 10, 1988.

16. Prasert Chittiwatanapong, "Japanese Official Development Assistance to Thailand," p. 11.

17. See *IECA Outline and Activity*, 1986.

18. Keidanren, "Keidanren International Cooperation Project," February 1, 1989.

19. Karel Van Wolferen, *The Enigma of Japanese Power*, pp. 110–111.

20. Prasert Chittiwatanapong, "International Conflict and Japanese Decision-making: Perspectives from Thailand," Thammasat University, Bangkok, Thailand. manuscript, p. 13.

21. Figures provided by the Ministry of Foreign Affairs, Japan.

22. Correspondence with OECF official stationed in Southeast Asia.

23. Nissho Iwai, "ODA: Hatten Tojokoku no Jizokuteki na Keizai Seicho o Kanonishi sono Saimu Hensai Noryoko o Kojo saseru tame ni Koso" (Making Economic Growth Possible through Improving Debt Repayment Capacity), *Tradepia*, interview with Hisao Misawa, Director of Nissho Iwai's office of Economic Cooperation, April 1989, p. 13.

24. "GEC wins Japan-backed signal deal with Thailand," p. 1, and "Breaking the Japanese stranglehold," *Financial Times* (London), January 20, 1989, p. 6. Also, "GEC signs record rail contract: Mitsui beaten for OECF loan," *Nation* (Bangkok), January 20, 1989, p. 13.

25. Interview with Prasert Chittiwatanapong, February 28, 1989.

4. Translating the Policies: Regional and Multilateral Bank Emphasis

1. Yasutomo, *The Manner of Giving*, p. 91.

2. Ministry of Foreign Affairs, *Wagakuni no Seifu Kaihatsu Enjo*, 1989 (Our Country's Official Development Assistance), hereafter cited as *Wagakuni*. . . .

3. Hugh Borton, *Japan's Modern Century*, p. 324.

4. The United States, West Germany, and Japan were among the last western powers to establish relations with the People's Republic of China. Great Britain did so in 1950 and France in 1964.

5. For a comprehensive discussion of the conflicting issues in Japan's China policy, see Wolf Mendl, *Issues in Japan's China Policy.*

6. William L. Brooks, "Japanese Economic Assistance to China." Brooks suggests that since Japan's relations with China are of political importance to the entire region, then all aid to Beijing has strategic implications.

7. Greg Story, "Japan's Official Development Assistance to China: A Survey" (Australia–Japan Research Centre, Pacific Economic Papers), No. 150, p. 9.

8. U.S. Congress, *Legislation on Foreign Relations Through 1985*, vol. 1, p. 171.

9. Brooks conference paper, p. 12.

10. Ibid., p. 13.

11. Yasutomo, p. 91.

12. Susumu Yamakage, "Japan and ASEAN: Are They Really Becoming Closer?," p. 311.

13. "Boei.Enjo Setto ron no Kangaegatta" (The Concept of Defense and Aid as a Pair), *Yomiuri Shimbun*, March 1, 1987, p. 3.

14. Hiroshi Matsumoto, "Japanese ODA to ASEAN Countries," conference paper presented at ARSPP Tokyo Symposium: Japan-ASEAN Trade and Economic Relations in the Coming Decade (Tokyo, Japan, Institute for International Affairs, February 5, 1987), p. 5.

15. Yasutomo, p. 95.

16. "Aid for Asian Nations Export Industries Urged," *Japan Times*, October 4, 1986, p. 6.

17. "MITI Minister Tamura Pledges Increased Aid to Indonesia," *Asahi Evening News*, January 13, 1987, p. 1.

18. "ASEAN Accuses Japan of Not Doing Enough," *Daily Yomiuri*, June 24, 1987, p. 4.

19. "Keizai Kyoryoku ni wa Nihon Shijoo Kaihoo wo" (Economic Cooperation and the Need to Open Japanese Markets), *Yomiuri Shimbun*, February 14, 1987, p. 3.

20. "ASEAN Yuushi e Shinkikin" (New Financing Fund for ASEAN), *Nihon Keizai Shimbun*, April 20, 1987, p. 2.

21. Former Foreign Minister Okita Saburo expressed concern over this issue in a January 1, 1989, *Japan Times* interview.

22. *Wagakuni . . .* , 1989 vol. 2, see pp. 62–76.

23. Ibid.

24. Interview with OECF official, August 8, 1987, Tokyo, Japan.

25. Bruce Koppel et al., "Japan–U.S. ODA Cooperation: Perspectives from India, Indonesia and the Philippines," p. 4.

26. "Japan Balks at Indonesian Debt Plan," *Asahi Evening News*, June 8, 1988, p. 4.

27. Figures provided by the Ministry of Foreign Affairs, Japan, and USAID.

28. Koppel, "Japan-U.S. Aid Cooperation . . . ," p. 12.

29. Yasutomo, p. 93.

30. Quoted in Bruce Koppel, "Cooperation or Co-Prosperity? Asian Perspectives on Japan's Ascendancy as an ODA Power," p. 13.

31. Yasuo Muramatsu, "Hi Seiken wo Sossen Shien" ([Japan] Aggressively Supports Philippines Leadership), *Asahi Shimbun*, January 19, 1985.

32. Robert M. Orr, Jr., "Japan Beefs Up Its Aid to Asia," *PHP Intersect*, October 1985, p. 16.

33. "Gov't Snubs Call for Aid Money Audit," *Japan Times*, April 24, 1986, p. 1.

34. Yuji Suzuki, "Rethinking Japanese Foreign Aid," *Japan Times*, June 30, 1986, p. 8.

35. Interviews with USAID and State Department officials, June 23–July 1, 1986, in Washington, D.C.

36. "Gov't Will Pledge Special Loan of Y40 Bil. to the Philippines," *Asahi Evening News*, November 5, 1986, p. 1.

37. "Wakaoji Released in Suburban Manila, to Fly Home Today," *Japan Times*, April 2, 1987, p. 4.

38. Koppel, "Japan–U.S. ODA Cooperation . . . ," p. 17.

39. Ibid.

40. *Wagakuni* . . . , 1989 vol. 2, p. 120.

41. Nigel Holloway, "Muted Harping," *Far Eastern Economic Review*, March 16, 1989.

42. Interviews with Ministry of Foreign Affairs and Ministry of Finance officials, Tokyo, Japan, March 1989.

43. See Hosup Kim, "Policy-Making . . .".

44. Interview with high-ranking official in the Economic Cooperation Bureau, Ministry of Foreign Affairs, Japan. Tokyo, February 10, 1987.

45. Kim, p. 182. Also, interview with Ministry of Finance official, February 23, 1987.

46. Foreign Broadcast Information Service (FBIS), April 29, 1982, p. C1.

47. Yasutomo, p. 53.

48. Isami Takeda, "New Factors in Japan's ODA Policy," pp. 5–6.

49. Ibid.

50. *Wagakuni* . . . , 1989 vol. 2, p. 747.

51. Isami Takeda, "South Pacific as Testing Ground," *Japan Times*, January 18, 1987, p. 6.

52. "Japan–Aussie Meet Ends with Pledge of 'S. Pacific Axis' " *Japan Times*, January 10, 1987, p. 1.

53. Isami Takeda, "Kawaru Nihon no Taigai Enjo to Minami Teiheiyo Chiiki" (Japan's Changing Foreign Aid Policy to the South Pacific Region), *Toa-Asia Monthly*, February 1987, p. 23.

54. "U.S. Pleased," *Japan Times*, January 16, 1987, p. 3.

55. "Minor Nations Want Major Power Respect: Vanuatu," *Japan Times*, January 16, 1987, p. 4.

56. "Soviets Slam Japan's S. Pacific Policy," *Japan Times*, January 16, 1987, p. 3.

57. Figures supplied by USAID.

58. Koppel, "Japan–U.S. ODA Cooperation . . . ," p. 30.

59. Juichi Inada, "Hatten Tojo Koku to Nihon: Taigai Enjo Seisaku no Henyo Katei" (The Developing Countries and Japan: Changing Foreign Aid Policy), in Akio Watanabe, ed., *Sengo Nihon no Taigai Seisaku* (Japan's Post-War Foreign Policy) (Tokyo: Yuhikaku, 1985) p. 306.

60. Yasutomo, p. 89.

61. Ichiro Inukai, "Japan in Africa," p. 4.

62. Kweku Ampiah, "A One-Sided Partnership," *West Africa*, November 28–December 4, 1988.

63. Yasutomo, p. 88.

64. Inukai, p. 10.

65. Joanna Moss and John Ravenhill, "The Emerging Japanese Influence in Africa and its Implications for the United States," p. 71.

66. Khalil T. Darwish, "Keizai Enjo to Nihon no Afurika Seisaku" (Economic Aid and Japan's Africa Policy), *Kokusai Mondai*, May 1987, No. 326, p.72.

67. Inukai, pp. 6 and 10.

68. Eileen Doherty, "Japan's Economic Relations with Africa," p. 5.

69. Moss and Ravenhill, p. 70.

70. Ibid.

71. Darwish, p. 75.

72. Inukai, p. 19. Also, see Darwish, p. 84.

73. Moss and Ravenhill, p. 72.

74. Yasutomo, p. 85.

75. Doherty, "Japan's Role in Multilateral Aid Organizations, p. 8.

76. Ministry of Foreign Affairs, *Japan's Official Development Assistance*, p. 56.

77. Nonetheless, the Japanese government operated with a surplus in the latter part of the 1980s.

78. Bernhard May, "Japans neue Rolle in der multilateralen Entwicklungspolitik" (Japan's New Role in Multilateral Development Policy), p. 530.

79. Ministry of Foreign Affairs, *Japan ODA 1988* Annual Report, p. 56.

80. Doherty, "Japan's Role in Multilateral Aid Organizations," p. 11

81. Rix, "The Philosophy of Japanese Foreign Aid."

5. *Foreign Pressure: The Role of the United States*

1. Interview, North American Division, Ministry of Foreign Affairs, February 9, 1987.

2. Chikara Higashi, *Reagan no tai Nichi Gaiko o Yomu* (Reading Reagan's Japan Policy) pp. 179, 180.

3. Seigen Miyasato, "Foreign Aid in Japan–U.S. Relations: The Japanese Perspective," p. 3.

4. Ibid.

5. Actually, today this is the norm rather than unusual. Under the Reagan Administration, only one aid appropriation bill has passed (1981). All U.S. aid has, in legislative terms, operated under Continuing Resolutions since then.

6. "New Directions" were amendments to the Foreign Assistance Act.

7. See David A. Stockman, *The Triumph of Politics* pp. 126–130, for a full discussion.

8. Interview, Budget Examiner for MOFA, MITI, and EPA, Ministry of Finance. When asked how often MOFA used foreign pressure as a weapon in aid budget negotiations with the Ministry of Finance, the response was, "Almost every time," March 19, 1987.

9. Interview, Second North American Division, Ministry of Foreign Affairs, February 9, 1987. Also, interview, Office of Japanese Affairs, Department of State, June 23, 1986.

10. Ibid.; the MOFA official interviewed commented "In MOFA, we must all specialize in U.S. affairs."

11. Ibid.

12. See Kent E. Calder, "Japanese Foreign Economic Policy Formation: Explaining the Reactive State," *World Politics*, July 1988.

13. See ch. 2 and conclusions in Paul A. Summerville, "The Politics of Self-Restraint."

14. Miyasato, p. 18. Also, see George Cunningham, *The Management of Aid Agencies*, p. 134.

15. Shigekazu Matsumoto, "Progress and Policy Formulation of Japan's External Assistance," p. 2.

16. Ibid. Also see Frank C. Langdon, *Japan's Foreign Policy*, p. 14.

17. Matsumoto; Langdon, p. 88.

18. Miyasato, p. 23. Also conference paper by Shigekazu Matsumoto.

19. Yasutomo, *Japan and the Asian Development Bank*, p. 67.

20. Miyasato, pp. 25, 26.

21. Ibid.

22. See Juichi Inada, "Hatten Tojo Koku to Nippon" (The Developing Countries and Japan), in Akio Watanabe, ed., *Sengo Nippon no Taigai Seisaku* (Japan's Postwar Foreign Policy), pp. 285–314.

23. I. M. Destler and Hisao Mitsuyu, "Locomotives on Different Tracks: Macroeconomic Diplomacy, 1977–1979," in I. M. Destler and Hideo Sato, eds., *Coping with U.S.-Japanese Economic Conflicts*, p. 253.

24. Miyasato, p. 31.

25. Interview with USAID official, June 24, 1986. Also, my personal recollection and notes as a former USAID official.

26. Miyasato, p. 33.

27. Interview, Economic Cooperation Bureau, Ministry of Foreign Affairs, May 1984.

28. Interview with USAID official, June 24, 1986, as well as my personal recollection and notes as a former USAID official.

29. Yasutomo, *The Manner of Giving*, p. 27.

30. Miyasato, p. 37.

31. National Security Council Directive, June 1981.

32. Interview with Office of Japanese Affairs officials, Department of State, June 23, 1986. Also, interview, Economic Cooperation Bureau, Ministry of Foreign Affairs, December 17, 1986.

33. Speech by Assistant Secretary of State for East Asia and Pacific Affairs, John Holderidge; Tokyo, Japan, November 1981.

34. Cable from U.S. Embassy/Tokyo to State Department/Washington, February 17, 1981.

35. Ibid.

36. Cable from U.S. Embassy/Tokyo to State Department/ Washington, March 5, 1981.

37. Ibid. Also, interview with Dr. Saburo Okita, former Japanese Foreign Minister, December 27, 1984.

38. Brooks and Orr, "Japan's Foreign Economic Assistance," *Asian Survey*, v. XXV, No. 3, March 1985, p. 333.

39. Bernhard May, *Reagan und die Entwicklungsländer: Die Auslandshilfepolitik im Amerikanischen Regierungssystem* (Reagan and the Developing Countries: Foreign Aid Policy in the American System), p. 49.

40. *Sankei Shimbun*, February 28, 1982, p. 1.

41. Cable from U.S. Embassy/Tokyo to State Department/Washington, March 2, 1982.

42. Cable from State Department/Washington to Embassies in Caribbean Basin region, March 30, 1982.

43. Cable from U.S. Embassy/Khartoum to State Department/Washington, June 11, 1981.

44. Letter from Japanese Foreign Minister Yoshio Sakurauchi to U.S. Secretary of State Alexander Haig, February 4, 1982.

45. Letter from Secretary of State Alexander Haig to Japanese Foreign Minister Yoshio Sakurauchi, February 11, 1982.

46. Akira Kubota, "Foreign Aid: Giving with One Hand?" *Japan Quarterly*, p. 142. Also, see Yasuo Muramatsu, "Philippine Seiken wo Sossen Shien: Seiji Fuan no Kaisho Nerau" (Willingly Supporting the Philippine Administration: Hoping to Prevent Political Instability), in the *Asahi Shimbun* series "Enjo Tojo Koku" (Aid Recipient Country), January 19, 1985.

47. Interview with high-ranking State Department official, June 30, 1986.

48. Interview, official in the Economic Section of the U.S. Embassy/Tokyo, April 21, 1987.

49. Interviews with USAID officials, June 24 and June 28, 1986. Also, interview, Economic Cooperation Bureau, Ministry of Foreign Affairs, December 17, 1986.

50. Yasutomo, *The Manner of Giving*, p. 84.

51. Cable from U.S. Embassy/Tokyo to State Department/Washington, December 4, 1981.

52. Ibid.

53. Interview, official in the Department of State, June 25, 1986.

54. Personal recollection of the meeting, February 4, 1982.

55. Stockman, pp. 126, 127, 128.

56. Lisa Myers, "Leak on Proposed Aid Cuts Stirs Sharp Reagan Reaction," *The Washington Star*, February 5, 1981.

57. Strobe Talbot, "Tokyo Protests Proposed Cut in Foreign Aid," *The Washington Star*, February 5, 1981, as well as Henry Scott Stokes, "Japanese to Double Foreign Aid Outlay," *The New York Times*, January 30, 1981. Also, cable from U.S. Embassy/Tokyo to State Department/Washington, January 30, 1981.

58. Interview, officials in the Office of Japanese Affairs, Department of State, June 23, 1986.

59. Karl Schoenberger, "Japan Aid Said to Worsen Trade Friction," *Asian Wall Street Journal*, December 12–13, 1986.

60. Press statement by Secretary of the Treasury James A. Baker, March 17, 1987.

61. *Nihon Keizai Shimbun*, October 8, 1986, p. 3.

62. Letter from Assistant Secretary of the Treasury David C. Mulford to Vice Finance Minister Gyohten Toyoo and Director General of the Economic Cooperation Bureau, Masamichi Hanabusa, March 5, 1987.

63. Baker press statement.

64. Ibid.

65. Interviews with high-ranking officials in the Aid Policy Division of the Economic Cooperation Bureau, June 23, 1987, and Ministry of Finance, October 21, 1988.

66. "Keizai Enjo o Zogaku: Bei Kokusai Kaihatsu Chokan ga Kaiken; Aite Koku

to wa Seisaku Taiwa" (Increase Economic Assistance: U.S. AID Administrator Interviewed; Should Establish Policy Dialogue with Recipient Countries), *Nihon Keizai Shimbun*, February 2, 1982, p. 3.

67. Yasutomo, *The Manner of Giving*, p. 104.
68. Interview, Economic Cooperation Bureau official, Ministry of Foreign Affairs, December 17, 1986. Also, discussion with USAID official, March 6, 1987.
69. Interview, U.S. Embassy, April 12, 1988.
70. Interview, USAID officials, June 24, 1986.
71. Inada, p. 304.
72. Discussion with USAID officials, November 18, 1982.
73. Cable from State Department/Washington to all USAID field missions, February 17, 1980.
74. USAID memorandum, February 1981.
75. Interviews with JICA, USAID, and Khon Kaen Dry Land Institute officials conducted during July 1984 in Thailand.
76. Interview with USAID official, Bangkok, Thailand, May 2, 1984.
77. Senator Charles Percy, "United States–Japan Relations," *Congressional Record*, March 23, 1982.
78. Cable from State Department/Washington to all USAID field missions.
79. Cable from U.S. Embassy/Rangoon to State Department/Washington.
80. Bruce Koppel and Seiji Naya, "ODA Management and Asia's Economic Development," pp. .
81. Michael Richardson, "U.S.–Japan Set Joint Efforts in Southeast Asia," *International Herald Tribune*, May 17, 1989, p. 7.
82. The U.S. House of Representatives passed H. Con. Res. 387 sponsored by Doug Bereuter (R–Nebraska) and the Senate passed S. Con. Res. 157 introduced by Bill Bradley (D–New Jersey).
83. "Nihon no Enjo: Nishi Gawa Senryaku Kinou Kyouka" (Japan's Aid: Reinforcing Western Strategy), *Yomiuri Shimbun*, February 5, 1989. Actually, the idea of combining Japanese aid with defense spending to calculate Tokyo's burdensharing role was broached in 1987. See "Boei-hi, Keizai Enjo: 'Wan Setto' Youkyu Bei no Tai Nichi Senryaku" (Defense Spending, Economic Aid: U.S. Strategy Toward Japan Is to Demand 'One Set'), *Yomiuri Shimbun*, February 25, 1987.

6. Conclusions: The Meaning of the Process

1. Ministry of Foreign Affairs, *Wagakuni no Seifu Kaihatsu Enjo*, vol. 1, p. 5.
2. Seizaburo Sato, "The Foundations of Modern Japanese Foreign Policy," in Scalapino, ed., *The Foreign Policy of Modern Japan*, p. 375.
3. Haruhiro Fukui, "Too Many Captains in Japan's Internationalization," p. 361.
4. Survey conducted by USAID in 1985.
5. For an interesting description of the impact of missionaries on U.S. foreign policy, see William L. Neumann, *America Encounters Japan*, pp. 139, 140. Neumann relates that President Woodrow Wilson felt that the American envoy to China should be an "evangelical Christian."
6. DAC standards refer to the terms of aid. The highest standard would be

untied grant assistance. The lowest would be tied loans at market interest rates and limited concessionality in the grace period.

7. Ministry of Foreign Affairs, *Japan's Official Development Assistance*, p. 10.

8. T. J. Pempel, "Unbundling 'Japan Inc.': The Changing Dynamics of Japanese Policy Formation," p. 303.

BIBLIOGRAPHY

Allison, Graham T. *Essence of Decision: Explaining the Cuban Missile Crisis.* Boston: Little, Brown, 1971.

Ambrose, Stephen E. *Eisenhower: The President,* vol. 2. New York: Simon & Shuster, 1988.

Angel, Robert C. "Explaining Policy Failure: Japan and the International Economy, 1969–1971." *Journal of Public Policy* (April–June 1988), vol. 8, no. 2.

Art, Robert J. "Bureaucratic Politics and American Foreign Policy: A Critique." *Policy Sciences* (December 1974), vol. 4.

Barnet, Robert W. *Beyond War: Japan's Concept of Comprehensive National Security.* Washington and New York: Pergamon Brassey International Defense Publishers, 1984.

Blaker, Michael. *Japanese Negotiating Style.* New York: Columbia University Press, 1977.

Borton, Hugh. *Japan's Modern Century.* New York: Ronald Press, 1970.

Brooks, William L. "Japanese Economic Assistance to China." Paper presented at conference–workshop on Japanese foreign aid sponsored by the Maureen and Mike Mansfield Foundation, Missoula, Montana, May 14–17, 1987.

Brooks, William L. and Robert M. Orr, Jr. "Japan's Foreign Economic Assistance." *Asian Survey* (March 1985), vol. 25, no. 3.

Calder, Kent E. "Elites in an Equalizing Role." *Comparative Politics* (July 1989).

———. "Japanese Foreign Economic Policy Formation: Explaining the Reactive State," *World Politics,* July 1988, Vol. XL, No. 4, pp. 517–541.

Caldwell, J. Alexander. "The Evolution of Japanese Economic Assistance Cooperation 1950–1970." In Harald B. Malmgren, ed., *Pacific Basin Development: The
American Interests*, pp. 61–80. Lexington, Mass.: Lexington Books, 1972.

Campbell, John Creighton. *Contemporary Japanese Budget Politics.* Berkeley: University of California Press, 1977.

Campbell, John Creighton. "Policy Conflict and Its Resolution Within the Governmental System." In Ellis S. Krauss, Thomas P. Rohlen, and Patricia G. Steinhoff, eds., *Conflict in Japan.* Honolulu: University of Hawaii Press, 1984.

Chittiwatanapong, Prasert. "International Conflict and Japanese Decisionmaking:
Perspectives from Thailand." Thammasat University, Bankok, Manuscript, 1987.

Chittiwatanapong, Prasert. "Japanese Official Development Assistance to Thailand: Impact on Thai Construction Industry." Thammasat University, Bangkok,
Thailand. Manuscript, 1988.

Cohen, Stephen D. *The Making of United States International Economic Policy.* New
York: Praeger, 1977.

Cunningham, George. *The Management of Aid Agencies.* London: Croom Helm,
1974.

Curtis, Gerald L. "Japanese Security Policies and the United States." *Foreign
Affairs* (Spring 1981).

Darwish, Khalil T. "Keizai Enjo to Nihon no Afurika Seisaku" (Economic Aid and
Japan's Africa Policy). *Kokusai Mondai* (May 1987), pp. 70–86.

Destler, I. M. "Comment: Multiple Advocacy—Some Limits and Costs." *American
Political Science Review* (September 1972), no. 66

Destler, I. M. *Making Foreign Economic Policy.* Washington, D.C.: Brookings Institution, 1980.

Destler, I. M., Priscilla Clapp, Hideo Sato, and Haruhiro Fukui. *Managing an
Alliance: The Politics of U.S.–Japanese Relations.* Washington, D.C.: Brookings
Institution, 1976.

Destler, I. M., Haruhiro Fukui, and Hideo Sato. *The Textile Wrangle.* Ithaca and
London: Cornell University Press, 1979.

Destler, I. M. and Hisao Mitsuyu. "Locomotives on Different Tracks: Macroeconomic Diplomacy, 1977–1979." In I. M. Destler and Hideo Sato, eds., *Coping
with U.S.–Japanese Economic Conflicts*, pp. 243–269. Washington, D.C.: Heath,
1982.

Destler, I. M. and Hideo Sato, eds. *Coping with U.S.–Japanese Economic Conflicts.*
Lexington, Mass.: Lexington Books, 1982.

Deutsch, Karl W. "External Influences on the Internal Behavior of States." In
Barry Farrell, ed., *Approaches to Comparative and International Politics*, pp. 5–
26. Evanston, Ill.: Northwestern University Press, 1966.

Doherty, Eileen Marie. "Japan and Subsaharan Africa: Economic and Political
Relations." *Japan Economic Institute Report* (September 19, 1986).

Doherty, Eileen Marie. "Japan's Economic Relations with Africa." *Japan Economic
Institute Report* (November 1986).

Doherty, Eileen Marie. "Japan's Foreign Aid Policy: 1986 Update." *Japan Economic Institute Report* (October 24, 1986).

Doherty, Eileen Marie. "Japan's Role in Multilateral Aid Organizations." *Japan
Economic Institute Report* (May 10, 1988).

Doi, Takeo. *The Anatomy of Dependence.* Tokyo: Kodansha International, 1971.

Dougherty, James E. and Robert L. Pfaltzgraff, Jr. *Contending Theories of International Relations*. New York: Harper & Row, 1981.

Dower, John. *War Without Mercy*. New York: Pantheon Books, 1986.

Drysdale, Peter and Hironubu Kitaoji, eds. *Japan and Australia: Two Societies and Their Interaction*. Canberra: Australia National University Press, 1979.

Dubin, Martin David. "Transgovernmental Processes in the League of Nations." *International Organization* (Summer 1983), vol. 37, no. 3.

Frost, Ellen S. "U.S.–Japan Security Relations in the 1980s and Beyond." Report prepared for the U.S.–Japan Advisory Commission, 1984.

Fukui, Haruhiro. "Too Many Captains in Japan's Internationalization: Travails at the Foreign Ministry." *Journal of Japanese Studies* (Summer 1987), vol. 13, no. 1.

Goto, Kazumi. "Aratana Enjo Gyosei o Motomete." *ESP* (published by the Economic Planning Agency), December 1982.

Halperin, Morton H. and Arnold Kanter. *Readings in American Foreign Policy: A Bureaucratic Perspective*. Boston: Little, Brown, 1973.

Hansen, Roger D. et al. *U.S. Foreign Policy and the Third World*. Washington, D.C.: Overseas Development Council, 1982.

Higashi, Chikara. *Japanese Trade Policy Formulation*. New York: Praeger, 1983.

Higashi, Chikara. *Reagan no Tai-nichi Gaiko o Yomu*. Tokyo: Toyodo Kikaku, 1983.

Higuchi, Sadao. *Seifu Kaihatsu Enjo*. Tokyo: Keiso Shobo Press, 1986.

Hoffman, Michael. "Japan's Development Assistance: A German View." Institute of Developing Economies, Tokyo, January 1985.

Hoptman, Sheri. "Japan's Foreign Aid Policy: 1985 Update." *Japan Economic Institute Report* (November 15, 1985).

Hosoya, Chihiro and Nagayo Honma. *Nichibei Kankeishi: Masatsu to Kyocho no 130 Nen*. Tokyo: Yuhikaku, 1982.

Iida, Tsuneo. "Taigai Enjo, Kore ga Jittai Da?" *This Is* (July 1986).

Inada, Juichi. "Nihon Gaiko ni okeru Enjo Mondai no Shosokumen." *Kokusai Mondai* (May 1987), no. 326, pp. 2–20.

Inukai, Ichiro. "Japan in Africa." Paper presented at conference–workshop sponsored by the Maureen and Mike Mansfield Foundation, Missoula, Montana, May 14–17, 1987.

Johnson, Chalmers. *MITI and the Japanese Miracle*. Stanford: Stanford University Press, 1982.

Johnson, Chalmers. "Tanaka Kakue, Structural Corruption, and the Advent of Machine Politics in Japan." *Journal of Japanese Studies* (Fall 1986), vol. 12, no. 4.

Kaiser, Karl. "Transnational Politics: Toward a Theory of Multinational Politics." *International Organization* (Autumn 1971), vol. 25, no. 4.

Kakazu, Hiroshi. "Japan's Economic Cooperation: History and Performance— Emphasis on the Philippines." *Asian Study Project*, 1982.

Kamo, Takehiko. "Japan's Security Policy: Continuity or Change?" Paper delivered at the Thirtieth Anniversary International Conference of the Japan Association of International Relations, September 4–8, 1986.

Kawai, Saburo. "Future Japan–ASEAN Economic Cooperation." *Asia Pacific Community* (December 1980).

Keidanren. "Keidanren International Cooperation Project Promotion System on the Establishment of the International Cooperation Project Promotion Company and International Cooperation Project Promotion Council." February 1, 1989.

Keohane, Robert O. and Joseph S. Nye, Jr. *Power and Interdependence: World Politics in Transition.* Boston: Little, Brown, 1977.

Keohane, Robert O. and Joseph S. Nye, Jr. *Transnational Relations and World Politics.* Cambridge: Harvard University Press, 1972.

Keohane, Robert O. and Joseph S. Nye, Jr. "Transgovernmental Relations and International Organizations." *World Politics* (October 1974), No. 27.

Kim, Hosup. "Policy-Making of Japanese Official Development Assistance to the Republic of Korea, 1965–1983." Ph.D. dissertation, University of Michigan, 1987.

Kindelberger, Charles and Bruce Herrick. *Economic Development.* New York: McGraw-Hill, 1977.

Kitazawa, Yoko. "The Japanese Economy and the Third World." *Ampo* (1984), vol. 15, no. 3–4.

Koppel, Bruce. "Cooperation or Co-Prosperity? Asian Perspectives on Japan's Ascendancy as an ODA Power." Paper presented at the Forty-first Annual Meeting of the Association for Asian Studies, Washington, D.C., March 17–19, 1989.

Koppel, Bruce, with the assistance of Hirohisa Kohama, Akira Takahashi, and Toru Yanagihara. "Japan–U.S. ODA Cooperation: Perspectives from India, Indonesia and the Philippines." Honolulu, Hawaii: East–West Center, Resource Systems Institute, 1988.

Koppel, Bruce and Seiji Naya. "ODA Management and Asia's Economic Development." Occasional Papers. Based on a conference sponsored by the East–West Center, Resource Systems Institute, Honolulu, Hawaii, May 10–12, 1988.

Krasner, Stephen D. *Defending the National Interest: Raw Materials Investment and U.S. Foreign Policy.* Princeton, N.J.: Princeton University Press, 1978.

Krauss, Ellis S., Thomas P. Rohlen, and Patricia G. Steinhoff, eds. *Conflict in Japan.* Honolulu: University of Hawaii Press, 1984.

Kubota, Akira. "Foreign Aid: Giving with One Hand?" *Japan Quarterly* (April–June 1985), vol. 22, no. 2

Langdon, Frank C. *Japan's Foreign Policy.* Vancouver: University of British Columbia Press, 1973.

Lerch, Hubert. *Die Japanische Bilaterale Entwicklungspolitik Am Beispiel Afrikas: Von den Sechziger Jahren bis Heute.* Munich: W. Angerer, 1984.

Matsui, Ken. *Keizai Kyoryoku: Towareru Nihon no Keizai Gaiko.* Tokyo: Yuhikaku, 1983.

Matsui, Ken. "Nihon no Enjo Seisaku #1: Enjo Hihanron no Keifu." *Kokusai Kaihatsu Journal* (March 1982).

Matsui, Ken. "Nihon no Enjo Seisaku #2: Enjo Futan Busoku e no Taiyo." *Kokusai Kaihatsu Journal* (April 1982).

Matsui, Ken. "Nihon no Enjo Seisaku #3: Kikin no Shishutsu to Haibun no Teki Seika." *Kokusai Kaihatsu Journal* (May 1982).

Matsui, Ken. "Nihon no Enjo Seisaku #4: Kikin no Koritsuteki Unyou." *Kokusai Kaihatsu Journal* (June 1982).

Matsui, Ken. "Nihon no Enjo Seisaku #5: Sengo Enjo Gaiko no Rekishi Tenkai." *Kokusai Kaihatsu Journal* (July 1982).

Matsui, Ken. "Nihon no Enjo Seisaku #6: Enjo Gaiko Seisaku no Zahyo Jiku." *Kokusai Kaihatsu Journal* (August 1982).

Matsumoto, Hiroshi. "Japanese ODA to ASEAN Countries." Paper presented at ARSPP conference sponsored by the Japan Institute for International Affairs, February 5, 1987.

Matsumoto, Kosaku. "External Elements of China's Eocnomic Policy and Japan's Financial Assistance to China." *China Newsletter* (1983), no. 42.

Matsumoto, Shigekazu. "Progress and Policy Formulation of Japan's External Assistance." Paper presented at "The U.S. Congress and the Japanese Diet: Conference on Comparative Studies in Foreign Policy." Honolulu, February 9–12, 1983.

Matsuura, Koichiro. "Japan's Role in International Cooperation." *National Development* (October 1981).

McDougall, Derek J., Rodney A. Martin, Gary K. Smith, and Bernard C. Tranter. *Foreign Policies in the Asian Pacific Region.* Sydney: Prentice Hall of Australia, 1982.

McNeill, Desmond. *The Contradictions of Foreign Aid.* London: Croom Helm, 1981.

May, Bernhard. "Japans Neue Rolle in der Multilateralen Entwicklungspolitik." *Europa Archiv* (September 25, 1988), no. 18.

May, Bernhard. *Reagan und die Entwicklungsländer: Die Auslandshilfepolitik im Amerikanischen Regierungssytem.* (Reagan and the Developing Countries: Foreign Aid Policy in the American System) Munich: R. Oldenbourg Press, 1987.

Mees, Charles L., Jr. *The Marshall Plan.* New York: Simon & Shuster, 1984.

Meltzer, Ronald I. "The Politics of Policy Reversal: The U.S. Response to Granting Trade Preferences to Developing Countries and Linkages between International Organizations and National Policymaking." *International Organization* (Autumn 1976), vol. 30, no. 4.

Mendl, Wolf. *Issues in Japan's China Policy.* New York: Oxford University Press, 1978.

Minor, Michael. "Decision Models and Japanese Foreign Policy Decision Makers." *Asian Survey* (December 1985), vol. 25, no. 12.

Miyasato, Seigen. "Foreign Aid in Japan–U.S. Relations: The Japanese Perspective." Paper delivered at a conference at the Georgetown Center for Strategic and International Studies (March 1985).

Morgenthau, Hans J. *Politics Among Nations: The Struggle for Power and Peace.* New York: Knopf, 1967.

Mosley, Paul. *Foreign Aid: Its Defense and Reform.* Lexington: University of Kentucky Press, 1987.

Moss, Joanna and John Ravenhill. "The Emerging Japanese Influence in Africa nad Its Implications for the United States." Report prepared for the U.S. Department of State, June 1983.

Neumann, William L. *America Encoutners Japan.* Baltimore: Johns Hopkins University Press, 1963.

Neustadt, Richard E. *Alliance Politics.* New York: Columbia University Press, 1970.

Nishihara, Masashi. *East Asian Security and the Trilateral Countries.* New York and London: New York University Press, 1985.

Nishihara, Masashi. "Japanese Role for Northeast Asian Security and Beyond." Paper presented at the Fourth Annual Meeting, International Institute for Strategic Studies, Kyoto, August 1986.

Nissho Iwai. "ODA Hatten Tojokoku no Jizokuteki na Keizai Seicho o Kanonshi
sono Saimu Hensai Noryoku o Kojo saseru tame ni koso." (Making Economic
Growth Possible Through Debt Repayment capacity) *Tradepia* (April 1989).

Nowels, Larry Z. "Foreign Aid: Budget, Policy,and Reform." Washington, D.C.:
Congressional Research Service, 1989.

Okita, Saburo. *The Developing Economies and Japan.* Tokyo: University of Tokyo
Press, 1980.

Okita, Saburo. *Japan's Challenging Years: Reflections on My Lifetime.* Winchester,
Mass.: Allen and Unwinn, 1985.

Orr, Robert M., Jr. "Japan's Foreign Aid Policy—Opinion." *Japan Economic Journal* (December 1985).

Orr, Robert M., Jr., "The Aid Factor in U.S.–Japan Relations." *Asian Survey* (July
1988).

Orr, Robert M., Jr., "The Politics of Japan's Foreign Aid." Paper presented at
conference–workshop sponsored by the Maureen and Mike Mansfield Foundation, Missoula, Montana, May 14–17, 1987.

Orr, Robert M., Jr., "The Rising Sun: Japanese Economic Aid to South Korea, the
Pacific Basin and ASEAN." *Journal of International Affairs* (Fall 1987), vol. 41,
no. 2.

Osamu, Muro. "Japan und International Entwicklungshilfe." *Vierteljahresberichte*
(September 1985), Nr. 101.

Ota, Hiroshi. "Sore Demo Keizai Kyoryoku wa Kakasenai." *This Is* (December
1986).

Ozawa, Norio. Paper presented at conference on Japan's Development Financing:
Opportunities for U.S. Business. San Francisco, California, and Orlando, Florida, May 1989.

Paper, Lewis J. *John F. Kennedy: The Promise and the Performance.* New York: Da
Capo, 1975.

Pempel, T. J. "The Unbundling of 'Japan, Inc.': The Changing Dynamics of Japanese Policy Formation." *Journal of Japanese Studies* (Summer 1987), vol. 13, no.
1, pp. 271–306.

Pharr, Susan J. "Japan's Foreign Aid." Testimony before the House Foreign Affairs
Committee, Subcommittee on Asia and Pacific Affairs. September 28, 1988.

Pharr, Susan J. and Takako Kishima. "Japan in 1986: A Landmark Year for the
LDP." *Asian Survey* (January 1987), pp. 23–34.

Pollock, Stephen. "Cohesion and Competition: A Study of Japan's Foreign Aid."
Senior thesis for Harvard College, June 1985 (unpublished).

Pollack, Stephen. "The Role of the Private Sector in Japan's Foreign Aid Program."
Paper presented at conference–workshop sponsored by the Maureen and Mike
Mansfield Foundation, Missoula, Montana, May 14–17, 1987.

Reischauer, Edwin O. *My Life Between Japan and America.* New York: Harper &
Row, 1986.

Rix, Alan. *Japan's Economic Aid.* New York: St. Martin's, 1980.

Rix, Alan. *Quantity versus Quality: Trends and Issues in the Japanese Aid Program.*
Canberra: Australian Development Assistance Bureau, 1987.

Rix, Alan. "The Future of Japanese Foreign Aid." *Australian Outlook* (December
1977), vol. 31, No. 3.

Rix, Alan. "The Mitsugoro Project: Japanese Aid Policy and Indonesia." *Pacific
Affairs.* (Spring 1979).

Rix, Alan. "The Social Basis and Philosophy of Japanese Aid." Paper presented at conference–workshop sponsored by the Maureen and Mike Mansfield Foundation, Missoula, Montana, May 14–17, 1987.

Rosati, Jarel A. "Developing a Systematic Decisionmaking Framework: Bureaucratic Politics in Perspective." *World Politics* (January 1981), vol. 33, no. 2.

Rourke, Francis. *Bureaucracy and Foreign Policy.* Baltimore: Johns Hopkins University Press, 1972.

Rubin, Barry. *Secrets of State.* New York: Oxford University Press, 1987.

Rubinstein, Gregg. "Facing the Challenge: Defense Technology Cooperation Between the United States and Japan." In Ronald A. Morse, ed., *Politics and High Technology in Japan's Defense and Strategic Future.* Washington, D.C.: Wilson Center, 1987).

Sato Seizaburo and Tetsuhisa Matsuzaki. *Jiminto Seiken.* Tokyo: Chuo Koron Press, 1986.

Sato, Seizaburo and Tetsuhisa Matsuzaki. "Party Leadership by the Liberal Democrats." *Economic Eye* (December 1984).

Scalapino, Robert A., ed. *The Foreign Policy of Modern Japan.* Berkeley: University of California Press, 1977.

Self, Peter. *Political Theories of Modern Government: Its Role and Reform.* London: Allen and Unwinn, 1985.

Spanier, John and Eric M. Uslaner. *American Foreign Policy Making and the Democratic Dilemmas.* New York: Holt, Rhinehart & Winston, 1985.

Stockman, David A. *The Triumph of Politics.* New York: Avon Books, 1986.

Story, Greg. "Japan's Official Development Assistance to China: A Survey." Australia–Japan Research Centre, Pacific Economic Papers, No. 150.

Sumita, Makoto. "Politics of Foreign Aid: Japanese Bureaucratic Politics." M. A. Thesis, George Washington University, June 1979.

Summerville, Paul A. "The Politics of Self-Restraint: The Japanese State, and the Voluntary Export Restraint of Japanese Passenger Car Exports to the United States in 1981." Ph.D. dissertation, University of Tokyo, March 1988.

Takeda, Isami. "New Factors in Japan's ODA Policy: Implications for Australia–Japan Relations." Paper presented at the AJRC–JARC Research Project on Australia–Japan Relations: Toward the Twenty-first Century, Australia National University, Canberra, August 18–19, 1986.

Takeda, Isami. "Kawaru Nihon no Taigai Enjo to Minami Taiheiyo Chiiki." *Toa-Asia Monthly* (February 1987).

Tanaka, Akihiko. "Long-Term Scenarios in Japan–U.S. Relations." Prepared for the U.S.–Japan Advisory Commission, September 1984.

Tanaka, Akihiko. "ASEAN Factor in Japan's China Policy? A Case Study: Japan's Government Loans to China 1979." Paper presented at the Dialogue Conference, October 27–29, 1986.

Toba, Kinichiro. "Japan's Peace Corps Turns Technical." *Japan Quarterly* (July–September 1985), vol. 32, no. 3.

Tsuji, Kazuto. "A Comparative Study of Administration in Two Foreign Aid Agencies: USAID and OECF." Unpublished paper, University of Michigan, June 1982.

Tsuji, Kiyoaki, ed. *Public Administration in Japan.* Tokyo: University of Tokyo Press, 1984.

U.S.–Japan Advisory Commission. *Challenges and Opportunities in United States– Japan Relations.* 1984.
Valeo, Frank and Charles Morrison. *The Japanese Diet and the U.S. Congress.* Boulder: Westview Press, 1983.
Van Wolferen, Karel. *The Enigma of Japanese Power.* London: MacMillan, 1989.
Wanner, Barbara. "Japan's Foreign Aid Policy: an Annual Update." *Japan Economic Institute Report* (September 2, 1983).
Watanabe, Akio, ed. *Sengo Nihon no Taigai Seisaku.* Tokyo: Yuhikaku, 1985.
Wheeler, Joseph C. *Development Cooperation.* 1986 DAC Review. Paris: Organization for Economic Cooperation and Development, 1987.
Yamakage, Susumu. "Japan and ASEAN: Are They Really Becoming Closer?" In Werner Pfennig and Mark B. Suh, eds., *Aspects of ASEAN.* Munich–Cologne– London: Weltforum Press, 1984.
Yamakage, Susumu. "Japan's Official Assistance to Southeast Asia and Comprehensive Security." In *Japanese-American Relations and Comprehensive Security.* Tokyo: Sekai Keizai Joho Service, 1985.
Yamamoto, Tsuyoshi. *Nihon no Keizai Enjo.* Tokyo: Sanseido Press, 1978.
Yasutomo, Dennis T. *Japan and the Asian Development Bank.* New York: Praeger, 1983.
Yasutomo, Dennis T. *The Manner of Giving: Strategic Aid and Japanese Foreign Policy.* Lexington, MA: Lexington Books, 1986.
Yoshitsu, Michael. *Caught in the Middle East: Japan's Diplomacy in Transition.* Lexington, MA: Lexington Books, 1984.

Government Documents

Economic Planning Agency. "Taiheiyo Jidai no Tenbou" (report). 1985.
Foreign Broadcast Information Service, monitored by the Central Intelligence Agency and distributed by the U.S. Department of Commerce.
Foreign Ministry of Japan. "Keizai Kyoryoku ni Kansuru Kihon Shiryou" (report). 1986.
Haig, Alexander M., Jr., Secretary of State. Letter to Foreign Minister Yoshio Sakurauchi and response concerning increasing aid to Egypt, February 4, 1982.
Haig, Alexander M., Jr., Secretary of State. Letter to Foreign Minister Yoshio Sakurauchi, February 6, 1982.
Holderidge, John H., Assistant Secretary of State for East Asia and Pacific Affairs. Statement before House Subcommittee on East Asia Pacific Affairs, Washington, D.C., March 1, 1982.
House of Councillors, Foreign Affairs Committee. "Sogo Anzen Hosho ni Chosa." Tokubetsu Iinkai Kaigi roku Dai 5 gou, May 16, 1984.
International Engineering Consultants Association Outline and Activity. Thirtieth Anniversary, Tokyo, 1986.
Japan Engineering Consulting Firms Association. *Annual Report.* Tokyo, 1986.
Ministry of Foreign Affairs. "Keizai Kyoryoku no Rinen: Seifu Kaihatsu Enjo wa Naze Okonau no ka." Keizai Kyoryoku Kenkyusha, 1981.
Ministry of Foreign Affairs. *Wagakuni no Seifu Kaihatsu Enjo,* vols. 1 and 2. Tokyo: Association for Promotion of International Cooperation, 1988 and 1989.
Ministry of Foreign Affairs. *Japan's Official Development Assistance.* Tokyo: Association for Promotion of International Cooperation, 1988.

National Security Council. "Directive on U.S.–Japan Relations." August 18, 1982.
ODA Jisshi ni Koritsuka Kenkyukai. "Seifu Kaihatsu Enjo no Kokateki Koritsuteki Jisshi ni Tsuite." December 1985.
Overseas Economic Cooperation Fund. "Beikoku Kokusai Kaihatsu-Cho." 1984.
Overseas Economic Cooperation Fund. *Kaigai Keizai Kyoryoku Kikin 20 Nenshi.* 1982.
Report from U.S. Embassy/Tokyo to State Department. "Deployment of U.S.–Japan Collaborative Projects." September 1982.
Sakurauchi, Yoshio, Minister of Foreign Affairs. Message to delegates of the third Japan–U.S. Aid Policy Consultations, February 1982.
Selected Cable Traffic (unclassified) between U.S. Embassy/Tokyo, Washington, and several field missions concerning Japanese foreign aid, 1979–1987.
Shultz, George, Secretary of State. Speech before the sixth Shimoda Conference. United States Information Service, American Embassy, press release, September 2, 1983.
Sigur, Gaston, Assistant Secretary of State for East Asia and the Pacific. "Sigur sees Japan, U.S. Headed in Right Direction" (speech). United States Information Service, American Embassy, press release, June 2, 1986.
Sutter, Robert G. "Dealing with Japan: Policy Approaches for a Troubled Alliance." Congressional Research Service, May 28, 1982.
U.S.A.I.D. Press Release. "United States and Japan to Undertake Foreign Aid Projects Jointly in Thailand." June 18, 1982.
U.S. Congress. House and Senate. Committee on Foreign Affairs, Committee on Foreign Relations. *Legislation on Foreign Relations Through 1985*, vols. 1 and 2. Washington, D.C.: GPO, April 1986.
U.S. Congress. House. Committee On Foreign Affairs. *Government Decisionmaking in Japan: Implications for the United States.* 97th Congress, 2d session, 1982.
U.S. Congress. House. Committee on Foreign Affairs, Subcommittee on International Economic Policy and Trade: Subcommittee on Asian and Pacific Affairs. 97th Congress, 2d session: "Hearings on United States–Japan Relations," March 1, 3, 9, 17, 24; April 27; June 2, 5; August 4, 1982. Washington D.C.: GPO.
U.S. Congress. Senate. Senator Charles Percy speaking on U.S.–Japan Relations. 97th Congress, 2d session, *Congressional Record*, March 23, 1982.

Interviews and Assistance

Aichi, Kazuo. Member of the Diet.
Aki, Yoichi. Overseas Economic Cooperation Fund.
Alton, Charles. U.S.A.I.D.: Khon Kaen, Thailand.
Anderson, Desaix. Deputy Chief of Mission, U.S. Embassy/Tokyo.
Armacost, Michael. Undersecretary of State for Political Affairs.
Banyat, Surakanvit. Thammasat University.
Bloch, Julia C. Assistant Administrator for Asia and the Neareast, U.S.A.I.D.
Brooks, William L. Chief Japan Analyst, Bureau for Intelligence and Research, Department of State.
Brown, Fred. Senate Foreign Relations Committee Staff.
Chinworth, Michael. MIT Japan Science and Technology Program.
Chittiwatanapong, Prasert. Thammasat University.
Corbett, William. Office of Japan Affairs, Department of State.

Domichi, Hideaki. Economic Cooperation Bureau, Ministry of Foreign Affairs.
Enoki, Yasukuni., Economic Cooperation Bureau, Ministry of Foreign Affairs.
Fascell, Dante. Member of U.S. House of Representatives, Chairman of the Foreign Affairs Committee.
Foley, Cora. ASEAN Analyst, Bureau for Intelligence and Research, Department of State.
Forman, Lori. U.S.A.I.D.
Foster, James. U.S. Embassy/Tokyo.
Foti, John. U.S.A.I.D.: Bangkok, Thailand.
Fuji, Makoto. Budget Examiner, Ministry of Finance.
Gibbons, Sam. Member of U.S. House of Representatives, Chairman of the Subcommittee on Trade.
Goodman, Margaret. House Foreign Affairs Committee Staff.
Goto, Kazumi. Overseas Economic Cooperation Fund.
Greenleaf, Charles. Assistant Administrator for Asia and the Near East, U.S.A.I.D.
Halligan, Robert. Former Mission Director, Thailand U.S.A.I.D.
Higashi, Chikara. Member of the Diet.
Hirono, Ryokichi. Professor, Seikei University.
Hubbard, Thomas. Director, Office of Japanese Affairs, Department of State.
Ishii, Ijiji. Member of the Diet.
Karu, Hiroshi. Keizai Doyukai.
Kato, Koji. House of Councillors Legislative Bureau staff.
Kawakami, Takao. Deputy Director General, Economic Cooperation Bureau, Ministry of Foreign Affairs.
Kirkpatrick, Jeane J. Former U.S. Ambassador to the United Nations.
Klemm, Hans. U.S. Embassy/Tokyo.
Kobayashi, Shoichi. Engineering Consulting Firms Association of Japan.
Kumagai, Akira. Japan International Cooperation Agency.
Koppel, Bruce. East–West Center.
Ludden, Kenneth. Senate Foreign Relations Committee Staff.
Matsumoto, Hiroshi. Executive Director, Association for the Promotion of International Cooperation.
Matsuura, Koichiro. Director General, Economic Cooperation Bureau, Ministry of Foreign Affairs.
Matsuyama, K. Economic Planning Agency.
Morinobu, Shigeki. Ministry of Finance, Development Assistance Division.
McPherson, M. Peter. Administrator, U.S.A.I.D.
Mineshima, Toshiyuki. Director, International Finance Bureau, Ministry of Finance.
Mineta, Norman Y. Member of U.S. House of Representatives.
Moriga, Akira. Economic Cooperation Bureau, Ministry of Foreign Affairs.
Naya, Seiji. Vice President, East–West Center.
Nishie, Akira. International Finance Bureau, Ministry of Finance.
Nowels, Larry. Congressional Research Service.
Nogami, Yoshiji. Economic Counselor, Japanese Embassy/Washington.
Nishihara, Masashi. Professor, National Defense University.
Nakamura, Yoshio. Keidanren.
Okita, Saburo. Former Foreign Minister of Japan.

Ota, Hiroshi. Deputy Director General, Economic Cooperation Bureau, Ministry of Foreign Affairs.
Peasley, Carol. U.S.A.I.D.: Bangkok, Thailand.
Pharr, Susan J. Director, U.S.–Japan Relations Program, Harvard University.
Rix, Alan. University of Queensland.
Sakaue, Marlene. U.S. Embassy/Tokyo.
Sakanaka, Tomohisa. Aoyama Gakuin.
Sato, Seizaburo. Tokyo University.
Seligmann, Albert L. Japan Representative, Asia Foundation.
Shiina, Motoo. Member of the Diet.
Sherry, Jerome. U.S.A.I.D.
Solarz, Stephen. Member of U.S. House of Representatives, Chairman of Subcommittee on Asian and Pacific Affairs.
Tanabe, Yoshio. Economic Cooperation Bureau, Ministry of Foreign Affairs.
Tanaka, Hitoshi. Director, Second North American Division, Ministry of Foreign Affairs.
Taniuchi, Michiru. Economic Planning Agency.
Tomimoto, Ikufumi. Japan International Cooperation Agency.
Triplett, William. Senate Foreign Relations Committee Staff.
Uchida, Tomio. Ministry of Finance.
Watanabe, Akio. Tokyo University.
Wheeler, Joseph. Chairman, Development Assistance Committee, Organization of Economic Cooperation and Development.
Yonekawa, Yoshinobu. Department of Technical Cooperation for Development, United Nations.
Yamada, Akira. Economic Cooperation Bureau, Ministry of Foreign Affairs.
Yamada, Eugene. Asian Productivity Organization.
Yamakage, Susumu. Tokyo University.
Yasutomo, Dennis. Smith College.
Yokota, Katsuhiro. Director, Economic Cooperation Department, Ministry of International Trade and Industry.

Newspapers and Magazines Consulted

Asahi Evening News
Asian Wall Street Journal
Asahi Shimbun
Bungei Shunju
Business Week
Daily Yomiuri
Far Eastern Economic Review
Financial Times of London
Foreign Service Journal
International Herald Tribune
Japan Economic Journal
Japan Times
Journal of Commerce
Mainichi Daily News
Nation
Newsweek
New York Times
Nihon Keizai Shimbun
PHP Intersect
Sankei Shimbun
Sekai
Tokyo Business today
Tokyo Insider
Wall Street Journal
Washington Post
Washington Star
West Africa
Yomiuri Shimbun

INDEX

Abe Shintaro, 85, 98, 125
Africa, 37, 52, 55, 93–96, 130
Agriculture, Forestry and Fisheries, Ministry of, 20, 48
Allison, Graham, 8
Amae (dependence), 5
"Amakudari," 64
ANZUS, 90
Aquino, Corazon, 82–83, 142
Armacost, Michael, 120, 130
ASEAN, 75–84, 120, 142. *See also* Southeast Asia
ASEAN–Japan Development Fund, 78
Asia, 4–5, 55, 69, 103, 110, 141
Asian Development Bank, 45–46, 99
Association of South East Asian Nations. *See* ASEAN
Australia, 66, 89–90
Ayuthaya History Study Center, 64

Baker, James A., 127
Bandar-Khomeini Petrochemical Project, 93

Bangladesh, 91, 135
Baraclough, William, 114
Basic Human Needs projects, 20, 37, 56
Bloch, Julia, 135
Bolivia, 97
British Consulting Firms Association, 66
British Crown Agents, 29, 94
Brunei, 79
Budget Bureau, 32, 34, 132
Budgets, 10, 21, 24, 31, 34
"Burden sharing," 3, 89, 136
"Bureaucratic politics" model, of decisionmaking, 4, 7–10, 12–13, 31
Burma, *see* Myanmar
Bush, George, 133, 136

C. Itoh, *see* Itoh, C.
Cabinet, composition of the Japanese, 10–11
Cambodia, 53, 122
Caribbean, 97–98

Caribbean Basin Initiative, 97, 116, 143
Carter, Jimmy, 14, 111, 112
Charity, 54
Chiang Kai-shek, 71, 109
China, People's Republic of, 16, 53, 58, 71–75, 129
Cho Shin Yongi, 88
Chun Do Hwan, 88, 113
Clayton, William, 2
Colombo Plan, 53
Comprehensive Security Council, 24
Construction industry, 61–62
Consultations, 14, 39, 128–31
Consulting firms, 66
Cooperation Development Division, 39–41
Country Development Strategy Statement (CDSS), 101, 135
Cuba, 58, 121

"Dango," 62–63
Dean, John Gunther, 133
Debt problems, 78, 80, 97–98
Decisionmaking process, models of, 6–10, 12–13
Defense Agency, 14
De Gaulle, Charles, 109
Deng Xiaoping, 73
Destler, I. M., 16–17
Development Assistance Committee (DAC), 3, 19, 54, 56, 107, 125, 127, 139
Development Assistance Group, see Development Assistance Committee
Diet, role in foreign aid policy, 11, 140, 141
Differentiated discount rate (DDR), 125–127
Disbursement difficulties, 47, 75, 80, 92, 96
Douglas, William, 133
Dulles, John Foster, 53

East-West Center meetings, 135
"Economic cooperation," use of term to describe Japanese foreign aid, 53
Economic Cooperation Bureau, 39–44, 107

Economic Planning Agency, 3, 20, 44–45, 48–49
Ecuador, 97
Education, Ministry of, 15
Egypt, 94, 118, 141
Embassies, role of in foreign aid administration, 44, 134–35
Emigration policy, 97
Engineering Consulting Firms Association (ECFA), 28, 63
Enjo zoku (aid caucus), 22
European Recovery Program, 2
Expert missions, 80–81, 83
Export-Import Bank, see Japan Export-Import Bank
Export promotion, 38, 53–54, 59, 112
External Economic Assistance, Special Committee for, 22

Factions, in Japanese politics, 10–11, 23
Fiji, 89
Finance, Ministry of, 3, 14–15, 20, 30–34, 47, 55–56, 98–99, 128, 141–142
Fiscal Investment and Loan Program, 33, 47
Food aid, 37, 95
Foreign Affairs, Ministry of (MOFA): conceptions of foreign aid of, 20, 26–27, 39, 44, 55–56, 58, 102, 111–12, 141; interministerial relations and, 14–15, 17, 33–34, 38–39, 49, 56, 86, 128, 137–38, 146; organizational structure of, 39–44; role of, 3, 20, 78, 107, 115–16, 128–29, 144–45; see also National security
Foreign aid: definition of, 2; as foreign policy instrument, 55–56, 58, 105–6, 130, 139, 141; motivations for, 37–39, 52–54, 141; policy formation for, 6, 19–21, 42–43, 56–59, 137–38; public support for in Japan, 25–29; public support for in the U.S., 27, 105; regional distribution of, 55, 69; and trade relations, 13, 17, 59, 107, 126–28, 143
Four-ministry system, 3, 6, 20, 29, 34, 137–38; see also individual ministries, e.g., Finance, Ministry of

FSX aircraft negotiations, 14–15
Fujita Kimio, 129
Fukuda Takeo, 55, 76, 110–11
Funso shuhen koku (countries border-
ing conflict areas), 111

Gaiatsu (foreign pressure), 5, 17, 107–
9, 113, 134
General Electric Company, 67
Giinrenmei (parliamentary friendship
leagues), 23, 142
Gotoda Masaharu, 42–43
Gramm-Rudman legislation, 124
Grant aid, 3, 20, 29–30, 140; *see also*
Japan International Cooperation
Agency
Green Corps, 95
Gyoten, Toyoo, 126–27

Haig, Alexander M., Jr., 114, 118–19
Hanabusa Masamichi, 126–27, 130
Health and Welfare, Ministry of, 20
Higuchi Sadao, 6
Holderidge, John, 115
Honduras, 97
Hosomi Takashi, 47

Ikeda Hayato, 109
Implementing agencies, 3, 45, 60, 139
India, 53, 91, 135
Indonesia, 38, 53, 77–81, 132, 135
Interest groups, 28–29
Intergovernmental Group for Indone-
sia (IGGI), 80
International Cooperation Day, 26
International Development Agency,
126
International Engineering Consultants
Association (IECA), 63
International Trade and Industry, Min-
istry of (MITI), 3, 15–16, 20, 24,
30–31, 35–39, 48, 54–56, 78–79, 86,
142
Iran, 56, 93
Iraq, 92–93
Ishihara Kaneo, 47
Ishihara Shintaro, 142
Israel, 55, 93
Ito Kosuke, 25

Ito Masayoshi, 114, 124
Itoh, C., 61, 66

Jamaica, 98, 113–16, 141
Japan: defense relations with the U.S.,
5, 13–14; foreign aid policies of, 3,
37–39, 42, 52–54, 56–59, 141; foreign relations with China, 74–75;
foreign relations with Taiwan, 71–
72; foreign relations with the U.S.,
5–6, 71, 100, 139, 145; influence of
U.S. on foreign aid policy of, 3–4,
14–18, 53, 56, 82, 97–98, 103–4,
107–13, 143–45; ranking of foreign
aid of, 1–3, 52, 89; trade relations
with the U.S., 5–6, 13, 15–17, 126–
28, 143
Japan Emigration Services, 49
Japan Export-Import Bank, 3, 29, 45,
128
Japan Federation of Construction Contractors (Nikkenren), 63
Japan Federation of Economic Organizations (Keidanren), 63
Japan International Cooperation
Agency (JICA), 3, 24, 29–30, 42–43,
47–50, 140; *see also* Grant aid
Japan International Development Organization (JAIDO), 63–64
Japan Overseas Volunteers Coopera-
tion, 30, 95
Japan–U.S. Security Subcommittee,
14
Johnson, Lyndon B., 8, 109–10
Joint projects, 131–33, 143
Jordan, 92

Kaifu Toshiki, 98
Keidanren, *see* Japan Federation of
Economic Organizations
Kennedy, John F., 104–5, 109–10
Kiribati, 89
Kishi Nobusuke, 23, 45
Korea, Republic of, 87–89, 109, 113–
14
Krasner, Stephen D., 7
Kubota Minoru, 135
Kuranari Tadashi, 90, 121
Kurofune (black ships), 16, 144

Laos, 53, 58
Latin America, 55, 97–98
Least developed countries (LLDCs), 29, 37, 52
Less developed countries (LDCs), 32, 35, 37
Liberal Democratic Party (LDP), 10, 21–22, 63
Loan aid, 3, 20, 29, 30–31, 46–47, 57, 77, 80, 109, 140; see also Overseas Economic Cooperation Fund

Malaysia, 81
Mansfield, Mike, 110
Marshall Plan, 2, 104
Matsuura Koichiro, 41, 124
McPherson, M. Peter, 122–23, 129–30
Mexico, 97
Middle East, 37, 92–93, 106
Miki Takeo, 14, 55, 76
Ministries, powers of, 11–12, 31; for individual ministries see under first significant word of title, e.g., Finance, Ministry of; see also Four-ministry system
Missionary activities, 54, 139
MITI, see International Trade and Industry, Ministry of
Mixed credits, 17, 125–26, 144
Miyazawa Kiichi, 11
Mohammed, Abdullah Zawawi, 78
Mongolia, 58
Mosley, Paul, 2
Mulford, David C., 126–27
Multilateral development banks, 98–102
Murata Ryohei, 130
Myanmar (Burma), 53, 84–86, 134

Nakasone Yasuhiro, 11, 14, 23, 64, 74, 77, 82, 88, 98, 114, 118, 125, 127–28
National security, links with foreign aid, 2, 6, 56, 91–92, 111–12, 117–19
National Security Directive of 1981, 112–13, 117, 136
Natural resources, see raw materials
Nenjikyoyokoku (recipients of consistently high levels of Japanese aid), 76, 113

Nepal, 91
New Asian Industries Development Plan (New AID Plan), 38, 77–78
"New Directions" policy, 108
Newly industrialized economies (NIEs), 29, 32
New Zealand, 90
Nicaragua, 123, 129, 143–44
Nikkenren, see Japan Federation of Construction Contractors
Nishihara loans, 71
Nixon, Richard L., influence on Japanese decisionmaking, 16, 72
Nongovernmental organizations (NGOs), 27, 42

Ogiso Motoo, 133
Ohira Masayoshi, 24, 49, 76, 111
Oil crisis, 54–55
Okita Saburo, 78, 115
Oman, 92–93
"Omiyage gaiko," (souvenir foreign policy), 24, 98
Ongpin, Jaime, 83
Oni (good/evil devil), 5, 16
Organization for Economic Development (OECD), 3, 54
Overseas Construction Association, 62, 65–66
Overseas development assistance, see foreign aid
Overseas Economic Cooperation Fund (OECF), 3, 24, 33, 39, 45–47, 50, 63, 67, 82, 96, 139; see also Loan aid
Overseas Technical Cooperation Agency, see Japan International Cooperation Agency

Pacific region nations, 89–91, 121
Pakistan, 91, 111, 141
Papua New Guinea, 89
Paraguay, 97
Peace Corps, 105
Pempel, T. J., 13, 15
Percy, Charles, 133
Persian Gulf, 93
Philippines, 24, 53, 81–84, 120, 131–33, 135, 142

Pluralist model, of decisionmaking, 7–8
Policy Research Council, 22
Politicians, role formulating in foreign aid policy, 21–25, 140
Posts and Telecommunications, Ministry of, 15
Prime Minister, powers of Japanese, 10–11, 23–24
Private sector, 4, 28–29, 59–65, 95–96, 99–100, 140
Project evaluation, 57, 101, 139
Public opinion, of foreign aid, 25–28, 95

"Rational actor" model, of decisionmaking, 6–7
Raw materials, 37, 53, 55, 75, 94, 97
"Reactive vs. interpretive state," 108
Reagan, Ronald, 14, 73, 106, 112–14, 118, 120, 123, 125
Recruit Cosmos scandal, 21
Reparation payments, 3, 23, 53
Rix, Alan, 6, 20, 46, 57, 101
Rusk, Dean, 8

Sadat, Anwar al-, 118
Sakurauchi Yoshio, 117, 119, 122, 142
Sato Ekisaku, 109–10
Sato Hideo, 16–17, 137
Sato Seizaburo, 4, 137
Saudi Arabia, 92
Scandals, 21, 24, 28, 42, 82
Seaga, Edward, 114, 116
Sejima Ryozo, 88
Shultz, George, 90, 121
Singapore, 81
Solomon Islands, 89
Sonoda Sunao, 87, 111
South Africa, Republic of, 96
Southeast Asia, 53, 109; see also ASEAN
South Pacific Axis, 90
Soviet Union, 56, 75, 89–91
Sri Lanka, 91–92
Staffing: assignment of ministry personnel to agencies, 41–42, 45, 47, 49–50; levels and qualifications of,

28, 47, 59, 80, 83, 91, 95, 99–100, 136
Stockman, David A., 124
Sudan, 117–19, 141
Suzuki, Zenko, 24, 56, 77, 88, 98, 112–13

Takgai Keizai Kyoryoku Tokubetsu Iinkai, see External Economic Assistance, Special Committee for
Taiwan, 71–72, 109
Takeshita Noboru, 23, 85–86
Tamaki Kazuo, 42
Tamura Hajime, 38
Tanaka Kakuei, 23, 72, 76
Technical assistance, 30, 49
Technical training, 96
Thailand, 64, 67, 79, 132–33
Tian-an-mien Square, 74–75
Tied aid, 33, 52–53, 62, 65–68, 110–11, 125
Trade relations, 5–6, 13, 15–17, 126–28, 143
Trade surplus, recycling of, 33, 98, 110, 127–128, 143
Trading companies, 60–61, 96
Training programs, 49, 96, 131
Transgovernmental relations, 4, 12–18, 145
Truman, Harry S., 8
Turkey, 92, 111

United Nations, 100
United States: defense relations with Japan, 5, 13–14; foreign aid policies of, 2, 104–6, 144; foreign relations with Japan, 5–6, 71, 100, 139, 145; influence on foreign aid policy of Japan, 3–4, 14–18, 53, 56, 82, 97–98, 103–4, 107–13, 143–45; trade relations with Japan, 5–6, 13, 15–17, 126–28, 143
U.S. Agency for International Development (USAID), 24, 59, 66, 104–5, 107, 134–36, 144
U.S. Foreign Assistance Act, 21, 73, 104
U.S.–Japan Mutual Security Treaty, 13, 145

Vanuatu, 89–90
Vietnam, 37, 58, 105, 121–122, 142

Wakaoji Nobuyuki, 82
Watanabe Michio, 85
World Bank, 29, 84, 99–100

Yamaguchi Mitsuhide, 47
Yamamoto Tsuyoshi, 38

Yanagi, Kenichi, 122–23, 129
Yanai Shinichi, 114, 120, 129
Yasutomo, Dennis, 6
Yemen Arab Republic, 92
Yen, appreciation of the, 65–66, 77–78
Yen loans, *see* loan aid
"Yosei shugi" (request basis) policy,
    60
Yoshida Shigeru, 53, 109